INFANTRY
OF THE SECOND WORLD WAR
TACTICS

OSPREY
PUBLISHING

INFANTRY
OF THE SECOND WORLD WAR
TACTICS

STEPHEN BULL & GORDON L ROTTMAN

First published in Great Britain in 2008 by Osprey Publishing,
Midland House, West Way, Botley, Oxford OX2 0PH, UK.
443 Park Avenue South, New York, NY 10016, USA.

Email: info@ospreypublishing.com

Previously published as Dr Stephen Bull, Elite 105: *World War II Infantry Tactics: Squad and Platoon*; Dr Stephen Bull, Elite 122: *World War II Infantry Tactics: Company and Battlion*; and Gordon L Rottman, Elite 124: *World War II Infantry Anti-Tank Tactics*

© 2008 Osprey Publishing Ltd

A CIP catalogue record for this book is available from the British Library

ISBN-13: 978 1 84603 282 0

Cover and page layout by Myriam Bell Design, France
Index by Alan Thatcher
Typeset in Adobe Garamond and Helvetica
Originated by PPS Grasmere Ltd, Leeds, UK
Printed in China through Bookbuilders

08 09 10 11 12   10 9 8 7 6 5 4 3 2 1

For a catalogue of all books published by Osprey please contact:

NORTH AMERICA
Osprey Direct, c/o Random House Distribution Center
400 Hahn Road, Westminster, MD 21157, USA

E-mail: info@ospreydirect.com

ALL OTHER REGIONS
Osprey Direct UK, P.O. Box 140, Wellingborough, Northants, NN8 2FA, UK

E-mail: info@ospreydirect.co.uk

www.ospreypublishing.com

Osprey Publishing is supporting the Woodland Trust, the UK's leading woodland conservation charity, by funding the dedication of trees.

Front cover: Image © akg-images, map courtesy University of Texas Libraries

Endpapers: © Stephen Bull

Back cover: Brian Delf © Osprey Publishing Ltd

Editor's Note

Photographs without credit lines indicate those from public domain sources, primarily the US National Archives and the US Army.

While weapons calibres are given in either imperial or metric according to official usage, and armour penetration figures are denoted in metric, the rest of the measurements in this book are provided in imperial only. For exact conversion to metric equivalents note:

feet to metres = multiply feet x 0.3058   yards to metres = multiply yards x 0.9114

CONTENTS

INTRODUCTION

Infantry must in the end confirm all success in war. Infantry compels the withdrawal or surrender of the enemy and holds the objectives which have been secured, or the points of importance which have to be protected, as a base for further action. It is the most adaptable and the most generally useful of all arms, since it is capable of operating over any ground by day or night and can find or make cover for itself more readily than the other arms.

Such was the opinion expressed in the *British Operations* manual of September 1939, and although many things have changed, this statement probably remains as true today as it was then.

There have been many books on weapons of war, but surprisingly few on tactics, and on the human organization necessary to use those weapons effectively. This work seeks to help redress that imbalance by a detailed look at infantry tactics in World War II, with the focus on the British, American and German forces at squad and platoon levels (Part 1), then at company and battalion levels (Part 2). Part 3 will also explore the specific demands of anti-tank (AT) tactics, and broaden the analysis of this particular type of warfare by including Japanese and Soviet tactics. The sources used are threefold: contemporary manuals, memoirs and secondary works. In the manuals we see what soldiers were taught to do or should have done, and the theory behind the tactics. About a hundred manuals have been consulted, including such minor classics as the German Dr Reibert's *Dienst Unterricht Im Heere* ('Service Instructions in the Army'); the *British Infantry Training, 1944*; and the US manual *Scouting, Patrolling, and Sniping, 1944*. Yet what should have happened did not always come to pass in practice, and

Compared with the armies of World War I, the infantrymen of 1939–45 represented a far smaller proportion of the millions swept up by mass conscription, although they suffered the bulk of the casualties; and in some armies it was decided to mark the status of the battle-tried footsoldier by special insignia. This Obergefreiter of a German mountain unit wears on his left breast the *Infanterie-Sturmabzeichen* ('Infantry Assault Badge'), instituted in December 1939 to recognize participation in at least three actions on different days. The peculiarly dangerous nature of infantry work was recognized by the US Army in late 1943 by the Combat Infantryman Badge, which carried additional pay of $10 per month. (Stephen Bull)

it is individual memoirs and oral history that provide eyewitness testimony. The secondary sources used here are diverse, comprising unit and official histories and recent specialist studies. Among these last must be noted particularly J. English, *A Perspective on Infantry*; T. H. Place, *Military Training in the British Army*; A. Farrar-Hockley, *Infantry Tactics*; J. Ellis, *The Sharp End*; J. Balkoski, *Beyond the Beachhead*; and S. Ambrose, *Citizen Soldiers*.

PART 1
SQUAD & PLATOON

THE SOLDIER'S EXPERIENCE

CASUALTY RATES

The idea that infantry combat in World War II was relatively far less costly in casualties when compared with World War I is widely believed – but largely erroneous. The US infantry divisions that fought in North-West Europe between D-Day on 6 June 1944 and VE-Day on 8 May 1945 had an average manpower turnover of approximately 100 per cent. In the extreme instance of the US 4th Infantry Division the gross turnover was in excess of 35,000 men – or almost two and a half times its original strength of about 14,000. Even units that were only at the front for a month had significant casualties: the 86th Division took 1,233 battle and non-battle casualties in just 34 days at the end of the war. The 17th Division, joining the fray on Christmas Day 1944, had 4,000 casualties of all types in 45 days.

Combat infantry company losses could be cataclysmic. A study of G Co, 3rd Battalion, 328th Infantry Regt, in the 26th ('Yankee') Division, shows a unit with an establishment of 187 other ranks and six officers, through which passed

An all-out bayonet charge across open ground, demonstrated by British infantrymen of the Loyal Regiment for publicity purposes, late 1930s. Such unsophisticated tactics became increasingly rare in Western Europe, although odd instances were recorded almost until the end of the war. (Stephen Bull)

625 men in just eight months. Of these, 51 were killed in action and a further six died of wounds. A total of 183 men were wounded in battle; of these 51 returned to duty, ten of them to be wounded a second time. Illness, trench foot and frostbite added a further 143 losses by the company, and eight self-inflicted wounds were reported. The experience of the 26th Division was little more than average: no American infantry company that landed in France in the summer or autumn of 1944 would have many of the same men left by the time the unit celebrated the end of the war in Europe.

British and German examples may be less obvious, since there was a greater propensity to rotate or even to disband weakened formations rather than keeping them in the line with successive drafts of replacements. Yet at times – as in Normandy, and on the German border – the attrition rate rivalled or even surpassed that of the Great War. In 1944 New Zealand casualties in Italy reached roughly double the original ration strength. Proportionately, Canadian losses on the Scheldt in 1944 marginally exceeded those at Passchendaele in 1917. Among British units, the 1st Bn Norfolk Regt in NW Europe suffered almost 70 per cent casualties, and over 17 per cent actually died. In one of the worst instances, the 6th Bn Duke of Wellington's Regt – badly mauled by elements of the Panzer Lehr and 12. SS-Panzer 'Hitlerjugend' divisions at Le Parc de Boislond – lost 16 officers and 220 men in two days. With a new commanding officer and second-in-command and raw replacements in the ranks, they were again ordered forward, only to be heavily mortared. After more than another hundred casualties, LtCol Turner was pleading to be taken out of the line: no one knew each other, the battalion was 'jumpy', and there was 'no esprit de corps' – he twice had to rally men at revolver point. The battalion was disbanded.

Quite a few men were pleased to be wounded: for the British this was the familiar 'blighty one', for the Americans the 'million dollar wound', for the Germans the very literal *Heimatschuss*, the shot that sends you home. Lt Peter White, a platoon commander in 4th Bn King's Own Scottish Borderers (KOSB), 52nd (Lowland) Division, noted that in the comparatively short period between October 1944 and May 1945 his little command suffered 42 casualties killed, wounded or otherwise incapacitated. A majority of these were the result of shell and mortar fire – some of it 'friendly'. Others fell to snipers and machine guns, but some defied simple categorization. Among these was a bad case of frostbite; two cases of 'bomb-happiness', or shell shock; and a man who was blown up by his own load of mortar bombs. One had a self-inflicted wound, another was injured while cooking. Only four men in the original platoon were unscathed throughout, with a further three early replacements who also survived uninjured. Allowing for those who returned very quickly or were wounded twice, the total turnover was about 100 per cent. The experience of the KOSB was widely replicated.

As in World War I, junior officers fared particularly badly in NW Europe: in the 15th (Scottish) Division officer casualties exceeded 72 per cent, with almost 29 per cent killed. Things were probably worse in the 51st Highland Division, already veterans of North Africa: Maj Martin Lindsay noted one battalion in which all 20 rifle company officers were casualties or replaced. The adjutant of the 1st Gordon Highlanders offered the remarkable statistic that of the officers serving in the 20 rifle company appointments, nine had been killed and 30 wounded.

Soldiers were not stupid, and soon recognized the comparative risks they ran from particular causes. A US poll asked a large sample of GIs which weapons they feared most: almost half picked the 8.8cm gun, with dive-bombers, bombers, mortars and machine guns in the runner-up positions (and this at a time when the number of German level bombers was negligible – a reminder of the high perceived and actual threat from friendly aircraft). Bayonets, although widely carried, featured relatively slightly in either fact or imagination. The US 90th Division was probably fairly typical, in that out of a total of 20,000 casualties just 13 were recorded as being caused by bayonets. Official statistics for the British Army over the course of the whole war state that 75 per cent of battle wounds were occasioned by shells, bombs and mortar rounds. Bullets and AT shells accounted for 10 per cent, the same figure as for mines and booby-traps. The remaining 5 per cent were caused by a miscellaneous range of crushings, chemical burns, and 'other' injuries.

Shelling, particularly prolonged bombardment, was the sternest test of infantry morale. As a soldier with the US 90th Division recorded:

The footsoldier learns to listen to the rustling sound made by a shell passing overhead. If the rustling diminishes in the direction of the enemy, it is caused by a friendly, or outgoing shell. If it diminishes in the direction of our rear, it is unfriendly or incoming. We were not particularly upset by shells that passed overhead and rustled on to our rear, for that was where the various headquarters lay, and we took some satisfaction from imagining the discomfiture of higher headquarters… Incoming shells that land among the forward troops arrive suddenly without warning. There is a shriek and a bang. The best thing to do is drop to the ground and crawl into the steel helmet. The helmet was of a shape and size to fit the head, but one tends to shrink a great deal when shells come in. I am sure I have gotten as much as eighty per cent of my body under my helmet when caught under shellfire.

Infantry officer, Italy, 1944: Maj Anandro Kadam of the Indian Army's 3/5th Mahratta Light Infantry poses with a captured German MP40 submachine gun, a popular weapon among Allied patrol leaders. He retains his regulation holstered revolver, but such weapons were almost useless at more than hand-to-hand range. (Stephen Bull)

A private of the Worcesters was shocked to see the effects of a direct hit that blew the victim into 'tiny little bits'. All that was left was 'a booted foot, a section of the human cranium, a bunch of fingers' and 'a bit of clothing'.

COMBAT FATIGUE

'Exhaustion' was a widely acknowledged phenomenon. Yet this was not always directly related to losses: as Capt Alastair Borthwick of the 5th Seaforths put it: 'nervous strain cannot be assessed by counting casualties, and nervous strain is what matters at the end of the day'. Generals came to realize that the soldier went through a cycle of efficiency. Untrained, a man was next to useless. When trained, but untried, formations could often be almost suicidally brave while still inexperienced in the finer points of combat. The first action was a vital test of mettle, which could prove a unit's worth or lead to dramatic collapse. Having seen combat, but still being fresh, a unit was likely to be at a peak of effectiveness. True veterans tended to suffer fewest casualties, but this was in part because they took the fewest risks. Maj Benson saw this cycle repeated in the 1st Black Watch:

> We generally found that newly joined drafts of officers and Jocks, provided they survived the first three weeks, had a much better chance of surviving. They got battle experience in simple things and … learned a lot by talking to their NCOs and fellow Jocks. Quite a lot had only staff experience, not having been at the 'Sharp End'. But proper battle experience could only be gained … under active service conditions.

When the point of nervous exhaustion was reached the Allied armies were ostensibly more humane than in World War I, and the ultimate sanction of 'shooting at dawn' a man whose nerves broke down was unknown in this war. Only in the German forces was execution 'for cowardice' the norm; this was partly the result of a more repressive society, but it was also the case that the German soldier was expected to spend longer and longer in the line as reserves dried up. In the British Army there was an emphasis on 'keeping the man in the line'. Commanding officers differed in their approach, some recording that men could often return to duty after a few nights' unbroken sleep in the unit rear area. A man's immediate superiors and comrades had no difficulty distinguishing between a good soldier who had reached the end of his mental strength, and an habitual shirker. In the 51st Highland Division the 'cure' could be drastic, nevertheless, as recounted by Pte Whitehouse:

This portrait of a war weary sergeant is typical of a tanker in the ETO in the winter of 1944/45. Note the connector jack on his right shoulder, hanging from his helmet; this connector pulled out easily if a crew had to abandon a burning tank in a hurry. Shortly after this photo was taken its subject, Sgt John H. Parks from Mill Creek, Indiana, was killed in action in Germany.

> 'Banger' Brown and Jock Harman were the first 'trotters' [deserters]. The Corps of Military Police caught them, returned the couple to Stan's platoon both handcuffed. They had then been taken out on patrol, still manacled, into 'No Man's Land', and then a second patrol. On their return, during the night a supporting tank had pulled into the platoon position by mistake and one track went over the prisoners…'

Lt Otts of the US 26th Division saw his first case succumb to 'exhaustion' under sporadic shellfire in November 1944:

> About the middle of the night we had our first case of battle fatigue – in other words, the first man to crack mentally. His was the most violent case I was to see. A couple of men brought him into the Command Post and laid him on a mattress on the floor. For the rest of the night he lay there crying loudly, laughing, screaming, or just

sobbing quietly. At times he would try to get up and run out, and it took several men to hold him down. I think that such a case is the worst thing that can happen for morale… The man himself is not to blame; it is all in the way one is made inside. Some men crack up very quickly, others last longer, and still others never crack. I saw some of the bravest men snap under the strain of too many days in combat.

Chemical sedation was a widespread palliative. The Americans jokingly named one tranquillizer the 'Blue 88', because it supposedly had the power of an AT shell.

PHYSICAL DEMANDS

Soldiers of all nationalities soon learned that there were gaps between what they had learned in training, and what happened in the field. In terms of clothing and equipment, peacetime theory and wartime practice could be poles apart.

The British manual writers were soon instructing the troops not to polish their 'brass', nor shine their boots; and officialdom joined the soldiery in accepting that the gas mask was just too big and awkward, introducing a lightweight model midway through the war. An *Army Training Memorandum* of 1944 suggested to baggage-laden British officers that they could limit their entire kit to 'valise, pack, and haversack' – and still not sacrifice their pyjamas. The Germans, with experience on many fronts, frequently wore their light fatigue uniform in warm weather, and discarded their old-fashioned Tornister or knapsack pack in favour of a small triangular canvas frame or 'assault pack'; the versatile rucksack issued to mountain troops was also popular with those who could get one.

For US units untried prior to D-Day the impact of reality was abrupt. The result, as one 90th Division commentator recorded, was a 'GI litter' of items shed by the wayside:

You must understand that planners decided the basic infantryman must have, besides his weapon, a shelter half (half of a pup tent), a blanket, a mess kit complete with knife, fork and spoon, a gas mask, an entrenching tool, a raincoat, a couple of hand grenades and bandoleers of extra ammunition. The uniform was steel helmets and chemically treated fatigues … more or less resistant to poison gas. The treatment rendered the clothing virtually impermeable. Hence, it was hot. As we plodded along we sweated excessively and began to feel the weight of all the 'essential' equipment.

When unchecked the jettisoning of kit could become an epidemic. While most naturally hung on to weapons, ammunition and digging tools, the blankets, raincoats and gas masks often disappeared. Some decided the mess kit was a luxury, though the spoon was generally kept. Even K-rations came in for rationalization, with men gobbling down as much as they could and throwing away surplus packaging. Some US units became wise to the dumping, and had a truck trail the marching men to pick up discarded items for reissue, with admonishments, later on.

The transformation from the neatly attired novice going into battle to the veteran coming out could be remarkable. Pfc Egger recorded his cold weather combat gear as consisting of raincoat or wool overcoat, boots with overshoes, gloves, wool underwear, shirt and uniform, helmet with liner, and scarf tied over the head. One golden rule was never to look like an officer. A lieutenant of the US 35th Division going into the line was puzzled to see the dishevelled men of the 29th ('Blue and Gray') wearing their field jackets inside out. The blanket cloth lining had a duller, darker surface than the exterior, and this odd fashion was improvised camouflage. Not infrequently the long canvas leggings, which

Ardennes, December 1944: coming in from manning a night roadblock, these three GIs (including two carrying bazookas) are lucky to have cold/wet weather footwear – in the foreground, four-clip M1942 overshoes. The man on the left wears the big fitted woollen anti-gas hood for warmth. From the diamond shape of the shoulder patch on the centre man's overcoat, these soldiers could be from the 5th or 26th Divisions.

were time-consuming to lace, were thrown away – but this occasionally proved dangerous, as the result could look like a loose-fitting pair of German fatigues.

What could be thrust into the pockets almost defied belief. Writing home on 28 January 1945, Egger examined the contents of his own, to find: a billfold, a pay book, two boxes of ammunition, two tooth brushes, water purification tablets, no fewer than eight bars of chocolate, a Bible, a can opener, cocoa powder, string, matches, a knife and 'other pieces of equipment'. The US Combat Infantry Badge was a proud but dressy novelty, so much so that many men mailed them home and never actually wore them in the field.

NATIONAL DIFFERENCES

It is frequently said that 'national characteristics' played an important part in determining the efficiency of the soldier. For example, there is an influential lobby which suggests that Germans simply make better soldiers; Col Dupuy has gone so far as to state that a quantifiable value can be given to the combat superiority of German troops. While ultimately successful, and respected for their defensive stubbornness, the British infantry are saddled with a plodding reputation. The Americans have been criticized for over-reliance on matériel. LtCol Ziegelmann, a staff officer with the German 352nd Division in Normandy, observed that 'With the exception of operations on a fairly small scale, the enemy in principle only committed his men to an attack if he was able to make use of his superiority in matériel before and during the attack… The enemy would have found himself in a predicament against an adversary equally strong in matériel.'

While there may be limited truth in such assertions, it has to be said that context, leadership, terrain, equipment and – vitally – tactics and training are more important determinants. As we shall see, Americans did not shoot more, and more randomly, because they were Americans, but because they were trained to do so. When German troops proved 'better' it was not because they were Germans, but because their tactics and experience fitted the circumstances precisely. When the British 'plodded' it was not because they were British, but because their officers were taught to be methodical and sparing of life. Lt Sydney Jary, who survived ten months of intensive action as a platoon commander in 4th Somerset Light Infantry, was adamant that his men were more aggressive and enterprising than any German troops they met. There is much to be said for the old adage that 'there are no bad soldiers, only bad officers'. Success or failure

A German patrol, lacking white camouflage clothing, darts from the cover of a ravine and out across a broad snowfield. Such actions were obviously dangerous, but soldiers often had no choice but to expose themselves in such a manner. They count on the enemy not opening fire due to their desire not to reveal their positions.

would often hang on whether troops were attacking or defending, on the quality of intelligence data available to them, on the weather and terrain, on sheer numbers and – of course – on blind luck.

Fitness and education did have a bearing: educational standards have historically been relatively high in countries such as Germany and Scotland, while city slum dwellers were seldom as physically fit as countrymen. The levels of selection and training applied to different populations were crucial. Expansion of the German Army commenced as early as the middle 1930s, and it is arguable that the many National Socialist paramilitary organizations, such as the Hitler Youth, made a significant contribution toward the militarization and fitness of the nation. Even in the Reich Labour Service there was drilling with spades, which, like rifles, had to be kept scrupulously clean. While SS recruiting literature was aimed specifically at the young as 'our front comrades of tomorrow', the Army made more traditional appeals for new officers, for example, to be 'a pattern and model of achievement for the men', in the highest and 'most fortunate' vocation.

In the pre-war Wehrmacht all soldiers underwent basic infantry training, ensuring that officer candidates were competent in the skills of leading infantry before they started any specialized training. As Siegfried Knappe recorded of his training in 1936:

> Often our three hours a day in the field would be infantry practice, for which we would wear our field uniforms, steel helmets, and gas masks… We did this to make sure that everyone knew infantry tactics even if he was in the artillery or Panzers, because tactics usually determined the outcome of a battle.

The German infantry of late 1940 was at a peak of efficiency and enthusiasm, having won substantial victories at limited cost. By the end of the war five million casualties, leading to increasing dependence on the young, the old, the sick, and disaffected foreigners, had taken their inevitable toll. The Scottish platoon commander Peter White, looking at German prisoners taken in late 1944, was surprised to find that:

> There seemed much more variety of type than among our chaps. Very old, very young, massive and brutish – the type one expected – or frail, wheezing, cold and frightened parodies, small and almost pitiful in jumbled ill-fitting uniform. Most carried lots of belongings and had discarded their steel helmets, almost invariably wearing instead their peaked caps, which called to my mind a group of vultures with their beaks twiddling this way and that as their heads swung. Also popular were cooking pots, mess tins, rye black bread, water bottles full of alcoholic drink and evil looking heavy sausages. Their tin shaped respirators were always in evidence. This latter point used to cause me thought at times, for our respirators were nearly always with 'B' Echelon some miles to the rear.

The experience of the democracies was very different. In America the major expansion of the army did not come until 1942. At least in the first instance a lower proportion of the total population was required for military service, so initially much greater levels of selectivity were possible. John Ellis records that about two million would-be draftees were excluded on psychiatric grounds alone. Even so, the US infantry got less than its fair share of talent, as those with relevant civilian specialist skills were sifted out for the supporting corps. As the official history has admitted, 'General service men were assigned to units irrespective of finer physical gradations … whether a man would engage in hand to hand fighting, march long distances on foot, carry a heavy pack, or go without sleep and food counted very little in his original assignment.'

On the plus side, the US Army was backed by growing industrial might, unhindered by bombing of the homeland or by the need to provide garrisons for conquered nations. Moreover, American troops enjoyed a good reputation and the children of the enemy learned to associate them with candy rather than atrocities. Eventually German soldiers would recognize them as a good bet to surrender to (although statistically the most scrupulous captors were the Canadians). Conversely, the US suffered from an early lack of expertise and seasoned instructors, and many GIs remember training being delivered in large lecture halls by junior NCOs whose practical experience was limited. In the absence of

anything better, passages from manuals were sometimes learned parrot-fashion – though the story that rookie GIs in combat had to be prevented from bayoneting the enemy 'by numbers' is probably apocryphal.

In the British case, history and previous form were especially important. With the exception of the period 1916–18, Britain had no historical experience of conscript armies, and Britons regarded any militaristic culture with a healthy skepticism. The Royal Navy was indubitably the 'Senior Service' and, as in America, there was a feeling that the infantry did not get the best material. As MajGen Utterson-Kelso of 47th Division put it, the infantry was often regarded as 'the legitimate dumping-ground for the lowest forms of military life'. The appalling casualties of 1914–18 had led to a climate of public opinion in which the squandering of life would not be tolerated indefinitely. By 1944 the United Kingdom had been fighting for five years, facing many setbacks and often unfavourable odds. At least some of those generals who had reached the top (and more importantly, stayed there) were the most methodical and calculating, deeply marked by their experience as subalterns in World War I – Gen

Normandy, summer 1944: an officers' orders group at battalion HQ of the 29th Division (the censor's pen has scribbled over the right-hand man's patch). All wear the so-called 'tanker's jacket'; the man sitting in the middle has a fighting knife sticking out of his custom-made bucked leather legging. The kneeling man has British-made hobnailed boots, and an officer's bar painted on his helmet back; in the ETO all officers were supposed to have a 2in-wide white bar painted here, vertical for officers and horizontal for NCOs. While not universally applied, these were commonly seen throughout 1944/45.

Montgomery is perhaps the most obvious example. How the GI and his generals would have fought after five years can only be guessed at. Maj E. M. Llewellyn, editor of *Stars and Stripes*, was one who realized that there was a basic difference of viewpoint: 'The British believe that, regardless of mistakes made today and tomorrow, they will fight on courageously and win final victory. The Yankee feels that no power on earth can withstand his might…'

Britain's Empire and Dominions were a huge resource but a mixed blessing, as the advantages of manpower were sometimes offset both by her almost worldwide defensive responsibilities, and by communication and supply problems. Indian Army troops, who fought extensively in North Africa and Italy, were of variable quality, yet the best of them showed unequalled loyalty. The Canadians alone seem to have managed to blend the virtues of the American and British traditions without inheriting too many of their weaknesses. Yet important as these underlying factors were, it may be argued that it was doctrine, armament, training, organization and small-unit tactics that were the final arbiters of battle.

TRAINING – FIELDCRAFT & BATTLECRAFT

Though scouts and snipers learned camouflage and movement during World War I, the universal teaching of sophisticated skills was essentially a development of the interwar period. In the words of Basil Liddell Hart, protégé of the Great War training expert Gen Ivor Maxse and author of the 1921 edition of *Infantry Training and Science of Infantry Tactics*, the 'modern infantry soldier' had to be three in one: 'stalker, athlete, and marksman'. By World War II such concepts were accepted as defining features of the footsoldier. The US *Operations Manual* of June 1944 noted:

> Infantry can maneuver on difficult ground. Its ability to move in small and inconspicuous formations enables it to take advantage of covered routes of approach and minor accidents of terrain. It must utilize the terrain intelligently to attain maximum fire effect, to conserve personnel, to conceal movement, and to facilitate the maneuvre and employment of reserves.

Pre-war German training heartily embraced these precepts. Contrary to the common suggestion that cartoon-style manuals are a modern US innovation, they date back at least to World War I, and interwar German training literature frequently includes quirky or even comic pictures. Maj Bodo Zimmermann's *Die Soldatenfiebel* illustrated 'Bewegungen im Gelände' or stealthy 'field movement' by means of photographs and line drawings. Recruits were taught to 'kriechen' or creep forward with an elbow-and-knee movement approximating to the British 'leopard crawl', with the weapon held transverse in front of the

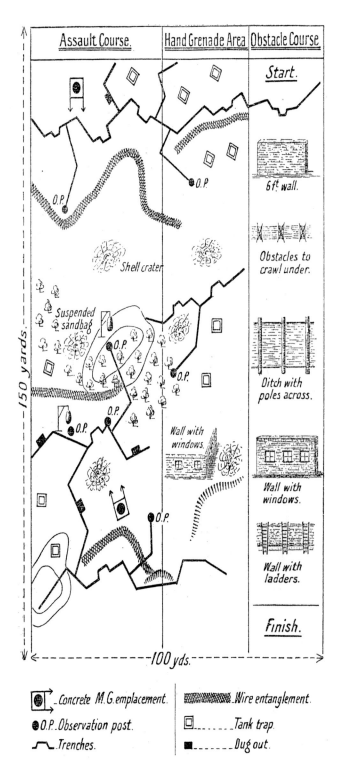

Assault Course. | **Hand Grenade Area** | **Obstacle Course**

Start.

6 ft. wall.

Obstacles to crawl under.

Ditch with poles across.

Wall with windows.

Wall with windows.

Wall with ladders.

Finish.

O.P.

O.P.

O.P.

Shell crater.

Suspended sandbag.

O.P.

O.P.

O.P.

O.P.

O.P.

— 150 yards.

←- - - - - - 100 yds. - - - - - - →

◻ ..Concrete M.G. emplacement.

● O.P..Observation post.

⌐_⌐.Trenches.

▒▒▒▒ Wire entanglement.

◻ - - - - - Tank trap.

■ - - - - - Dug out.

body or slung around the neck. A variation on the theme was 'gleiten' or gliding, pushing straight forward with the feet. Drawings were also used to show dispersal and use of cover.

Other sections dealt with personal camouflage and spade work, shooting from trees, the use of trunks as rests, and the importance of quick loading and sight-setting in any firing position. Another useful ruse depicted was lying under the camouflaged shelter-quarter to achieve near total concealment when shooting. 'Richtig' and 'Falsch' – 'Right' and 'Wrong' – line drawings were continued in Weber's *Unterrichtsbuch für Soldaten* ('Instruction Book for Soldiers') of 1938. Here wrong-headed characters had bucket-shaped heads and were seen committing cardinal errors, such as advancing nonchalantly across open ground, using obvious isolated cover and failing to observe. One of the worst sins was *zusammenballen* – 'bunching together' and offering an easy target.

Film was increasingly used as a supplement to exercises, lectures and manuals. While the US enlisted Hollywood and the Germans nationalized their film industry, even Britain made a remarkable range of film training materials. As early as 1 May 1942 there were 154 British training films, with a further 107 under production. These were in three main categories: basic training films; 'instructional' films on specific pieces of equipment; and 'background' films. While not to be treated as 'an alternative to Mickey Mouse', these were freely available to units from area 'Kinema Section Libraries'.

German instructions of the early war period suggested that an effective arena for realistic infantry training could be constructed on a piece of ground about 100 x 150 yards. Ideally this would be provided with 'ruins of walls, parts of buildings, tank traps, barbed wire defences, shell holes, frames with suspended sand bags, clumps of trees and bushes', and a hilly or uneven area would give particular flexibility. The training ground should comprise three sections, for an obstacle course, hand grenade practise and assault training.

On the obstacle course trainees learned to cross ditches and walls, and rush over planks and poles. Team efforts were encouraged for difficult crossings, while daring could be instilled with jumps from high walls. The hand grenade area was specifically for the teaching of throwing from various positions in close combat, but could also double for other weapons. The assault area applied the lessons to specific problems, dummies being used, often unexpectedly, to represent the enemy.

Opposite:
Typical German training area for close-quarter battle, as extracted from a semi-official German publication and translated in the *British Periodical Notes on the German Army* (1941). (Stephen Bull)

Bild 14

Bild 15

Bild 16

Left:
Throwing grenades in standing, kneeling and prone positions, from the 1937 German manual *Körperliche Grundausbildung* ('Basic Physical Training') – thus the thrower is shown as a semi-naked athlete, in a characteristically Nazi style of artwork. Distance marching, map reading, message running and shooting were all part of the Hitler Youth curriculum; the SA 'sport' qualification also included grenade throwing, and activities performed while wearing a gas mask. The aim was to provide a generation of fit and partially trained youths before they even reached the age for military conscription. (Stephen Bull)

Explosive charges and other devices were used to encourage the soldier 'to act not mechanically, but independently and on his own initiative'. Section assault training included attacking field works. Tactical training stressed the importance of speed and surprise: concentrating resources – moral, physical, and material – and ruthlessly exploiting success. Leaders at all levels were taught the importance of maintaining the initiative, keeping the objective in mind, and simplicity of planning which would ensure speed in execution.

A thorough appreciation of modern fieldcraft was given by the US *Scouting, Patrolling, and Sniping* manual of 1944. This drew a particularly clear distinction between cover – which was a 'protection against hostile weapons'; and concealment – which was protection against observation, but not fire. Among the 'principles of individual concealment' were the need to remain motionless, the art of observation when prone and the skill of blending with backgrounds. Observation was preferable through or around objects, not over them, while shooting around the right side of an obstruction was best, as this tended to conceal the maximum area of the body. Personal camouflage received considerable attention. Covering equipment was encouraged, as was the improvisation of camouflage clothing from 'gunny sacks or sand bags'. Face camouflage was also explained:

> Paint splotches across the nose, mouth, cheeks and hands with lampblack, burned wood, cork, crankcase oil, grease paint or vaseline with soot on it. Remember that mud dries light and many black substances glisten and reflect light. Green grass crushed in the hands will make a stain that lasts for about ten hours. No exposed skin should be overlooked in splotch painting: back of the neck, chest, lower arms, and both backs and palms of the hands should be painted. For a position amongst rocks or in open terrain, tone the skin to a solid dark color.

When issue camouflage garments were not available scouts were expected to daub ordinary fatigues with 'irregular splotches' of paint, dye or oil. The helmet could be disguised with a net, mud or a helmet cover 'improvised from a piece of cloth or burlap, about 20 inches square, irregularly colored to blend with the background'. Helmet nets, or wire or twine substitutes, were to be garnished and draped so as to break up the dark shadow of the helmet visor. 'Plumes' of foliage sticking up were inadvisable as movement would be obvious.

Given the American emphasis on firepower, and the rarity of wounds inflicted with edged weapons, it is perhaps surprising that bayonet training continued to feature significantly. The point, however, was that bayonet training helped to foster a desirable level of willpower and aggression. As Patton's pithy maxim put it, 'Few men are killed by the bayonet; many are scared by it.' The 1943 US field manual *Bayonet* explained that:

> The will to meet and destroy the enemy in hand to hand combat is the spirit of the bayonet. It springs from the fighter's confidence, courage and grim determination, and is the result of vigorous training… The will to use the bayonet first appears in the trainee when he begins to handle it with facility, and increases as his confidence grows. The full development of his physical prowess and complete confidence in his weapon culminates in the final expression of the spirit of the bayonet – fierce and relentless destruction of the enemy. For the enemy, demoralizing fear of the bayonet is added to the destructive power of every bomb, shell, bullet and grenade which supports and precedes the bayonet attack.

FIG. 3.—THE WITHDRAWAL (USING FOOT)

From the British manual *Small Arms Training: Bayonet* (1942). 'The sole object of weapon training is to teach all ranks the most efficient way of handling their weapons in order to kill.'

The manual noted that the blade was actually preferable to other weapons in certain circumstances, e.g. during night infiltration, or in close combat when friend and foe were so mingled that grenades and bullets would be dangerous to one's comrades. US bayonet fighting was taught as a series of moves from the starting point of the 'guard' or the 'high port'. These included the 'whirl', by means of which the fighter about-faced, and the parry, to block the opponent. The aggressive actions included not only the long and short thrusts, but vertical and horizontal strokes with the rifle butt, and the 'smash' and 'slash'. The 'slash' was used when an opponent moved out of range of the rifle butt, or fell during combat, and consisted of bringing the rifle sharply round with a slashing motion aimed at the neck. Butt jabs were particularly useful when the opponent was too close to be bayoneted, and were profitably teamed with various unsporting moves: 'When using a butt stroke the fighter can often knee his opponent in the groin, trip him or kick him in the legs. Butt strokes and slashes lend themselves especially to fighting in trenches, woods and brush, or in a general melee when lateral movements are restricted.'

British training has been criticized as backward, on the grounds that the old *1937 Infantry Training* manual was not comprehensively updated until March 1944. While this is true, it has to be stated that the British approach to fieldcraft was far from stagnant, and in certain matters British tacticians learned from German methods. In 1941, for example, it was noted that the Germans stressed concealment in defence more than the British, and also that the enemy were firing machine guns through their own attacking infantry. Within a few months both these points were absorbed into official British teaching. The 'Battle School' and 'Hate Training' were also factors that pointed toward a growing seriousness of approach – though the former was undoubtedly more practical than the latter. Battle Schools were started as early as 1940, and it may be claimed that the Home Guard School at Osterley Park, founded in answer to the need for 'real training' and run by the World War I and Spanish Civil War veteran Capt Tom Wintringham, was one of the first. As an article in *Picture Post* in September 1940 explained, the men were taught 'confidence and cunning, the use of shadow and cover'. Lectures and demonstrations were given on 'Modern tactics in general, and German tactics present and future. The use and improvisation of hand grenades, land mines and AT grenades. The use of various types of rifles, shotguns, pistols, etc., camouflage, fieldcraft, scouting, stalking and patrolling. Guerrilla warfare in territory occupied by the enemy. Street tactics and defence of cities; the use of smoke screens…' The aim of the school was to teach members of the Home Guard to become 'first class' irregulars. Regular Divisional Battle Schools were in existence not long afterwards, perhaps the best known being that of the 47th Division at Chelwood Gate, which opened in July 1941. A Central Battle School at Barnard Castle in County Durham was established specifically to train the instructors needed in the divisional schools.

If Battle Schools were a significant factor in the improvement of tactics, 'Hate Training' was prone to degenerate into farce. During late 1941 and early 1942 students were shown photographs of German atrocities, and given tours of local abattoirs. They were urged to yell 'Kill! Kill!' and 'Hate! Hate!' during exercises, and sometimes animal blood was added to bayonet practice for

Suggestions for garnishing the British Mk II steel helmet for concealment in the field, from *The Organisation of Home Guard Defence* (1943). Note the rather fanciful idea of sticking discarded cigarette packets to the helmet for camouflage during street fighting. (Stephen Bull)

100

STEEL HELMET CONCEALMENT.

Ends of framework tied to lining

UNDERSIDE

KNOT

OVERHEAD

TWO TYPES OF STRING FRAMEWORK USING 3 YARDS OF STRING, *for use with or without netting.*

For use in BUILT UP AREAS

LIGHT CARDBOARD BOX. TIED TO HELMET WITH STRING AND TEXTURED & PAINTED TO SUIT SURROUNDINGS

CIGARETTE PACKETS, BITS OF CARDBOARD, BUNCHED PAPER, SHAVINGS ETC. TIED WITH STRING

BREAK ALL OUTLINES

THE EYE THROUGH CONSTANT REPETITION RECOGNISES CERTAIN SHAPES AVOID THIS THE SIMPLEST WAY BY BREAKING THE SHAPE & THE OUTLINE

HELMET OUTLINE IRREGULAR. BREAK LINE OF FACE BY TYING PIECES OF SCRIM RAG, CARDBOARD OR PAPER TO THE CHIN STRAP AND DARKEN ALL FLESH

FIG. 25.

extra realism. The idea was to acquaint the soldier with, and harden him against, the reality of battle; but the unreality of these 'blood and hate' scenarios could seldom survive the British sense of humour and, under opposition from senior commanders, they were officially dropped in May 1942. (Nevertheless, similar ideas would later resurface, as for example during SAS training.)

In addition to these activities, the 'provisional' *Instructor's Handbook on Fieldcraft and Drill* of October 1942 was a significant advance. Though lacking the polish of later publications, it was a substantial booklet of almost 200 pages. Its messages were carried by means of diagrams, detailed exercises and cartoons. Moreover, though the words 'instructor's', and 'provisional' suggested limited application, no fewer than 175,000 copies were put into circulation – against 300,000 of the definitive 1944 *Infantry Training*.

GERMAN INFANTRY BATTLEFIELD POSITIONS, 1939–45

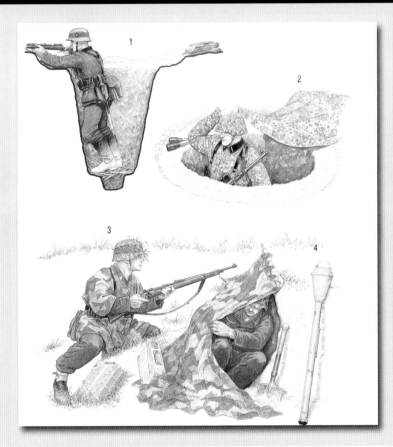

Protection and concealment were literally a matter of life and death to the infantryman in battle. (1) Profile view of a textbook *Schützenloch* or rifle pit, as originally depicted in Weber's 1938 *Unterrichtsbuch*. It features both an elbow rest round the rim, and a sump covered with brush to improve drainage.
(2) An oblique view of a similarly 'textbook perfect' foxhole occupied by an SS-Sturmann in c. 1944. Note how the camouflage-printed *Zeltbahn* could be pegged down and folded at one side, to be pulled forward above the hole for total concealment or to keep out rain.
(3 & 4) Tactical use of a roadside embankment or hillside, c. 1944 – (surrounding vegetation has been omitted for clarity). Infantryman (3) maintains tactical mobility below the cover of the bank, camouflaged by his *Zeltbahn* and with matching local foliage in his helmet net. The Panzergrenadier (4) has dug a burrow into the reverse slope, covered and concealed with his pegged-down *Zeltbahn*. In bad weather he would normally bring the head of his Panzerfaust anti-tank weapon under cover against the damp. (Mike Chappell © Osprey Publishing Ltd)

'PREPARE FOR BATTLE'

HELMET
Hessian knots plus natural garnish to break the dome and shadow under the rim.

FACE, NECK, AND HANDS
Highlights darkened with camouflage cream, soot, dark blanco, or cocoa.

RIFLE
Darken shiny metal with matt paint. Dark hessian cover conceals shiny butt-plate.

WEBBING
Dark blanco No. IA or 3. All brass painted with dark paint.

HAVERSACK
String holds hessian. Knots, plus natural garnish, to destroy square shape.

RESPIRATOR
Dark blanco.

BOOTS
Dubbined.

The British infantryman prepared for battle, from *Infantry Training* (1944). (Stephen Bull)

Other pamphlets were similarly widely applied. *Notes on Camouflage* (1939) stressed that 'concealment is a matter of common sense and good discipline' – explaining that the soldier 'must be able to hide himself if he is to have any chance of surprising his enemy and if he is to prevent the latter from making full use of his weapons.' Movement, particularly in the open, was to be avoided; when unavoidable it was to be irregular, so that no formation appeared to give away the unit. *Notes on Camouflage* also contained a series of line drawings showing the importance of avoiding isolated cover, crest lines and moving foliage to incongruous locations, and the use of shadow. *Surprise: The First Principle of Attack* (1941) was a handbook illustrated in cartoon style specifically for NCOs. Despite the title it was essentially a ready reference for fieldcraft and camouflage. *Individual Battle Practices* (March 1943) gave five short exercises to teach the use of ground and shooting in likely battle scenarios. In an exercise called 'The Stalker' the soldier was taught to advance stealthily, against the clock, for about a hundred yards, before engaging a man-shaped target placed in a battle position. Frightening realism could be added by instructors observing the trainee through a periscope and firing 'a round of ball or blank' whenever he was visible.

The basics of fieldcraft had a remarkably universal quality. Certain passages from the official German infantry manual *Ausbildungsvorschrift für die Infanterie* (1941; 'Training Regulations for Infantry') are translated almost word for word in the US manuals of 1942 and 1944. British publications such as *Notes on Camouflage* contain sections that are virtually interchangeable with both German and US documents. The German *Manual of the British Army* (1942) specifically claimed 'imitation of German methods', while one British *Army Training Memorandum* told officers to avoid using German tactical terms. Even the Home Guard had several remarkably modern fieldcraft manuals. One of the most detailed was the privately produced *Home Guard Fieldcraft Manual* by Maj John

Langdon-Davies, first published in 1942, 'based upon practical experience as Commandant of the South Eastern Command Fieldcraft School'. Despite the title this volume was also intended to supplement the materials available to army cadets and regulars. In addition to the now familiar content on camouflage, natural cover, movement and defending against paratroops, it contained useful hints on urban concealment and sniping.

By 1942 British training recognized several ways of moving about the battlefield:

The Walk. When not actually engaged, soldiers were encouraged to keep the head up, observing 'all the while' during movement. Riflemen were to keep the rifle ready for action, in the left hand across the body or poised in two hands. The weapon was to look as though it was 'part of you – not just an umbrella'. Walking was to be well balanced and fluid, allowing the soldier to freeze instantly and avoid jerkiness that would attract the eye.

The Leopard (or Stomach) Crawl. To be executed with the rifle held forward, or in the left hand with the small of the butt under the right armpit. In a 'Russian' version the muzzle cap was grasped in one hand and the rifle rested on the opposite forearm. Other crawl variations for two-man Bren teams included taking one end of the weapon each, or hooking the bipod legs through the equipment on the back of one of the team while the other kept the butt off the ground. One man could also side-crawl slowly with the Bren, resting it on the instep of the lower leg.

The Cossack Crawl. Advertised as 'convenient for moving behind low cover', this was done from the squat, moving one leg at a time around the side to the front, with the other knee taking the weight on the ground.

The Monkey Run. A hands-and-knees movement with clenched fists, this was best done as fast as possible. To avoid exhaustion the monkey run was in short bursts of 15 yards, followed by dropping flat and a pause before continuing.

The Roll. This allowed the man to get out of sight quickly if spotted when prone. It could be done with the rifle in hand but off the ground, so as to keep it clear of mud.

Running. This was perhaps most difficult for Bren gunners, who could put the weapon over the shoulder, carry it between two men, or better still port it on a sling to allow for firing on the move.

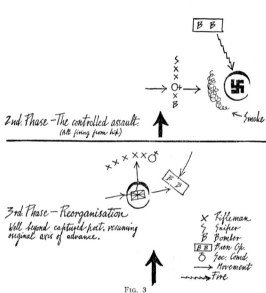

Fig. 3

(5) "ENEMY" is represented by a flag in the middle of the parade ground.
(6) Distance between men throughout will be five yards. They will fall in at five-yard intervals.

British squad assault drill for practice on the parade ground, from the *Instructor's Handbook* (October 1942). The squad is still shown as eight men, distinguished between 'riflemen', 'sniper', 'bomber' and a two-man Bren group. (Stephen Bull)

The infantryman's personal equipment of belts and pouches was scientifically designed to carry the ammunition and small equipment items which it was anticipated he would need. In practice, because expenditure of ammunition was faster than allowed for, and new items were repeatedly added to the squad or platoon's inventory, the load-bearing equipment always lagged behind the fast-evolving reality of the battlefield. Extras had to be accommodated by festooning soldiers with bandoliers, slung musettes and satchels (often improvised for new purposes), and even sandbags and bits of string. This 1944 GI is also wearing an inflatable lifebelt for beach landings.

The Ghost Walk, Cat Walk, and Kitten Crawl. These were specifically adapted for use by night when stealth and quietness were more important than speed. In the Ghost Walk the legs were lifted high and moved slowly, avoiding long grass and obstacles. The Cat Walk was a very slow hands-and-knees advance, using the hands to avoid twigs or noisy debris. The Kitten Crawl was even more tiring, being effectively a stomach crawl in which the body was kept clear of the ground with toes and forearms.

The opposite side of the game from avoiding being seen was skill in detecting the enemy, and various observation drills, with and without field glasses, were used. An interesting practice for 'eye and ear' was an exercise colloquially known as 'Crack and Thump'. Hidden riflemen fired over the heads of the trainees, who learned to distinguish the 'thump' of discharge from the 'crack' of the passing bullet. By listening for the discharge and looking for wisps of smoke it became possible to locate even well-concealed shooters. For cases of desperate necessity, methods of drawing fire were also taught. In one technique a sniper fired into likely spots while others waited ready to respond to return fire. In another, more hair-raising variation a man would jump up, run a few yards and throw himself down again, trusting that such brief exposure would not give an enemy time to aim properly.

'Battle inoculation' was a significant, if risky, concept employed in the training of British infantry. The purpose was to make men 'accustomed to the noises and shocks of war by reproducing these things as realistically as possible' (an idea which had in fact been employed as early as the 16th century – though primarily on cavalry horses). Not content with using live ammunition in as much training as possible, the *Instructor's Handbook* suggested that marksmen be deployed to fire live rounds over trainees' heads during exercises; pyrotechnic 'thunder flashes' should be used to represent enemy mortar fire; and low-flying aircraft should appear. In perhaps the hardest test, the trainees dug weapons pits and were overrun by tanks. They would understandably 'regard this experience with considerable misgivings', but on discovering that a tank could do no harm if they lay at the bottom of the pit they would eventually gain confidence. It is interesting that Guy Sajer, serving with the German 'Grossdeutschland' Division, described an almost identical exercise:

> As we had already been taught to dig a foxhole in record time, we had no trouble opening a trench 150 metres long, half a metre wide, and a metre deep. We were ordered into the trench in close ranks, and forbidden to leave it no matter what happened. Then four or five Mark III [tanks] rolled forward at right angles to us and crossed the trench at different speeds. The weight of these machines alone made them sink five or ten centimetres into the crumbling ground. When their monstrous treads ploughed into the rim of the trench only a few centimetres from our heads, cries of horror broke out…

Typically, the 51st Highland Division added another twist to the idea. In its version the Vickers guns of the Middlesex machine gun battalion fired live over the Highlanders, and then Canadian tanks were used to run over the Middlesex 'while lying in their trenches'. Nevertheless, troops got used even to this treatment. As the *Instructor's Handbook* put it, 'Generally the final attitude of the troops should be that they are bored and "fed up" when they see tanks and aircraft and take no notice at all of noises or of live ammunition passing close to them. On no account try to frighten the men; that would entirely defeat the whole object of battle inoculation.'

As far as detailed tactics were concerned, British training methods stressed the importance of the 'battle drill' – simple set procedures which everyone was taught in order to deal with a specific problem. This had the ready advantage of giving conscripted citizen soldiers a swift grounding in the basics of combat, and made panic less likely. Nevertheless, battle drill was regarded as merely the start. As the *Instructor's Handbook* explained, 'It does not, if properly taught, cramp initiative nor lead to stereotyped action regardless of the circumstances… Rather it gives the junior commander a firm base on which to develop his individual initiative, much in the same way that the young cricketer is taught the basic principles of stroke play on which later he develops his own style.'

Unarmed combat and knife fighting, developed as skills for raiders and scouts during the Great War, were relatively neglected prior to 1939. Thereafter they underwent a revival – partly through necessity as special forces skills, but also symbolically as a sign of acceptance of 'total war'. In the wake of Dunkirk new British interest was signalled by an *Army Training Memorandum* of July 1940. Here the object of unarmed combat training was explicitly defined as to 'inculcate the spirit of self confidence, initiative, and determination', even though the soldier

Disarming an enemy, from the US manual *Bayonet* (September 1943). (Stephen Bull)

found himself in 'the most desperate of situations'. War being a matter of 'life and death' there was to be no scruple about the use of 'complete ruthlessness'. Though kicking and eye-gouging, for example, were 'foreign and detestable to the Britisher', they were to be used without compunction, while the value of a 'good solid punch' was not to be underestimated. The steel helmet could likewise become a weapon for a head butt, or held in the hand as a parrying or smashing device.

Such bulldog sentiments doubtless inspired the privately produced manuals of the period. These included such gems as Bernard's 'Key to Victory' publication *Commando and Guerrilla Warfare: Unarmed Combat*, for 'Home Guard and service use', which promised the secrets to holds, releases, silent killing and the 'extraction of information'. Among the less useful moves were one for preventing a Nazi pulling your hair; and a means of securing a German soldier to 'any pole or street lighting standard', using only his legs to form a 'self locking grape vine hold'. At the other end of the spectrum was the best known and most successful of the genre, Capt W. E. Fairbairn's *All In Fighting* of 1942. Overcoming the 'cricket mentality', this was designed to teach the soldier to act 'instinctively and automatically' with a well-illustrated series of blows, holds and kicks. Most famously, it contained a section on knives, including the new Fairbairn Sykes fighting knife and the Smatchet. (Nevertheless, it also repeated the anti hair-pulling stunt.)

Interestingly, the prime objective of US unarmed combat, as outlined in the manual *Bayonet*, was becoming armed. The GI whose weapon was lost or useless was supposed to do one of two things. Ideally he should gather up a discarded weapon and continue the fight but, failing this, he should attempt to take one from an opponent. The main moves were intended to wrest a rifle or knife from an enemy's grasp; in the process the soldier was encouraged to kick, jab at the eyes or throat, elbow, punch or throw things, as opportunity allowed.

THE SQUAD ETHOS

The squad or section of ten or a dozen men was the basic building block of the infantry and its smallest tactical body – what some German instructions called the 'fire unit'. Just as importantly, it was the cornerstone of morale. Few veterans cite patriotic idealism, still fewer a political creed, as the impulse that made them pull the trigger or march the extra mile; almost invariably, they talk of the fear of letting their comrades down. As signaller Ronald Elliott of the 16th Durhams put it, the motivation was respect for yourself and 'for your mates'. The Americans, who usually worked in pairs, have referred to the importance of 'foxhole buddies': what Maj Dick Winters of 101st Airborne Division called the 'very unusual bond' of the combat veterans. It was what one recent American commentator has called 'a deadly brotherhood'. British manuals made explicit reference to this vital cement. As *Infantry Training* (1944) explained, the section was 'the team'; its personnel were to be altered as little as possible, and everything was to be done to foster 'group morale'. Shared experience was a major part of this powerful bonding process. For Lt Peter White of KOSB this was a life 'so departed from known values' as to be unreal: a world in which one could be huddled together with friends for animal warmth one moment, and stacking their frozen bodies an hour later. In this insane situation, where near-children had machine guns, and civilians and animals were in the line of fire, White believed that he and his 'Jocks' had a unique opportunity of 'getting to know our real selves'.

For the Germans, all this translated as *Kameradschaft* – comradeship. As Unteroffizier Friedrich Bertenrath put it, 'The worst thing that could happen to a soldier was to be thrown into a group in which he knew no one… We were

Kameradschaft – men of a German infantry *Gruppe* led by an Unterfeldwebel (right) photographed near Kiev, Russia, 1941. The Wehrmacht veteran Günter Koschorrek wrote that after men had been at the front for a while, 'You no longer fight for *Führer, Volk und Vaterland*. These ideals have long gone. And no one talks of National Socialism or similar political matters. From all our conversations, it is quite obvious that the primary reason we fight is to stay alive and help our front line comrades to do the same. But we often also fight for a superior, such as our Oberleutnant, who through his exemplary attitude manages to instil spirit into dog-tired and almost indifferent warriors.'

comrades, and always came to the rescue. We protected our comrades so that they would go home to wives, children and parents. That was our motivation.' Guy Sajer, with the 'Grossdeutschland' Division, heard a sergeant explain that it was only the soldier's life that brought men close together in 'absolute sincerity'. The Wehrmacht soldier Harry Mielert philosophized that the front was a sort of 'homeland' in its own right, where a 'solidarity of fate' actually led to 'higher ethical values'. It is interesting that Hitler made explicit political capital from the parallel between 'soldierly comradeship' and 'national comradeship' – *Frontgemeinschaft* and *Volksgemeinschaft*. In this way he sought to graft Nazi values on to a pre-existing military ethos, in a corruption of an essentially generous and unselfish impulse.

Loyalty to the squad was of similar, if not greater, significance to the American GI. It was all the more remarkable in an army drawn from so many different backgrounds, although it should be noted that African-Americans were still segregated. (This separation could have bizarre consequences, as when German prisoners were allowed into 'white' mess halls from which black GIs were excluded.)

A potential weakness in the US system was the method by which replacements were fed in to a unit in action, like so many individual spare parts. Green soldiers, plunged into their first experience of combat as recent additions to an inward-looking group of veterans, often suffered accordingly. The British system was not perfect, but at least those in authority were aware of this problem. For example, Gen Montgomery wrote addressing the concerns of Col Cooper of the Border Regiment on 16 July 1944, assuring him that 'every regard possible in the circumstances shall be paid to regimental affiliations, and that where possible officers and men will be posted together in units, in parties approximating to a platoon in size'. The Germans similarly intended that replacements for field formations should be trained up in *Ersatz* or 'supplementary' units from the same home area, although this was not always possible in practice.

A veteran German Unteroffizier squad leader, armed with an MP40 submachine gun, pictured on the cover of the Munich *Illustrierter Beobachter* of 7 October 1943. His decorations include two tank destruction bars, and the *Nahkampfspange* ('Close Combat Clasp'); the latter was awarded in bronze, silver and gold classes for 15, 30 and 50 days in close combat. (Stephen Bull)

THE SQUAD LEADER

The junior NCO who led the squad or section was of central importance. The 1942 US *Infantry Field Manual: Rifle Company, Rifle Regiment* gave one of the most demanding squad leader job specifications. He was to be responsible for 'discipline, appearance, training, control, and conduct' of the squad, enforcing proper standards of hygiene, sanitation and weapon cleaning, and leading from the front in combat. Ideally he would control fire, although it cannot always have been practicable to 'shift the fire of all or part of the squad from one target to another' as the manuals hoped.

The leader of the German *Gruppe* (squad) bore similarly heavy responsibility:

> The group leader must be an example – and a combat example – to his men.
> The most effective means for gaining the confidence and respect of subordinates and
> for getting the most out of them is to set an example. But in order to set an example,
> the squad leader must have a stronger will than his men, must do more than they do,
> and must always discharge his duties and obey orders cheerfully… In order to be a
> leader in the field, a superior must display an exemplary bearing before his men in the
> moment of danger and be willing, if necessary, to die for them.

Interestingly, the role of the section commander was not quite as strongly stressed in British literature, although he too was seen as controlling and leading in battle. The 1938 pamphlet *Infantry Section Leading* has been described as a weak document for its relative lack of tactical detail. Even so, there was a growing appreciation of the importance of the junior NCO, and the section leaders' course was an established part of training. According to the British manual *Application of Fire* (1939), one of the section leader's prime duties was fire control. He would specifically direct the light machine gun (LMG), give snipers their tasks and control the rifles 'according to circumstance'. Fire could be concentrated or distributed depending on the target. The grimmer language of the 1942 edition said that one of the leader's most important jobs would be to determine when to hold fire in order to maintain maximum surprise, and to 'ensure killing of the enemy'.

All this may sound superfluous, until one remembers that most units had chronic 'non-firers'. As a frustrated Lt Dick Hewlett of the Durhams remarked, 'One is inclined to freeze up so that you can't do anything – but the only thing to do is fire.' Post-war American research would identify not only men who would not shoot, but many who shut their eyes when they did.

SQUAD ORGANIZATION & WEAPONS

The idea of small groups living and fighting together is long established. As early as the 17th century 'files' of men from larger units are recorded as acting under a 'file leader' or junior NCO, who was responsible for their conduct in battle or billet. Yet it was not until the early 20th century that the squad achieved tactical significance. Arguably this began when various types of weapon were grouped as far down the chain of organization as the company, so making a range of tactics viable. By 1916 the platoons of many nations contained a mixture of rifles, grenades and light machine guns. By the end of World War I platoons were considered viable units in their own right, and there were even instances of the use of rifles and light machine guns in mixed squads.

According to the manual *Rifle Company* (1942), the US squad comprised 12 men: the sergeant squad leader; a corporal who acted as his assistant and AT rifle grenadier; an 'automatic rifle team' of three – the BAR man, his assistant and an ammunition carrier; and seven riflemen. Of these last, two were designated as scouts. The German squad or *Gruppe* underwent particularly significant changes over time. Interwar German training literature, such as Zimmermann's *Die Soldatenfiebel*, regarded the squad as composed of two sub-sections: the machine gun *Trupp* (squad) and the riflemen of the *Schützentrupp* (rifle squad). By 1939 it had been realized that close integration was tactically most effective, and the distinction was abandoned. The wartime *Gruppe* was therefore very much a machine gun based unit. The notional complement was ten for much of the war: the NCO squad leader; his deputy; the three-man light machine gun team comprising the firer, his assistant and an ammunition carrier; and five other riflemen. *German Infantry in Action: Minor Tactics* (1941) suggests a scheme of

Nine of the most important hand command signals shown in the German 1941 *Ausbildungsvorschrift für die Infanterie*. (1) Lie down, (2) Go right, (3) Fall in, or Speed up, (4) Dig in, (5) Clear the street – take cover from air attack, (6) Adopt next stage of operational readiness, (7) Ammunition to the front, (8) Area not cleared or impassable, (9) Put on gas masks. (Stephen Bull)

equipment for a model squad. The squad leader is equipped with a machine pistol with six magazines, field glasses, wire cutters, compass, whistle, sun glasses, torch and map case in addition to his basic equipment. Two of the three machine gunners carry pistols, the third a rifle, and the team carry three ammunition boxes between them. The six riflemen carry extras such as an MG tripod mount, grenades and explosive charges as needed. The official German *Ausbildungsvorschrift* adds details such as the carrying of a drum magazine on the LMG, and a belt of armour-piercing ammunition by the second gun number.

An order for the creation of 'new type' divisions came in October 1943. Within these '1944 type' infantry divisions the squad was reduced to nine, the complement of weapons being six rifles, two submachine guns (SMGs), the LMG and a pistol. In the last year of the war there were two further permutations which co-existed for some time. The Volksgrenadier divisions of late 1944 were effectively ordinary infantry divisions following rebuilding and re-organization. In these, although there were still nine men to the squad, these were either 'rifle' or 'submachine gun' squads. In the rifle squads the armament remained the same as previously, while SMG squads were supposed to be armed entirely with that weapon. The exception to the rule was to be one squad within each SMG platoon, which carried three rifles and five SMGs in addition to the LMG and pistol; presumably the idea was to give the SMG units some longer range firepower, but shortage of automatic weapons may also have played a part.

Armoured infantry or Panzergrenadier squads conforming to the 1944 establishment were more powerfully armed, and even more machine gun oriented. Among the 11 men riding in a half-track or truck there were supposed to be no fewer than three LMGs. One of these remained mounted on the transport in the care of the driver and his assistant, who were also supposed to have a rifle and a machine pistol. The other two machine guns moved with the nine-man team when they dismounted. Four men made up the two machine gun teams, with four riflemen and the leader completing the squad.

It should be recalled that at this date a progressive attempt was being made to replace both the K98k single-shot bolt-action rifle and the MP40 submachine gun with the MP43/StG44 series of selective fire semi-/fully automatic weapons, whose designation was changed from 'machine pistol' to 'assault rifle' for essentially political reasons. The final '1945 type' infantry divisional organization would aspire to have roughly half of the infantry armed with the Sturmgewehr assault rifle; theoretically each company was to have two *Sturm* ('storm') platoons. Squads armed with weapons which had the mid-range firepower of semi-automatic rifles, and the close-range impact of SMGs, were potentially revolutionary, but the change was never fully implemented. Sniper rifles were now fixed at six to the company. Presumably some of these were of the G43 semi-automatic variety, a type of weapon already listed in small numbers on the inventory of 'Field Replacement' battalions.

The British section was originally planned to have a reserve, as was explained in *Army Training Memorandum 38* (1941):

Although the scene is posed for the camera, this is a good study of a US infantry squad BAR man – in this case Pte Edward McCabe, from 29th Division, shortly after the capture of Julich on the Roer River in late February 1945. Note a second BAR man at the corner behind him; by 1945 it was not uncommon for a squad to have two automatic riflemen.

The size of the infantry section on the higher war establishment is one corporal and ten men. The battle strength of the section is one corporal and seven men. The three additional men were provided by the higher establishment to ensure that the basic strength of one corporal and seven men can be maintained during the absence of personnel due to sickness, leave and other causes. In battle the section should not exceed one corporal and seven men; the additional men may be employed on working parties and other duties.

An interesting picture of the ideal eight-man fighting section and its equipment is drawn in the *Light Machine Gun* manual (1942):

Section commander, with machine carbine [Thompson SMG] and six magazines, two Bren magazines, wire cutters, 'matchet' [machete] or knife, and whistle; weight carried, 65lb. [Typically the corporal would also carry a mapcase and torch.]

No.1 Rifleman, sniper rifle, 50 rounds, bayonet, four Bren magazines; weight, 61lb

No.1 Bomber, rifle, 50 rounds, bayonet, one Bren magazine, two No.36 grenades, two smoke grenades; weight, 60lb

No.2 Rifleman, rifle, 50 rounds, bayonet, four Bren magazines; weight, 61lb

No.2 Bomber, rifle, 50 rounds, bayonet, three Bren magazines, two No.36 grenades; weight, 60lb

Second-in-command, rifle, 50 rounds, bayonet, two Bren magazines, two smoke grenades; weight, 65lb

No.1 Bren, Bren gun, four Bren magazines plus 50 rounds, spare parts wallet; weight, 75lb

No.2 Bren, rifle, 50 rounds, bayonet, four Bren magazines in two 'utility' pouches; weight, 63lb. [Oddly, the Bren No.2's 'holdall' with spare barrel and cleaning tools is not listed – this would add about another 12lb to his load.]

Such an arrangement was intended as a guide, to be modified for specific tasks. Nevertheless, it shows a section of only eight carrying a total of 1,250 cartridges, and eight grenades. The majority of the ammunition is ready to be fed to the LMG. Interestingly, the average weight carried is 62lb, or a fractionally heavier load than the textbook soldier of 1914.

By 1944 the formal distinction between 'riflemen' and 'bombers', with its echoes of World War I, had disappeared, and *Infantry Training Part VIII: Fieldcraft, Battle Drill, Section and Platoon Tactics* (1944) lists the section as ten strong:

Section commander, Sten SMG and five magazines, two grenades, wire cutters, 'matchet' and whistle

German soldiers readying their MG34 squad light machine gun, c. 1939. For some reason the No.1 has raised the top cover plate and is repositioning a partly expended belt in the action to bring the next cartridge up against the feed stop. Normally a new belt was simply pulled through the action by its feed tag, without lifting the top cover, and a single crank on the cocking handle made the gun ready for firing. Note that the empty metal clips are still attached – the belt is not made up of 'disintegrating link'. The excellent MG34 was arguably the world's first true 'general-purpose machine gun', equally practical as a bipod-mounted assault weapon, tripod-mounted for sustained fire, and clamped to a vehicle mounting. (Stephen Bull)

No.1–No.6 Riflemen, each with rifle, bayonet, 50 rounds plus one grenade and two Bren magazines in basic pouches, plus 100 rounds in two cotton bandoliers
Second-in-command, with rifle, bayonet, 50 rounds in pouches plus 50-round bandolier, four Bren magazines in utility pouches [At various dates the machete also became part of his load, to clear fields of fire for the Bren.]
No.1 Bren, Bren gun, four Bren magazines, spare parts wallet
No.2 Bren, rifle, bayonet, 50 rounds plus two grenades and one Bren magazine in basic pouches, plus four Bren magazines in utility pouches, plus one 50-round bandolier, spare barrel holdall.

The total of small arms ammunition is thus 2,260 rounds, plus ten grenades. The intention was that when opportunity offered, the Bren No.2 would move around the riflemen, collecting their Bren magazines and handing out empty ones, which the riflemen would refill from their extra bandoliers. In the late stages of the war it was not unknown for the section to carry two Brens. The burdens had increased all round; in practice there was no set limit to the extra weight of ammunition, grenades and bombs for the platoon mortar which the infantryman might have to carry into the line, and by 1944 the section also carried up to five large General Service shovels and two picks. This increase in personnel and the equipment they carried was particularly marked in the 'assault' divisions detailed to make the initial landings in Normandy on D-Day, but the burdens remained heavy until the end of the war.

WEAPONS

Weaponry was a significant factor in the differences between the minor tactics of the various nationalities. In the US Army the squad was very much a group of riflemen with light support. According to Gen Patton, the M1 Garand semi-automatic rifle with which the majority of GIs were armed was the 'greatest battle implement ever devised'. It was certainly the general issue weapon with the greatest firepower. Using full size .30-cal cartridges loaded in a complete eight-round en bloc clip, it was accurate to about 600 yards and capable of about 30 rounds per minute. The drawbacks were few, and essentially minor: topping up the magazine part way through a clip was not possible, and when the last round was expended the clip itself popped out with a distinctive 'ping' – audible to the enemy if he was close enough. The fumble-fingered loader could also get 'M1 thumb' if he did not remove his digit fast enough when the bolt slammed forward.

The Browning Automatic Rifle (BAR) provided only light support. Weighing just over 20lb, it used the same .30-cal rifle ammunition, and could be fired from the support of its muzzle bipod (although this was often discarded). Theoretically it had a high rate of fire, but it did not have a quick-change barrel, and this lack, plus its 20-round box magazines, limited it in practice to short bursts. The result was an 'automatic rifle' that could be used in a very agile manner, from the hip on the move or even from the shoulder when standing, but it was unusual for it to lay down more than about 60 rounds per minute. Nevertheless, the value placed upon the BAR was underlined by the fact that in many squads a second weapon was carried, a practice that was officially recognized late in the war. Taking the Garand and BAR together, it is clear that the US squad had good firepower, with fairly even distribution throughout the group.

The German MG34, and its MG42 successor to an even greater extent, were genuine multi-role, general-purpose machine guns with high rates of fire. With cyclic rates of 900 and 1,200rpm (MG34 and MG42 respectively) they could fire off a 250-round belt in 30 seconds even in measured bursts, the main limitation being simply the number of belts carried. High rates of fire made engaging fleeting targets and delivering anti-aircraft fire practical propositions. They could fire from a bipod in the light role, and from the hip, sometimes fed from 50- or 75-round 'assault' drums. For sustained fire an excellent tripod mount was provided with telescopic sights, in which case engagements at 3,000 yards were possible. With 13 or more machine guns per infantry company, an effective fire screen could be maintained even if the unit was only at half strength.

The MG42's high rate of fire created a distinctive ripping noise that veteran Allied infantry learned to recognize. Whatever their precise designation, Allied troops tended to refer to German machine guns generically as 'Spandaus' –

US infantry squad and platoon weapons. (1) .30-cal Browning Automatic Rifle M1918A1; (2) .30-cal Garand M1 rifle; (3) .30-cal M1 carbine; (4) .45-cal M3 submachine gun; (5) 60mm M2 mortar; (7) Mk IIA1 fragmentation grenade; (8) Mk IIA1 in the Grenade Projector Adapter that fitted to the rifle muzzle; (9) Mk IIIA2 'offensive' grenade, with a fibreboard rather than a steel casing, relying on the blast effect alone; (10) .45-cal Colt M1911A1 semi-automatic pistol. (Mike Chappell © Osprey Publishing Ltd)

probably because during World War I many machine guns had been made at the Spandau arsenal and bore that name stamped into their metalwork. The name spread unease, as Capt Alistair Borthwick of 5th Seaforth Highlanders recalled:

> There was something much too personal about a Spandau. It did not aim at an area: it aimed at you, and its rate of fire was prodigious. It had a vindictive sound. Each burst began with an odd hiccup before getting into its stride, so that the crack of the first round was distinct and all the others ran together like the sound of tearing calico. Their pup-turrrr, pup-turrrr was the most distinctive noise on any battlefield…

One who heard the sound of distant German machine guns firing short bursts high over his head thought the sound reminiscent of hundreds of crickets.

British Commandos had a training exercise during which various weapons were fired to attune the ear for identification. An official army film, *Under Fire*, gave some hint of the noises of modern battle. (US accounts talk of a number of distinctive types of weapon sound: the swishing noise of mortar bombs, which was like 'passing telephone poles in a fast moving automobile', and the dreadful

The soldier's best friend – his rifle. This German soldier is cleaning his five-shot, bolt-action K98k, which remained the most numerous arm available to the Wehrmacht despite increasing issues of automatic weapons; total K98k production is thought to have been well in excess of ten million. (Stephen Bull)

'Screaming Meemie' or Nebelwerfer multiple rocket launcher. The '88', by contrast, had a 'peculiar whine' – like the scream of a madwoman, so it was said.) Sound sensitivity was useful; but there are recorded instances when US Rangers, for example, used captured weapons only to come under fire from their own side.

Compared to the veritable hail of bullets that the German machine guns could put down, the standard K98k rifle was a relatively modest contributor to the firefight. It featured the classic Mauser bolt action with a fixed five-round magazine: that is, after each shot the firer had to work a bolt-like lever to eject the empty case and feed another cartridge up into the chamber, so it was not usually fired at a rate of much more than ten aimed rounds per minute. Given that the *Gruppe* was usually smaller than the US squad, and that the MP40 or any other submachine guns available were essentially short range, the picture is of high firepower very unevenly distributed.

In terms of distribution of firepower the British section lay somewhere between the two extremes. The Bren gun was very accurate at normal battle ranges and weighed only slightly more than the BAR, but had a quick-change barrel and took 30-round box magazines. It was therefore almost as handy as a BAR, but capable of a greater concentration of fire. As a position weapon it was not capable of the annihilating curtain laid down by the belt-fed MG34 and MG42, since its cyclic rate of fire was 30 to 50 per cent slower, and changing magazines slowed it further. While it could be tripod-mounted, and with virtually the same muzzle velocity it was capable of comparable maximum range, the tripod and sights were much less sophisticated and gave less accuracy.

British thinking was that the Bren was the heart of the section, around which much of the action would revolve. As early as 1937 the small arms training manual *Application of Fire* was stating that the LMG was the 'main fire-producing weapon', while designated snipers were the skilled shots. The other riflemen were there essentially to augment fire 'in an emergency' or protect the Bren. While the Bren was a robust and popular weapon, the British rimmed .303in cartridge – in contrast to the rimless American .30in and German 7.92mm – put a premium on careful loading of magazines, and could cause feed stoppages if magazines were roughly handled.

The British SMLE (Short Magazine Lee Enfield) No.1 rifle, and its slightly modified No.4 offspring of the later war years, similarly lay somewhere between the K98k and Garand in terms of firepower and efficacy. Both British rifles were bolt-action, but with a ten-round detachable magazine they were capable of 15 or slightly more aimed rounds per minute. Rifle training at the outbreak of war aimed at producing a 'steady and accurate shot', quickness in engaging

A Waffen-SS junior NCO in the Ardennes, wearing the jacket of the 1944 camouflage-printed SS combat uniform and armed with the revolutionary Sturmgewehr 44, capable of selective semi- and fully automatic fire; note the large curved magazine pouches. The key to this new 'assault rifle', planned to take the place of both the K98k and the MP40, was an intermediate 'short' cartridge less powerful than the existing 7.92mm rifle round but more powerful than the 9mm pistol ammunition used in the submachine gun. This sequence of photos taken at Poteau on 18 December 1944 shows men of 2. Kompanie, SS-PzGren Regt 1 from Kampfgruppe Hansen, around vehicles abandoned earlier by the US 14th Cavalry. (Stephen Bull)

unpredictable and fleeting targets, and – perhaps most significantly – 'a handyman with the rifle, able to fire bursts [sic] of five to ten rounds at a rapid rate.' Reloading was practised 'in the shoulder', that is with the rifle still levelled and aimed toward the target; and in an army with a strong musketry tradition, practised men took pride in their rapid aimed fire, sometimes working a well-eased bolt with thumb and forefinger and the trigger with the second finger. Obviously the bolt-action Enfields, reloaded with the thumb from five-round 'stripper' clips, could never compete with the much more modern semi-automatic Garand in terms of volume fire. The overall result was a British rifle squad centred on the LMG, with considerable flexibility, but less concentrated firepower in absolute terms than either the German or US equivalents.

The SMG, or 'machine carbine' in British official literature, was commonly issued to section commanders, and on a larger scale in certain formations (e.g., as already mentioned, in German Volksgrenadier divisions). The British Sten and German MP38 and 40 were similar in that they were 9mm fully automatic weapons with 32-round box magazines, accurate to about 50 yards. In detail there were significant differences. The Sten was as cheap and light as possible – as crude as a piece of cheap plumbing, but simple for even a novice to assemble and dismantle. The side-mounted magazine could be clumsy, but had the significant advantage that it was easy to use lying down. The German MP38/40 series was a much more refined piece of work, machined to high standards rather than welded up from cheap steel pressings; but it too was best fired in very short bursts to maximize accuracy and avoid jams, and its bottom-mounted magazine made prone firing awkward. British weapons training in 1944 – of which 'the sole objective' was to 'teach all ranks the most efficient way of handling their weapons in order to kill the enemy' – stressed the SMG's value in street fighting and other enclosed environments at ranges under 100 yards. Firing was taught in short bursts and single shots. The SMG was at its best in circumstances where the enemy 'may appear suddenly at close range and in different directions, and can be attacked immediately by fire from the shoulder without using the sights, or from the waist'.

SMGs were not standard issue to the ordinary US infantry squad, but were used by specialists and special forces. The .45in US Thompson and M3 'grease gun' had great stopping power, but were at opposite ends of the scale in weight,

GERMAN 5CM LIGHT MORTAR TEAM, 1940–43

Issued on a scale of one per platoon, the leichte Granatwerfer 36 was a 5cm smoothbore mortar. By June 1943 approximately 30,000 of these weapons had been made, and they were very widely used. (1) Two of the three-man lGrW 36 detachment are seen here; the third man, the Truppführer detachment commander, is nearby, observing targets and directing his team. The No.1 holds the levering handgrips to adjust the aim as required; the No.2 loads the bomb. (2) Detail of the pack frame and harness worn by all three members of the team; this example is loaded with the base plate (which could also be carried in one hand by its integral handgrip). (3) A light mortar pit dug according to the 1940 field fortification manual. (Mike Chappell © Osprey Publishing Ltd)

quality, and expense. The elderly Thompson, dating from 1928, was superbly engineered but heavy and costly. The M3 was cheap, simple and never very popular. SMGs were ideal for enclosed spaces, trenches, street fighting and dense vegetation. In open areas they were not of much use: a US 29th Division joke that circulated in 1944 suggested that the M3 would be handy if they happened to find 'a Kraut in a closet'. Hollywood has given a misleading impression of the American usage of SMGs; more reliable is, for instance, the 45th Infantry Division history, which records that in Italy there were just 90 SMGs with the entire division of 14,000-plus men, at a time when the establishment table listed more than 6,500 rifles.

If the SMG's value was limited to close-quarter battle, pistols were the weapon of last resort. Many officers and senior NCOs carried them, but squad leaders had pistols only as a back-up to another arm. Semi-automatic P38 Walther or P08 Luger pistols were standard issue to German machine gunners and mortar men, and were used essentially at point-blank range for self-defence when the main weapon was out of action. The 9mm Parabellum cartridge was common to both, and was a sensible compromise in that it was powerful enough for most purposes, yet not so violent as to be unmanageable even for occasional shooters. Sensibly, German instructions were that 'the pistol is always to be treated as loaded'; the basic posture taught was a two-handed grip, with the muzzle pointed downwards to the front unless actually firing. Undoubtedly one of the best combat pistols was the .45in US M1911A1 ('Army Colt'), which combined excellent stopping power with the speed of the semi-automatic action and a seven-round box magazine.

The British battalion *Provisional War Equipment Table* of September 1941 shows that each rifle company was entitled to five issue .38in No.2 revolvers, with a further 22 at company headquarters; many officers also possessed privately purchased alternatives. Semi-automatic 9mm Brownings also saw significant use by special forces. While acknowledging that its use was rare, British training literature stated that the pistol, used with 'cunning, initiative and determination', was handy for close-quarter fighting in enclosed environments such as buildings, woods and trench systems. Although it was very occasionally possible to hit something at greater distance, under battle conditions the pistol – particularly the .38in revolver – was normally useless at more than 25 yards, and required considerable talent and practice (rare among infantrymen) to hit a man-sized target consistently even at that range. Except when firing from cover men were not taught to use the sights, but to point and shoot instinctively – commonly, two swift shots at a time.

SQUAD TACTICS

OFFENSIVE TACTICS

The basic aggressive squad tactics of all nations were devised with similar ends in mind: they were solutions to the problem of how to advance by means of fire and movement, and dislodge the enemy from his position. The achievement of these aims was combined with a desire to minimize casualties, while maintaining unit effectiveness and control. The specifics varied with arms, numbers and the subtleties of doctrine, but there were obvious similarities in method.

The German squad would play its part by winning the *Feuerkampf* or firefight, and occupying key positions. It was enjoined to remain well concealed unless active in the firefight or advancing to contact, but never to hesitate on the battlefield so as to become 'mere targets'. The machine gun team and the rifles were not separate entities, but part and parcel of the *Gruppe* even though the men would generally be firing at will. Victory was likely to go to the side achieving the most concentrated rapid fire on target. Usually troops were instructed to hold their fire until 600 yards or closer. Even then only large targets would be engaged; individuals would not normally be shot at until within 400 yards.

When moving on the battlefield the German squad had two main formations. Advancing in the *Reihe* or loose single-file formation, the squad leader took the lead, followed by the machine gunner and his assistants; these were followed by the riflemen, with the assistant squad leader bringing up the rear. The *Reihe* was highly practical for moving along tracks, presented a small target from the front, and allowed the squad leader to take decisions, directing the squad as needed. In some circumstances the machine gun could be deployed while the remainder were held back. In all instances the men were to take advantage of terrain, keeping behind contours and cover, and rushing across exposed areas when alternatives were lacking. As Wilhelm Necker observed in *The German Army of Today* (1943), loose formation was important to 'avoid losses', and 'clustering' around the machine gun was to be avoided, but 'connection' had to be maintained.

From the *Reihe* the squad could easily be deployed into the *Schützenkette* or skirmish line. With the machine gun deploying on the spot, the riflemen could come up to the right, left or both sides, bringing their weapons to bear. The result was a ragged line with the men about five paces apart, taking whatever cover was available. The advance to contact was in bounds from one visible objective to another, with a new objective specified as soon as the leaders had

The march appears casual, but this early war *Propaganda Kompanie* photo shows a German squad advancing in the textbook *Gruppe* in *Reihe* formation – 'squad in column'. Seen here is the machine gun No.1 gunner or *Richtschütze*, followed by his No.2 with the spare barrel case and an ammunition box; the *Gewehrschützen*, riflemen, bring up the rear. (Stephen Bull)

reached the first. Where resistance was serious the advance became fully fledged 'fire and movement', either with a whole squad taking part, or a machine gun team down and firing while others advanced. However, instructions cautioned squad commanders not to open fire with the machine gun until forced to do so by the ground and enemy fire; Weber's 1938 *Unterrichtsbuch* stated that in the assault the machine gun was to open fire 'as late as possible'. The objective of the fire fight was not simply destruction of the enemy, but *Niederkampfen* – to beat down, silence or neutralize them, thus ensuring the success of close assault.

As described in the 1941 manual *German Infantry in Action: Minor Tactics*, the final phases of aggressive squad action were the firefight; advance; the actual assault; and occupation of a position:

> *The Firefight.* The section is the fire unit. When fire has to be opened, the section commander usually opens fire with the LMG only. He directs its fire. When good fire effect is possible and when plenty of cover exists, the riflemen take part early in the fire fight. The majority of riflemen should be in the front line and taking part in the fire fight at the latest when the assault is about to be made. They usually fire independently, unless the section commander decides to concentrate the whole of their firepower on to one target.
>
> *The Advance.* The section works its way forward in a loose formation. Within the section the LMG usually forms the spearhead of the attack. The longer the riflemen follow the LMG in narrow, deep formation, the longer will the machine guns in the rear be able to shoot past the section.
>
> *The Assault.* The section commander takes any opportunity that presents itself to carry out an assault and does not wait for orders to do so. He rushes the whole section forward into the assault, leading the way himself. Before and during the assault the enemy must be engaged by all weapons at the maximum rate of fire. The LMG No.1 takes part in the assault, firing on the move. With a cheer, the section attempts to break the enemy's resistance, using hand grenades, machine pistols, rifles, pistols and entrenching tools. After the assault the section must reorganize quickly.
>
> *Occupation of a position.* When occupying a position

The method for deploying the German squad column into the extended order or *Kette* ('chain') formation for action to the front, and the same manoeuvre to one flank, as depicted in *German Infantry in Action: Minor Tactics* (1941). Neither the squad column nor the chain are rigid lines, but loose tactical deployments. (Stephen Bull)

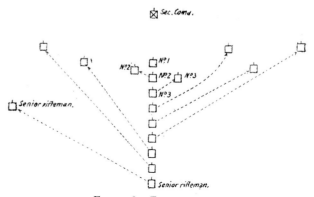

FIGURE 3.—EXTENDED LINE.

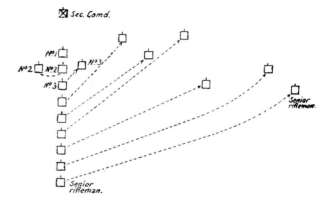

the riflemen group themselves in twos and threes around the LMG in such a way that they are within voice control of the section commander.

The *Ausbildungsvorschrift* adds significant additional colour on the assault phase, first noting that it is 'self confidence' in overcoming the enemy that makes the soldier successful in close combat. The LMG assault posture is specified as with the hand around the pistol grip, with the weapon couched under the right arm and held close to the body. The left hand clutches the feet of the bipod, so as to hold the muzzle down on firing, or ready to set up the weapon on arrival at the position. Riflemen are also enjoined to indulge in assault firing, the best method being to cant the rifle on to its left-hand side at the hip, with bayonet fixed, and to let fly at just 5–10 yards range. The soldier then wades in, able to use both arms to full effect in any ensuing hand-to-hand fighting with bayonet and butt.

Although grenades were best thrown from behind cover they could also be used on the move. The soldier was instructed to grasp his rifle in the left hand and the grenade in the right, using the fingers of the hand holding the rifle to

Men of the German 71st Infantry Division moving up to the front in trucks. The 71st fought in France in 1940, but was later destroyed in Russia; this photograph was taken by Johannes Heinrichs, listed missing at Stalingrad in January 1943. Even in Panzergrenadier units, armoured personnel carriers were in short supply, and were usually only available for the first battalion of each regiment. The great mass of the unmotorized infantry moved longer distances by railway or truck as available; otherwise they marched on foot, usually accompanied by horse wagons for much of their heavy gear. (Stephen Bull)

pull the fuse cord at the opportune moment. In circumstances where showers of grenades were needed the order 'Handgranaten!' from the squad leader would prompt the men to throw.

＊　　＊　　＊

Basic American squad formations as described in the *Rifle Company* manual of 1942 were remarkably similar to the German equivalents. The US 'squad column' saw the squad strung out, with the leader and BAR man to the fore, and the remainder in file to the rear to a length of roughly 60 paces. Such a formation was 'easily controlled and maneuvered', and 'suitable for crossing areas exposed to artillery fire, for utilizing narrow covered routes, and for movement in woods, fog, smoke, and darkness.'

The 'skirmish line' was similar to the *Schützenkette*. The squad was deployed in a rough line about 60 paces long; the skirmish line was of benefit in bringing all weapons to bear, and useful for short rapid dashes, but not so easy to control. An alternative was the 'squad wedge', suitable for ready movement in any direction and when emerging from cover or a defile. More vulnerable than a skirmish line, wedges were best used beyond the range of effective rifle fire. Once under fire the US squad was taught to advance either by short rushes, or by 'creep' and 'crawl', taking advantage of cover. Although it may only rarely have been practicable, a detailed scheme of 'fire distribution' formed part of squad training for the firefight:

Each member of the squad fires his first shot on that portion of the target corresponding generally to his position in the squad. He then distributes his next shots right and left of his first shots, covering that part of the target on which he can deliver accurate fire without having to change position. The amount of the target which one man can cover will depend upon the range and position of the firer. Frequently each man will be able to cover the target with accurate fire; this should be done whenever possible. Fire is not limited to points within the target known to contain an enemy; on the contrary, all men space their shots so that no portion of the target remains unhit. Automatic riflemen fire bursts of about five rounds at the slow cyclic rate (in about one second). This

The US 'diamond' eight-man patrol formation, from the official 1944 manual. One man of each of the leading pairs observes for ground targets while his buddy scans trees for snipers. At the rear, one man looks backwards while the other covers his flank, and checks the movements of the patrol leader. The patrol is well spread out, but visual contact is maintained. (Stephen Bull)

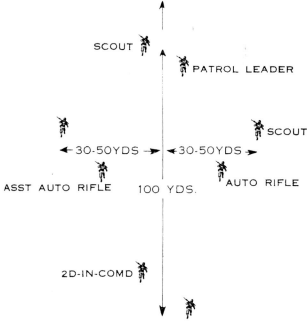

method of fire distribution is employed without command. The squad leader observes the fire to insure that the entire target is kept under fire. If other targets appear, he announces such changes in fire distribution as are necessary.

Even if the niceties were ignored, the implication is inescapable: the US infantryman was taught to treat the enemy position as an area target, to be evenly filled with lead whether or not specific individuals could be seen and hit. Frequently this is exactly what was done; it was definitely no mere 'theory'. A letter of instruction issued in April 1944 by Gen Patton to his unit commanders in US Third Army specifically stated that 'If you cannot see the enemy, you can at least shoot the place where he is apt to be.' According to Patton's opinion fire was better aimed short than long in cases of doubt, since 'ricochets make nastier sounds and wounds'.

For the textbook attack, US squad leaders were enjoined to give specific orders to individuals and as much information as possible about what was intended. The squad would then move forward, 'fire and movement' being employed when 'fire action' became necessary to cover the advance. At the first firing position the squad attempted to gain superiority of fire over the enemy – this being achieved 'by subjecting the enemy to fire of such accuracy and intensity that his fire becomes inaccurate or so reduced in volume as to be ineffective'. In order to maintain this superiority it would often be necessary for some squad members to remain in position, putting down large volumes of fire, while others moved forward to new positions, from which they in turn would take up the firefight. Suitable cover, including rises and depressions, could allow short moves at small hazard, but open areas would need longer rushes prepared by commensurately greater applications of fire. The BAR man was best placed to support the advance from a flank, husbanding his fire to the needs of the situation so as not to exhaust his ammunition prematurely.

Again, Patton's Third Army instructions of 1944 had an even more aggressive tone, and encouraged even heavier use of fire. It was to be seen as integral to movement: 'Infantry must move in order to close with the enemy. It must shoot in order to move.' Moreover, 'marching fire' was to be encouraged as the infantry went in, since it increased confidence and unsettled the enemy. 'To halt under fire is folly. To halt under fire and not fire back is suicide. Move forward under fire.'

In some circumstances, especially where a US squad was acting independently to seize an enemy position, the squad leader might decide to fight as sub-teams. 'Team Able', comprising the two rifleman scouts, would locate the enemy; 'Team Baker', with the BAR and three rifles, would put down fire; and 'Team Charlie', the five remaining riflemen and the squad leader, carried out the actual assault. In such conditions the squad leader would have his work cut out – leading a specific part of the squad, communicating with the platoon leader, or moving from man to man to give instruction or encouragement. Here the assistant squad leader would come into his own, leading whatever part of the squad was not in the immediate control of the leader. The actual assault was to be delivered at 'the earliest moment that promises success and without regard to the progress of adjacent squads.' At this moment the squad was to advance, bayonets fixed and dodging from cover to cover, to move 'rapidly toward the enemy and fire as they advance at areas known or believed to be occupied by hostile personnel. Such fire is usually delivered from the standing position and is executed at a rapid rate.' On taking the enemy position the squad leader would reorganize the squad to defend, or resume the advance.

*   *   *

British methods, as outlined in *Infantry Training* (1944), show significant improvement in both theory and practice since the start of the war. Formations were to depend 'chiefly on the ground and the type of enemy fire to be encountered.' Five formations were recognized: 'blobs', single file, loose file, irregular arrowhead and extended line. The term 'blob', first used in this context in 1917, now referred to ad hoc gatherings of between two and four men, hidden as best they were able, in a manner calculated to give concealment and control. Ordinary single file was fit only in certain circumstances, as for example when the section was advancing behind a hedgerow, and was not good for producing fire. Loose file denoted a slightly more scattered line, suitable for rapid movement and control, but vulnerable. Arrowheads allowed rapid deployment to either flank, and were difficult to spot from the air. Extended line was the ideal for the final assault, but had drawbacks in terms of control, and was vulnerable if fired on from a flank. In all formations except 'blobs' it was expected that intervals of about five yards would be maintained between individuals.

Chillingly, attacks were to be launched not just to take ground, 'but also to kill all enemy holding that ground.' Covering fire on the way in was seen as essential, and the transition between fire and physical assault was to be seamless: if an interval occurred the enemy would be able to start shooting again. As the manual put it, 'remember that if the enemy is dug in, covering fire seldom kills him; it merely makes him keep his head down so that he is unable to shoot back.' As the prime fire producer the Bren gun was critical to the advance to contact, and was best worked as far as possible around a flank so as to threaten the enemy rear. This had three advantages: ensuring 'the extermination of the enemy';

preventing enemy reinforcement; and the psychological impact of a threatened encirclement, which might induce retirement or surrender.

BRITISH SECTION FLANK ATTACK, 1944–45

A typical British 'battle drill' for attacking an enemy position from the flank. The red arrows indicate the movement of the 'Bren group', the blue arrows that of the 'rifle group' – the remainder of the section led by the NCO armed with a Sten gun. As soon as the advancing section comes under fire from the enemy-held copse the Bren group deploys under cover (red 1). The riflemen also drop to fire from cover. The section leader assesses the situation and orders a flanking manoeuvre. Taking advantage of the covering fire from the Bren group, he leads the rifle group in working its way through cover around one side (blue 1). Once the riflemen have reached their second position behind the enemy flank (blue 2), the Bren group can also move round to a position where it can give effective support to the assault. When the Bren group is in position to open fire from the flank (red 2), smoke bombs are dropped by the platoon 2in mortar to mask the rifle group's assault. The rifle group now dashes forward to the assault. Once the rifle group is fully engaged the Bren group can no longer support them safely, and so moves rapidly to its third position behind the enemy (red 3), in order to cut off any who try to disengage. With the attack successfully concluded, the section re-forms well beyond the enemy position (blue 3) to resume the advance.
(Brian Delf © Osprey Publishing Ltd)

Commonly the British section would break into two for the attack. The 'Bren group' – the two-man Bren team and the second-in-command – formed one element, and the main body of riflemen with the section commander the other. The larger group with the leader bore main responsibility for closing with the enemy, and would advance at the double when under threat. In the event of coming under effective fire the riflemen would go over to fully fledged 'fire and movement'. Falling to the ground 'instantly as if shot', the men were ordered to crawl rapidly sideways or forward to a good firing position, taking rapid aim and firing independently until the section leader shouted the command to stop. In some circumstances it was also deemed necessary for the Bren group to advance by bounds to a position where they could pour in fire, preferably at an angle of about 90 degrees to the main attack. In this case the two groups would give each other covering fire alternately. The final rush on to the enemy position was to be made by the riflemen 'firing from the hip as they go in'.

A more complex variation on the theme was to allow full-strength sections to form three groups, thereby achieving the maximum tactical dispersion. In this scheme one man in each sub-section took his orders from the leader, reducing the burden of command. The way this was supposed to work was a remarkable statement of the group ethos of comradeship: 'Groups are formed from friends as far as possible, in order that friends keep together and fight together. One man

A British patrol moves briskly across an open space in a wrecked Italian town abandoned by the Germans. Such patrols became routine as the Allies pursued the withdrawing enemy, and it took concentration not to relax security. These soldiers have dumped their web equipment but have plenty of firepower. The patrol leader, with a Thompson SMG, is followed by a rifleman, another Tommy-gunner and an LMG team with a Bren and a rifle.

in each group which is not commanded by an NCO acts as leader. He should be chosen because of his natural gifts of leadership and because the rest of the group look to him as leader. This leader can be changed whenever considered necessary.'

The assault was horribly frightening but often exhilarating, almost to the extent of temporary insanity. The most successful infantrymen were often those who succeeded in entirely suspending their view of the enemy as fellow humans, and functioned almost automatically according to a long-familiar choreography of combat. Once raised to the frenzy of battle, disengagement was by no means easy. Pte Dennis Bowen of the 5th East Yorkshires remembered of Normandy:

> If a German soldier appeared everybody fired at him. It was no bother, we didn't think of them as human beings … everybody is shouting and screaming and suddenly you see this figure. In the excitement you fire at him … a man at 100 or 150 yards is an awful big target … Some Germans were trying to surrender but in the excitement we fired at them before they had any chance… I don't think our lads were saying, 'Well, I don't care if that man wants to surrender'… I don't think that was in anyone's mind. I think it was the excitement of constantly stuffing fresh ammunition into the magazines and blazing away. A lot of men were just firing from the hip as we walked forward… There was a lot of small arms fire, more than you would think.

DEFENSIVE TACTICS

German squad defensive methods stressed the importance of integration with larger plans, and the principles of posts scattered in depth. The individual *Gruppe* was expected to dig-in on a frontage of 35 or 45 yards, this being the maximum that a squad leader could effectively oversee in a defending battle. Major landmarks such as single trees or crests were best shunned as too attractive to enemy fire. During the digging one member of the squad was to stand sentry, preventing surprise from ground or air. Gaps between squads might be left, although covered by fire. Key to the defence was the location of the machine gun, which would be given several alternative positions, perhaps 50 or more yards apart, that were identified from the outset. It would cover longer range targets, while the riflemen – who might well be held further back – were concerned mainly with sweeping the terrain at close and very close range.

The usual deployment would see the men of the squad in pairs in foxholes, trenches or ditches, posted close enough to communicate with their partner. These little sub-section nests would be slightly separated, echeloned, or at different levels, thus decreasing the effect of enemy fire. In the event that the enemy attack did not materialize immediately, the second phase of construction would see the digging of trenches behind the main line in which much of the squad could be kept back under cover until needed. Good camouflage was complemented by the avoidance of any obvious movement to attract enemy observation. The defensive firefight was commenced by the machine gun at effective range, riflemen remaining concealed until the enemy attacked, at which all were to open fire regardless of cover. Hand grenades falling on the position were to be dealt with either by the men diving away into cover, or by picking up the grenade and throwing it back. The latter was obviously a particularly dangerous game: US sources speak of casualties minus a hand or foot where grenades had been tackled with a return throw or kick.

In the latter part of the war there was particular emphasis on resistance to armour. Ideal defensive positions were therefore on a 'tankproof obstacle'; equipped with at least one AT weapon; capable of all round defence, and having artillery support directed by a forward observer. Active patrols with AT weapons, as small as a single squad, were to be encouraged to intercept enemy tanks probing a defence.

The most basic and perhaps most typical of all hasty defensive positions on the battlefield: a German soldier takes advantage of the cover and concealment of a natural earth bank in heathland, rapidly improved by a few moments' work with the entrenching tool. He waits with his rifle at the ready, and 'egg' and 'stick' grenades laid at hand for close defence. (Stephen Bull)

Some squads would be detailed to act as *Vorposten* or outposts beyond the main line. Acting as defensive 'door bells', they might also contain observers and listening posts. Such details were given advance orders as to what to do in specific eventualities, for example when to fall back on the main line. The job of the *Vorposten* was made slightly more secure by preplanned artillery support, numerous dummy positions to distract attention, and identified safe routes away from the front. According to the 1943 British publication *Regimental Officer's Handbook of the German Army*, advanced posts were commonly within range of close support weapons such as mortars and infantry guns, and were thus to be found within about 2,000 yards of a main position.

*   *   *

In defence the American squad was usually seen as playing a part in the overall plan laid for the platoon. The duty of the squad leader was to explain the larger picture, and position his squad, starting with the BAR. Generally the men would go prone, at least 5 yards apart, to cover predetermined sectors of fire. If time allowed, the squad would then dig-in, camouflage the position and clear any obstructions in the field of fire. The squad leader would then prepare rough sketches of the sector for reference both by the platoon commander and himself. Under bombardment the squad was supposed to take cover in its holes, peering out to adopt firing positions as soon as the shelling or bombing ceased. No shooting would be allowed until the enemy troops had approached within 500 yards, and then in accordance with the squad leader's directions. In the event of enemies overrunning the position, 'they are driven out by fire, grenades, and the bayonet.'

British instructions for defence were similar, with the section commander placing and concealing the men, taking the trouble to view the potential fields of fire 'with the eye close to the ground'. Weapons pits or 'hasty' defences were dug whenever possible, but *Infantry Training* (1944) placed particular stress on the value of 'improvement of natural cover'. Banks, hedges and ditches were to be used as a matter of course. Sunken roads and railway cuttings could also be useful, but had a tendency to become 'shell traps', so were best used with excavations dug into the bank nearest the enemy. Walls and rocks were also possible cover, but had the potential disadvantage of splintering, or being obvious aiming points. The shell hole could be regarded as an instant weapons pit, but overcrowding was to be avoided, and when possible the shell holes were to be linked to provide communication.

FIELD WORKS

On battlefields swept by shells and machine gun fire there were really only two tactical options: swift and purposeful movement, or staying still under cover. Given the ingrained experience of World War I, it is not surprising that the British *Infantry Training* manual of 1937 stressed the importance of solid entrenchment, with 'extensive digging between platoons and company localities in both forward and reserve areas', concealment being a useful but secondary consideration. 'Effect before cover' was also a maxim that survived in official German manuals until at least 1941. Yet the speed of the movement of armies in the early stages of the war, and the destruction that could be brought down upon obvious fixed defences, soon led to a distinct change in emphasis. As the much improved 1944 British *Infantry Training* manual observed:

> An outstanding lesson of the present war is that, if their positions are accurately located, defending troops at the point of attack will be neutralized by overwhelming air, artillery or mortar bombardment. If, however, their positions remain undetected, the bombardment will be ineffective provided that their weapons slits are designed to afford reasonable protection.

For the infantry company in the field 'reasonable' protection was usually the 'foxhole' or 'weapons pit'. Although some early manuals show these

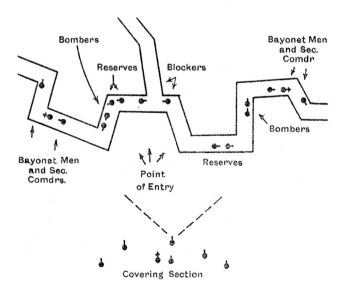

61

being joined into full-blown trench systems, in practice most remained small and – unless part of a major defensive line – were not normally expanded beyond squad- or platoon-sized battle positions. As the 1942 *Instructor's Handbook* explained, the weapons pit was 'comparatively safe against all forms of fire, except a direct hit from a shell or bomb.' This could be demonstrated to trainee soldiers by getting them to fire against dummies, petrol tins or balloons in dug-in positions, which would seldom be damaged. Nevertheless, it had to be remembered that any bombardment or suppressive fire would usually be followed by an attack. Therefore defenders of field works had to be trained to 'bob up at once' as soon as fire ceased, to take advantage of the last hundred or so yards of comparatively open ground the enemy had to cross.

According to Weber's *Unterrichtsbuch für Soldaten*, the ideal *Schützenloch* or rifle pit for a standing soldier was an excavation about 4ft 7in deep. It was shaped with a slight lip to provide an elbow rest, and a small deeper sump hole at the base to give some drainage. A small niche provided a handy ammunition store.

Day and night defensive deployments of US rifle platoons, from the manual of 1942. Note how the platoons are moved closer at night, and may be moved out of cover during the hours of darkness. (Stephen Bull)

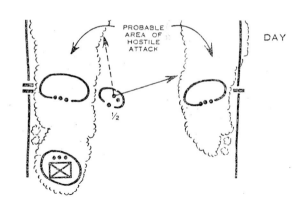

DAY LOCATIONS, SHOWING DISTRIBUTION OF RIFLE PLATOONS IN DEFENSE

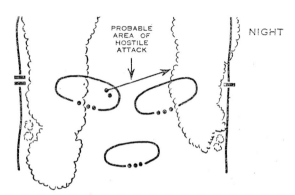

NIGHT LOCATIONS, SHOWING DISTRIBUTION OF RIFLE PLATOONS IN DEFENSE

The infantryman would peg his folded *Zeltbahn* or shelter-quarter to the rear of the hole in such a way that it could be pulled over the aperture to provide both concealment and protection against the elements.

A more elaborate machine gun nest or *MG-Stellung* could be dug in the field by two men, working to enlarge a hole while concealed by a camouflage net. The resulting position was about four times the size of a rifle pit, and was ideally provided with a flooring of brushwood or other means of keeping the floor well drained. Holes dug horizontally into the face of the excavation nearest to the enemy provided the crew with a sheltering *Fuchsloch* or foxhole, a munition store, and an *MG-Unterschlupf* – literally a 'machine gun refuge', a lined oblong cavity in which the gun could be stowed during bombardment or heavy rain. The somewhat simpler advice of the *Ausbildungsvorschift* could be summed up in relatively few words: 'deep and narrow' was best against artillery and aircraft.

Following experience in Russia in 1941/42, the 1942 German *Taschenbuch für den Winterkrieg* ('Pocket Book for Winter Warfare'), acknowledged that a totally different system of cover had to be used on ground frozen hard. Here logs could be cut and bound together in low walls to form a three-sided enclosure, pierced by one or more weapons slots. Drifting snow provided some additional protection but, more importantly, served to make the position difficult to see. White cloths or a *Zeltbahn* covered with snow completed the illusion. Similar effects could be created with sandbags sunk into holes dug down through the snow and placed directly on the frozen ground.

The ideal British weapons pit of 1944 was described as 'designed to hold two or three men and adapted to suit each particular site. Pits should be two feet wide at the bottom with sides as near vertical as the soil will allow … there should be no parapet or parados, all spoil being removed and well hidden, and elbow rests provided where needed by digging. Silhouetting of the occupants' heads should be avoided by siting against a suitable background.' Reverse slope positions were particularly advantageous, as they made works difficult to see and tended to improve drainage. Care was to be taken that pits were not betrayed by obvious paths; a 'track plan' made in advance would lead defenders in by discreet routes, perhaps around field boundaries or through hedges and ditches. The best pits were those that could be well revetted, using stakes and pegs to anchor the structure into the surrounding ground. Nevertheless, in cases of emergency or during a steady advance it was recognized that 'hasty defences' could be dug, which obtained their concealment by position rather than systematic removal or

Bild 63.

Recommended method of concealing German trenches with timber, brushwood and snow, from *Taschenbuch für den Winterkrieg* (November 1942). (Stephen Bull)

covering of the spoil. These improvisations would begin with 'the smallest hole in the ground that will give the occupants protection, and from which they can use their weapons.' It was perfectly feasible to start with a hole that catered for men in a sitting position, to be improved and deepened at a later stage.

In practice there were variations. In Normandy the 5th Bn, Seaforth Highlanders, constructed customized 'doovers' – a term borrowed from the Australians in the Western Desert, meaning a covered slit trench or foxhole. During a static phase of the campaign early in July, Capt Alastair Borthwick recalled:

> The firm clay of Normandy made good digging, and we soon learned to make ourselves snug. Although the basic model was only a pit six feet long by two and a half feet wide by four or five feet deep with a sheet of corrugated iron and a heap of earth on top, there were many things a man could do to improve it. There were

BRITISH 'WEAPON SLITS'

(1) This fully revetted 'two-man weapon slit' was illustrated in *Infantry Training* (March 1944), but in practice it was limited to units in home training. The ends of the pit are 4ft 6in deep from the parapet, with a 2ft drainage sump between them; solid stakes, braced with guy wires to tent pegs, give resilience, support the revetting of hurdles or brushwood, and allow the erection of overhead cover. Such elaborate constructions took time to build, and were very rarely seen on the more fluid battlefronts of 1943–45. (2) Typical of those later battlefields was the 'three-man V-shaped weapon slit', also 4ft 6in deep, and long and wide enough to accommodate the two-man Bren team and the section second-in-command. If there were time, all effort would be devoted to improvising some sort of overhead cover against mortar and artillery fragments. (Mike Chappell © Osprey Publishing Ltd)

doovers lined with parachute silk, doovers with electric light, mosquito-proof doovers with face veils over the entrances. Doors were lifted from their hinges and used to strengthen roofs (though some preferred earth-filled wardrobes), and few houses had a shutter left five minutes after the battalion moved into the area.

BRITISH ARMY HOUSE DEFENCE TACTICS

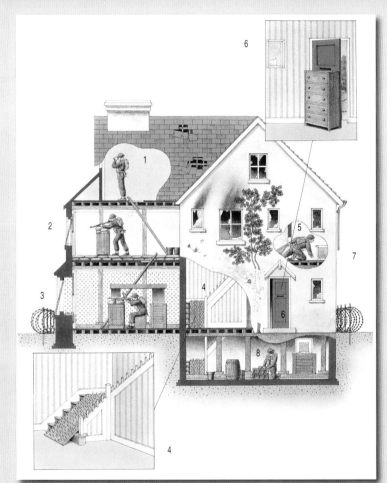

hatchway has been smashed through the floor and a ladder fitted. Windows not needed for fire or observation are blocked with planks, corrugated iron or anti-grenade netting. (3) Ground floor. 'Concertina' rolls of barbed wire all round the house keep the enemy back from the doors and windows, the latter being prepared as above; additional planks with exposed nails discourage climbing in over the window sills. Jammed and propped timbers again reinforce ceiling and floor, and also the lintels of interior doorways. Earth-filled furniture provides protected firing positions. (4) The staircase has the banisters broken away, and the treads and risers covered with nail-studded planks. One narrow gap is left until attack is imminent, then blocked with a last prepared plank. (5) Crawl-holes are knocked through interior partition walls throughout, so defenders can move freely through the house at floor level. The bath is filled with water for emergency use. (6) Ground-level doors to the exterior are barricaded with earth-filled furniture and sandbags, leaving only a narrow gap for observation and fire. (7) Down-pipes and climbing plants are removed above ground floor level, denying attackers any handholds if trying to reach the upper windows. (8) The cellar serves as a protected store for ammunition and other combat supplies. It is reinforced with wooden beams, and the stairway is prepared for blocking with nailed planks. (Brian Delf © Osprey Publishing Ltd)

(1) Attic post, with a few bricks and slates removed to provide loopholes for observation and sniping. (2) Upper floor. The floor and ceiling are reinforced with timber props and arrangements of 'capsills' and 'groundsills' at right angles to the joists; two layers of sandbags are laid over the floor. All window glass has been knocked out and anti-grenade netting fitted. Curtains of hessian or blankets obscure the top halves of the windows. A new

Note that in units which had not served in North Africa the term 'doover' was not current, 'slitters' – for 'slit trenches' – being the common slang.

Where hasty cover was needed the smallest hole or 'scrape' that would give some protection was dug immediately with the personal entrenching tool, which – unlike the large picks or shovels also carried by many British infantry – could be used while lying down or crouching. Failing this, the nearest natural ditch would do; around Anzio in Italy the ditches were never quite deep enough, and the US troops who spent time in them developed a cramped shuffle, long afterwards known as the 'Anzio Slouch'. For the GI in a real hurry instant cover could be blown with explosives. The approved method was to take a half-pound block of TNT, put it into a hole dug about a foot deep, and detonate it. The result was a pit just big enough for immediate requirements. In 1942 US doctrine called for individual foxholes, as providing smaller targets. By 1944 it was judged that the psychological isolation of one-man pits was a weakness, and that a two-man slit (in which one GI could try to rest while his buddy stood guard) was better for morale.

Yet even with American generosity of supplies, technical know-how and the encouragement of company a hole was still a hole, as Pfc Egger of 26th Division

A GI operates the air-cooled .30-cal Browning M1919 machine gun, fed by 250-round fabric belts. In the US infantry organization of 1944 two of these machine guns and three 60mm mortars formed a fourth 'weapons' platoon within each rifle company, its assets normally being dispersed to support the rifle platoons.

recorded of his two-man position in November: 'It was still raining and the water was rising. We kept throwing sods in the hole so we wouldn't be sleeping in water. By the time the leaks were stopped the hole was almost at ground level.' Lt Otts of the 26th recalled the situation a couple of weeks later near Giverycourt:

> The men set about digging two-man foxholes. It was raining as usual, so they improvised covers for them with whatever they could find. But they were far from leakproof; the water seeped in through the walls and the man on guard had to bail continually with his helmet. There was plenty of straw available and that helped to make the holes warmer and drier.

To be fair, Otts described himself as 'allergic to digging', with the result that in some sketchily dug foxholes he would find himself with limbs sticking out of the top. Nevertheless, by winter he was a veteran at the game, and found that snow was to be preferred to rain since it was less wet. Warmth was provided by a generous sandwich of shelter-halves and blankets in the hole, while he jammed on three sets of underwear – two winter and one summer; a sweater, field jacket ('Ike' jacket), combat jacket, two pairs of trousers and socks, gloves, a wool cap and his steel helmet. He drew the line at an overcoat, as being 'too bulky'.

The consequences of not digging-in properly could be catastrophic. Cpl Kenneth Lovell of the Durhams recalled remonstrating with two men who refused to dig deep, and returning later only to find them with 'their heads blasted off'. In Italy an entire heavy weapons company of 36th (Texas) Division paid the price, as Lt Trevor Evans recalled:

> There were bazookas and rifles hanging from the trees… Their faces had turned black and hard… They evidently had started to dig foxholes, but they were only three or four inches deep, and there were C-rations scattered around. My guess was that the battalion commander had felt sorry for them and failed to post security. Many had dug holes along the road where the digging was easier, but it was the wrong thing to do. The German tanks had just sprayed them with machine guns and then dropped their treads down off the road and crushed them in a long line.

THE PLATOON

The recommended formations for US platoon movement, from *Rifle Company* (1942). Left to right: platoon column; line of squads; two squads forward and one back; one squad forward and two back. Distances and intervals between squads and individuals are not to scale; and scouts are not shown. (Stephen Bull)

The platoon was the first level at which a junior officer would be expected to be in command, and at which the bureaucratic demands of record-keeping and contact with higher headquarters might intervene. It was also the first point up from the bottom of the infantry hierarchy at which a light mortar (and in the US Army, a .30-cal LMG) might be issued or attached, as well as – in 1943–45 – a man-portable AT weapon. The presence of several rifle squads within a platoon made possible the use of more complex tactics in which they could be manoeuvred together to achieve an objective.

The US Army platoon of 1944 consisted of three 12-man rifle squads and a 'command group', which included the platoon commander, platoon sergeant (second-in-command), guide sergeant and two messengers; in 1943 it had also

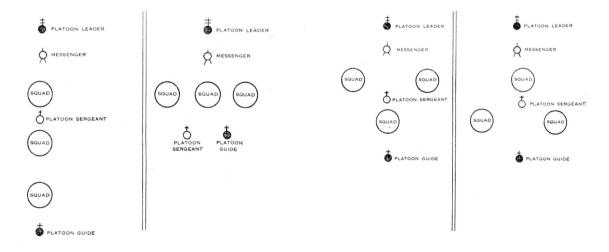

included extra privates detailed to act as replacements. The 41-strong platoon might also have attached to it a 60mm mortar and/or a .30-cal machine gun drawn from the rifle company's separate heavy weapons platoon, each with a three-man crew; and a two-man 2.36in bazooka team from the infantry battalion's AT platoon. An advantage was the presence of radio communication at platoon level in the form of an SCR-536 'handy-talkie'. This battery-powered transmitter/receiver weighed only 5lb, but its maximum range was only 1 mile; otherwise communication with company HQ was by running messenger. Like squads, platoons frequently carried far more firepower than allowed for in regulation 'tables of equipment'. Lt Otts recalled that though low on men, his platoon sometimes had two bazookas attached instead of the regulation one, and anything up to double the prescribed number of BARs. Conversely, the carrying of packs was discouraged in his unit, with necessities stuffed into pockets and pouches and inessentials thrown away.

According to *Rifle Company* (1942), the US platoon had four basic formations in the advance: 'platoon column'; 'line of squads'; 'two forward and one back'; and 'one forward and two back'. In 'platoon column' the formation strung out, one squad behind the next, over about 100 to 150 yards. Easily controlled and manoeuvred through gaps, woods and darkness, the column was vulnerable to fire from the front. 'Line of squads' abreast gave maximum firepower but was difficult to control. This formation was useful for short rushes to cross enemy fire zones that could not be avoided. The other two arrangements, with either one or two squads to the fore and the other/s behind, were intended to provide security to the front and flank while enabling flexible development. For the regulation of movement the platoon leader designated one squad as 'base squad' upon which the others would conform. In all instances it was usual for the platoon commander to lead, with a messenger close at hand, and for the 'guide sergeant' to follow up, preventing straggling and observing the situation on the flanks and rear. Where needed, scouts would be sent ahead, or the platoon commander would carry out his own reconnaissance.

Ideally, attacks were carefully preplanned and the squads briefed in advance. In many instances it was desirable to try to work either a squad or a selected group on to a flank, or close to the target, so as to provide covering fire for the main assault. Frequently one squad was kept in reserve, unless the firepower of all was needed from the outset. Before the attack squads would adopt the desired formation, usually with their scouts thrown out to the front. The platoon would then go forward with the leader seeking to

Original annotated return for II. Zug (second platoon), 10. Kompanie of a German infantry regiment 'in the field' (most likely on the Western Front), dated 1 April 1940. Total 'book' strength is 42 all ranks – one officer, five NCOs and 36 men. However, ten men are *kommandiert* or on detached duty, and seven sick, leaving a service strength of just 25. (Stephen Bull)

10. Kompanie Im Felde, den 1. 4. 19 40

	Off.	Unteroff.	Mannsch.	Sa.
Iststärke :	1	5	36	42
zum Dienst :	1	5	19	25
kommandiert :	-	-	10	10
krank :	-	-	7	7
Urlaub :	-	-	-	-

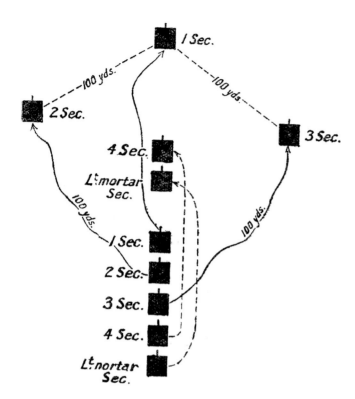

direct his main effort at weak points, on to which the reserve squad could also be brought up. Then:

When the platoon comes under effective small arms fire, further advance is usually by fire and movement. The enemy is pinned to the ground by frontal (and flanking) fire, under cover of which other elements of the platoon manoeuvre forward, using all available cover... In turn the original manoeuvring elements may occupy firing positions and cover the advance.

If resistance was weak the platoon would drive on into the enemy position in the same fashion. Where the enemy had strong positions, or nests to the flank or rear of the objective, it was necessary to build up an 'assaulting force' as close as possible to the point to be attacked. Other men, notably the BAR gunners, could be detached to give covering fire to the assault:

Forming the German platoon 'arrowhead' formation during the advance, from *German Infantry in Action: Minor Tactics* (1941). (Stephen Bull)

The assault may take place either on the orders of the platoon leader or as a part of the general assault ordered by the company or battalion commander. The attacking echelon of the platoon works its way as close as it can get to the hostile position without masking friendly supporting fires... For a platoon assault, the prearranged signal for the lifting of supporting fires is given by the platoon leader. A general assault is delivered at an hour fixed by the company or battalion commander or on his signal. Frequently in the heat of battle the assault is started on the initiative of a squad or even of a few individuals. Wherever and whenever the assault begins, it should receive the immediate cooperation of every individual and unit within sight. When the assault is launched, assault fire may be directed on the defender's position in order to keep it under fire and prevent the enemy from manning his defences.

Wherever possible, upon the capture of the objective the platoon leader was intended to make a quick assessment as to whether it was possible to press on any further. Platoons in the forefront of the attack were not supposed to linger to mop up every last vestige of resistance, this being left to those following up.

*   *   *

The German infantry *Zug* (platoon) had much in common with the US equivalent, although it saw considerable change over time. Under the organization pertaining from 1940 to the end of 1943, the Zug had four sections, a headquarters and a three-man 5cm light mortar section – a total of 49 personnel at full strength. Under the 1944 organization this was drastically reduced on a three-section model; so, even at maximum strength, the German platoon of the latter stages of the war was just 33 strong, with one officer and three NCOs (or four NCOs) and 29 other ranks. Nevertheless, their firepower was fearsome, with four LMGs, seven SMGs and 22 rifles. Although Volksgrenadier platoons had an establishment of only three LMGs from late 1944, Panzergrenadier platoons had many more, the full LMG establishment of the armoured infantry platoon being nine.

German officers were taught that inactivity and delay were greater crimes than the wrong choice of action. In specific cases where two solutions to a tactical problem offered equally good prospects of success, 'then the more aggressive of the two must be chosen'. Interestingly, exactly the same instruction was given to British officers in a *Training Memorandum* during the war, but this did not always square with the safer, more methodical train of thought detectable in *Infantry Training*.

March halt for a tired German platoon, 1940 or 1941; three men brandish stick grenades for their comrade's camera. The Tornister knapsack is not carried; among the scattered equipments are entrenching tools, mess tins, canteens, anti-gas capes, machine gun ammunition boxes and at upper left the 5cm light mortar. (Stephen Bull)

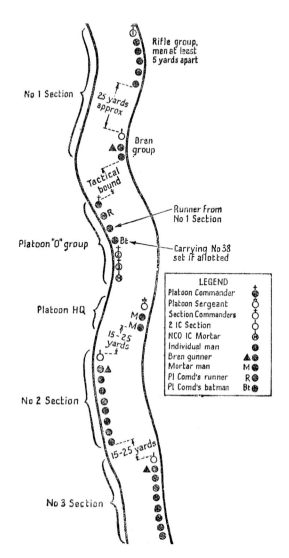

No 1 Section

Rifle group, men at least 5 yards apart

25 yards approx

Bren group

Tactical bound

Platoon "O" group

Runner from No 1 Section

Carrying No 38 set if allotted

LEGEND
Platoon Commander	✚
Platoon Sergeant	Ȯ
Section Commanders	Ο
2 IC Section	Ο
NCO IC Mortar	⊛
Individual man	●
Bren gunner	▲●
Mortar man	M●
Pl Comd's runner	R●
Pl Comd's batman	Bt●

Platoon HQ

15-25 yards

No 2 Section

15-25 yards

No 3 Section

British platoon movement along a road, from *Infantry Training* (1944). The distance between individuals is about 5 yards, to reduce casualties. No provision is made here for the two-man PIAT anti-tank team which was in practice almost invariably attached to each platoon at least from D-Day onwards. (Stephen Bull)

Commonly, the German platoon advanced in an 'arrowhead' formation, although both column, and line with sections forward and back similar to the US model, were also used. According to *Minor Tactics* it was up to the platoon commander to state the deployment areas and objective, to decide the formation, and to detail the sections to their tasks. Attacks would be carried out in bounds, with platoon commanders identifying weak spots in the enemy defence and deciding exactly where the blow would fall. Thereafter:

If the first assault is successful, even if penetration is made only on a narrow front, the attack must be pressed forward into the depth of the enemy position. At this moment the personal example of the platoon commander, who must concentrate on maintaining the momentum of the attack, is of great importance. Immediate pursuit at places where the enemy resistance weakens is therefore required. Premature movement to a flank before the enemy position has been completely penetrated is wrong. The flanks of attacking sections must be protected by troops in the rear. It is the duty of reserves following up the attack to destroy any centres of resistance which remain.

*　　*　　*

The British platoon organization as recommended in 1944 was three ten-man sections, and a platoon headquarters that comprised the commander, the platoon sergeant, a three-man 2in mortar team (who also carried rifles), a runner and the officer's batman/orderly. The standard platoon was thus 37 strong, armed with one light mortar, three Bren LMGs, five Sten SMGs and 29 rifles, as well as at least 36 grenades. This set-up was not intended as invariable, however, and could be altered according to the numbers available and the type of operation. In practice the headquarters group almost always included two men crewing one of the three AT weapons from company HQ (initially the .55in Boyes AT rifle, by 1943 the PIAT projector), and the orderly doubled as a runner or radio man. It must be borne in mind that once committed to combat, infantry platoons of all armies suffered casualties that took days, even weeks, to be replaced, often reducing platoons to a fraction of their establishment strength.

Communications were a vexed question for the British in 1944. The manpack No.38 wireless set had been partially introduced from 1943, initially to special forces but later more generally, to supplement at platoon level the No.18 sets carried by company HQs; but they were subsequently officially withdrawn from line rifle platoons. An *Army Training Memorandum* of January 1944 explained that this was because:

GERMAN DEFENSIVE POSITION; NORMANDY, JUNE–JULY 1944

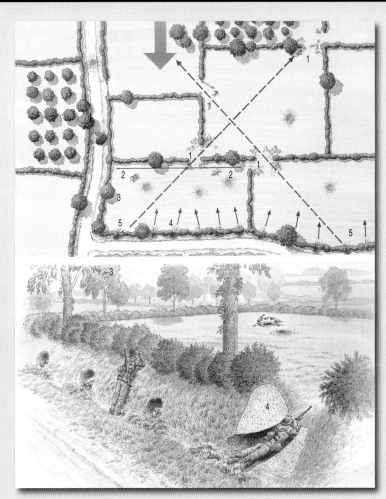

Based primarily on eyewitness sketches by men of the US 90th Infantry Division, this plate shows both plan (above) and oblique (below) views of a typical German squad position in the bocage countryside of Normandy. With its many trees, narrow sunken lanes, high banks and thick, centuries-old hedgerows, this terrain offered very limited visibility. Tanks were often ineffective, and normal infantry tactics had to be modified according to circumstances that usually favoured the defenders.

(1) Gaps have been deliberately cleared in some hedgerows for the interlocking fields of fire of machine guns located on the flanks, arranged obliquely to cover the natural avenues of advance. (2–2) A tripwire strung with noise-making tin cans is stretched low in the grass across a likely line of advance, to provide a warning and make the attackers pause. (3) The tree position of a sniper, forward of the main line of defence. His first shot or signal will alert the squad. (4) Riflemen occupy tunnels dug right through the base of the hedgerow bank, with a narrow aperture at the front; the rifle muzzle hardly protrudes and is masked by vegetation. (5) The MGs cover the front from different angles, and may also be positioned to fire from holes through the banks. Alternative positions will have been selected to sweep the lanes and potential enemy observation points, and guns can be moved to secondary positions in case of compromise or opportunity. (Brian Delf © Osprey Publishing)

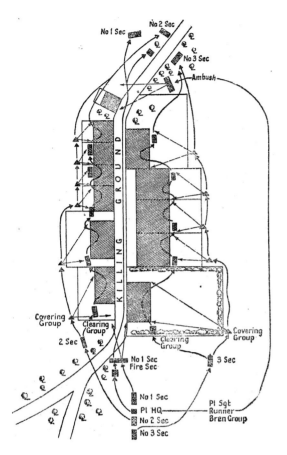

Clearing a village, from the British manual *Infantry Training* (1944). An 'ambush party' creeps around one flank to set up a stop line for any fleeing enemy. Meanwhile a 'fire section' takes up position with platoon HQ to cover likely windows and sweep the main street, which is designated as the 'killing ground'. The other two sections break into 'clearing groups' protected by 'covering groups'; they work their way from building to building down the rear of the gardens and houses. Doors, partition walls and ceilings are shot through before men enter, preceded by grenades as necessary. (Stephen Bull)

Their conspicuousness attracted fire from the enemy and frequently made it impossible for the man carrying it to remain with the platoon commander, when in close contact with the enemy. Consequently, the set was seldom available when most required. Moreover, the platoon commander had to make a difficult decision, whether to go and lead his platoon, which was his proper task, or to remain with his set in contact with his company commander. For these reasons, the platoon sets will not be available until a more inconspicuous set can be developed. Meanwhile each company is allotted two sets for its internal use.

In fact memoirs and photographs often give evidence of the continued use of No.38 sets by rifle platoons in NW Europe, but they were far from universal issue. With a range of about 4 miles, the set weighed 27lb, and was carried in a frontal webbing cradle and a separate haversack for the battery box; its throat microphones were popular, leaving both hands free.

Although the sections would go forward in blobs, files or arrowheads, it was up to the platoon commander to study the ground to decide which line of advance should be used; in building an attack he was to reconnoitre and then issue orders. He was to bear in mind that 'if the platoon is not put into battle properly, it will merely suffer a lot of casualties, however brave the men may be.' While 'battle drill must be our servant and not our master', different drills were taught as 'basic strokes' that could be modified and adjusted to circumstance. In moving across country, one possibility was to throw forward the first section in a rough arrowhead, behind which came the command group, and finally sections two and three in open line abreast. For a flanking move a good plan was to pin the enemy frontally with one section and the mortar (typically, under the direction of the platoon sergeant), while the others took advantage of any covered approach to move around the enemy. Smoke from the mortar would help make the flank attack a success.

For clearing small woods the Brens could be worked forward into positions outside or on the fringes from where they could cover escape routes; the sections then worked through the wood, strung out as 'beaters', with a 'support group' behind them. The beaters would move forward cautiously in rough lines, dodging from tree to tree and taking up one fire position after another. They would engage the enemy, and if the opposition stood to fight the support group would come up and attempt a flanking manoeuvre. If the enemy ran they would do so into curtains of Bren gun fire.

Though improvisation often occurred, some attacks were literally 'textbook', as related by Lt W. A. Elliott, a platoon commander of the Scots Guards in Italy:

Having halted my platoon just below the final ridge, I walked forward with my section commanders to site their new positions. In doing so I came over the brow where there were more rows of stone sangars [piled-stone positions] apparently deserted like the rest. Suddenly a white face topped by a mop of ginger hair appeared over a parapet only thirty yards ahead. We gaped at each other for a brief instant. Without a helmet the individual did not look a bit like a German. Then I quickly fired my tommy gun from the hip shouting 'hands up' in German; but my weapon jammed. Cursing I recocked it and fired one round, when it jammed again. Then there was a deafening crackle of German machine gun bullets all around my ears…

I leapt backwards into dead ground and retreated to rejoin my platoon while the rest of the company on the hill behind fired at German heads popping up along the line of the ridge. With a large audience now watching from all sides, I laid on a model battle drill attack 'according to the book' with one covering section, two flanking sections and 2-inch mortar smoke. Our battle school attack, however, was somewhat assisted by the complete withdrawal of the enemy…

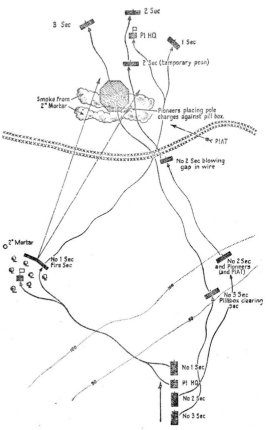

Attacking a strongpoint, from *Infantry Training* (1944). The British platoon breaks down into its composite sections, the first bringing the objective under heavy fire while it is blinded by smoke from the platoon HQ's 2in mortar. The second section is accompanied by assault pioneers and a PIAT from the unit headquarters assets. It closes in, blasting with the PIAT at close range, while the pioneers gap the wire with charges. Both second and third sections now rush the gap; the second secures the ground beyond the pillbox, taking any defensive trenches, while the third section attacks the objective with grenades. (Stephen Bull)

THE SNIPER

Sniping could be indulged in by virtually any soldier, but it would be entirely wrong to assume that it was a random activity, without theoretical background or specific training. Though somewhat neglected between the wars, the basic techniques had been evolved by 1918, and by WWII the deadly trade was a highly organized business. As Maj Nevill Armstrong of the Canadian Army observed in his unofficial 1940 publication *Fieldcraft: Sniping and Intelligence*, disorganized sniping was of little use, while properly deployed snipers could have

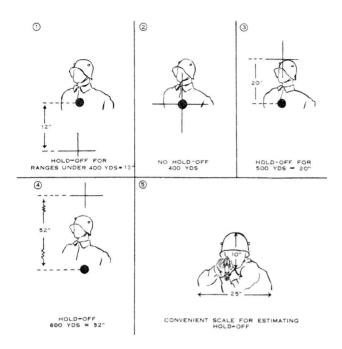

① ② ③

HOLD-OFF FOR
RANGES UNDER 400 YDS=12"

NO HOLD-OFF
400 YDS

HOLD-OFF FOR
500 YDS = 20"

④ ⑤

HOLD-OFF
600 YDS = 52"

CONVENIENT SCALE FOR ESTIMATING
HOLD-OFF

Aiming diagram from the US sniper manual of 1944. For the sake of speed, snipers were trained not to fiddle with sight settings for individual shots but to leave the weapon zeroed-in at 400 yards. If an enemy appeared at about this distance the sniper fired directly at the middle of his chest; if the target was closer he aimed about a foot lower, and at 500 yards the aiming point was the top of the head. In both instances sights set at 400 yards would bring the round back into the middle of the body mass. At 600 yards the ideal point of aim was 52in above the intended point of strike, but shooting at greater ranges was discouraged since hits were unlikely. (Stephen Bull)

a disproportionate effect in relation to their numbers. According to his rationale, the main purposes of sniping were to screen one's own positions and movements, kill enemy snipers and shake enemy morale. This would be achieved not merely by hitting as many of the enemy as possible, but by 'obtaining a superiority of fire' which would keep him down, and by 'visual reconnaissance' that would allow the gathering of information.

In the American synthesis scouting and sniping were similarly linked. In the US manual of 1944, sniping was described as specifically intended to pick off key enemy personnel, thereby softening his resistance and weakening morale. In US theory snipers were deployed in two distinct roles. Stationary two-man 'observer-sniper' teams occupied specific, well-camouflaged posts. These covered designated areas, preferably from more than one position, and the team took turns to observe with binoculars. To avoid fatigue, observation duty alternated every 15 to 20 minutes. Where possible range cards were drawn up for each post, showing landmarks and distances to designated points. These would allow for quick direction of the shooter to targets, and accurate shooting on known data. Concealment and patience were primary requirements for the observer-sniper team, with rifle barrels not to protrude beyond cover and smoking strictly forbidden. By contrast, the 'mobile sniper' was intended to be far more aggressive:

The mobile sniper acts alone, moves about frequently, and covers a large but not necessarily fixed area. He may be used to infiltrate enemy lines and seek out and destroy mobile targets along enemy routes of supply and communication. It is essential that the mobile sniper hit his target with the first round fired. If the sniper is forced to fire several times, he discloses his position and also gives the enemy time to escape. Therefore, although the mobile sniper must be an expert shot at all ranges, he must be trained to stalk his target until he is close enough to insure that it will be eliminated with his first shot.

Where snipers were acting behind the enemy line it was recommended that they carry a second weapon, such as a pistol, submachine gun or even an automatic rifle.

The US sniper was warned that 'the telescopic sight does not make the rifle or the firer more accurate' – accuracy depended on marksmanship. The telescope was mainly to allow him to pick up obscure targets, and perhaps enable him to engage targets that might otherwise have been out of range. Several men per platoon received sniper training, being selected for their ability to use map and compass and their physical agility as well as their potential with the rifle. Training stressed the importance of advanced marksmanship, range estimation, concealment, the identification of sounds, care and use of telescopic sights, and the study of trajectory and drift.

The basic sniper weapon was the highly accurate M1903 bolt-action Springfield rifle with telescopic sight, properly described as the 'US Rifle Cal .30, M1903A4 (Sniper's)'. Even so, the sniper manual observed that scopes would not always be mounted, and that in close country carbines might also be used. When weapons without telescopes were used at night it was recommended that a strip of white tape along the top surface of the barrel could be used as a primitive sight for close targets. In practice, e.g. in the case of the 29th Division, it was quickly observed that snipers with a well-developed sense of self-preservation discarded the relatively slow bolt-action rifle and its delicate scope in favour of the

A photo taken on the Russian Front in May 1943 by a man named Heuberger, from Propaganda Kompanie 666. The subject is a German sniper-observer team working from a prepared position; the sniper fires through – rather than over – the parapet.

semi-automatic Garand. Work was also done to fit telescopes to both the Garand and the M1 carbine. Official figures state that almost 7,000 Garand M1C sniper rifles were produced by the end of the war, although precious few actually made it to Europe.

Snipers could have a significant impact on the tactical battle; Bud McMillan of the 45th Divison recalled a German counterattack at Anzio:

> As soon as it got light, they started the artillery barrage all around and then started running across the open land... With my sniper's rifle, I was able to shoot the ones I thought were officers or NCOs. You pretty well had your choice of what to shoot at. Up to 400 or 500 yards, you could really pick 'em off. The enemy used fire and movement, where they'd run forward, hit the ground, roll, come up and run some more.

Most German snipers used bolt-action rifles, but examples of the semi-automatic G41 and G43 types were also fitted with telescope sights. In Normandy all types were an absolute plague for the Allies. As one US 90th Division platoon commander noted, a favourite enemy trick during the campaign was to take up positions in trees wearing 'camouflage suits for concealment'. These men were 'bothersome', until the American squads took to getting their BAR man to empty his magazine into the thickest parts of each suspicious tree. Some snipers had tied themselves in, and so were left hanging after they had been shot. Capt Marshall of the 7th Somerset Light Infantry recorded enemy snipers who lay in the mud of ditches or hid in haystacks. One determined character barricaded himself on the upper floor of a barn, and was only silenced by a Bren gun burst through the closed door.

German instructions from the latter part of the war stated that snipers should wear a camouflage smock or suit, but that if none happened to be available 'fatigue dress must be imprinted or sprayed with appropriate camouflage colours.' Where a belt was worn this should be of webbing rather than the more conspicuous leather. Helmet covers and nets were likewise to be worn as available, and the rifle wrapped in strips of canvas or hessian, the sniper's motto being 'Camouflage ten times, shoot once.' A recommended ruse was the 'camouflage fan': this was a natural branch about 16in long, to which end-pieces were attached so as to create a former over which camouflage netting covered with natural foliage camouflage could be placed. The result was a small portable hide from which the sniper could operate. Rather more elaborate was a 'grass mat' camouflage, created by binding together ordinary small camouflage nets and braiding them with appropriate local foliage. The sniper then put on the whole thing like a coat, with the upper third right over the head and loops around the arms and waist to hold the shapeless mass to his body. Some thought was applied to tree positions, slings and *Zeltbahn* shelter-quarters being used to make long occupation more comfortable and less obvious. Unobtrusive assistance to tree-climbing could be provided by banging spent cartridge cases into the trunk to give the feet a little additional purchase.

Patient observation was recommended, preferably by men working in pairs, but deceptions were also encouraged. Dummy heads were useful to attract attention, as were figures stuck up trees: the enemy would fire upon them, thus giving away his position. An improvement on the theme was to put a rifle in a dummy position, and have one of the team discharge it from a distance using a long cord. According to interviews with leading German snipers, the vast majority of shots were taken at under 450 yards, with priority targeting of enemy officers, observers and support weapon crews. In many instances snipers were deployed in front of their own lines, and would remain in position from dawn to dusk. A German sniper's sleeve badge, depicting an eagle's head and oakleaves, was instituted in August 1944; three classes were to mark 20, 40 and 60 kills respectively, but understandably these were seldom seen on uniform, particularly in the field.

Briefing scouts and snipers from the 10th Indian Division in Italy. The full panoply of camouflage kit can be seen: 'scrim' suits with hessian (burlap) strips sewn on, netting face veils, foliage on headdresses and tucked in to break up the body outline, and hessian wrapped around rifles. It is not immediately apparent that there are eight snipers in this photograph. (Queen's Lancashire Regiment)

British snipers used bolt-action rifles; at the beginning of the war the US-manufactured P14 fitted with a telescopic sight was termed the No.3 Mk I(T) in this role. By 1942 the new Enfield No.4 rifle was also modified for sniper use as the No.4 Mk I(T). A 'Sniping Wing' was set up at the old National Rifle Association grounds at Bisley, and new schools were later established at Llanberis in North Wales and on the Continent. Early British sniping methods differed relatively little from those of World War I, being summarized in 1940 and 1941 in *Notes on the Training of Snipers*. Eight men per battalion were designated as a sniper section, intended to operate either individually or as sniper-observer pairs. Rifles were best dulled with hessian wrapping, with brown paper or mud being emergency alternatives. Patience and observant stillness were important virtues – restless snipers were recommended to chew gum if they had to do something.

Many possible sniping posts were identified, the ideal being one that could be entered or left during daylight by means of covered approaches. Where time allowed, field positions could incorporate a dug-in sniper position, and 'mousetrap' observation loops consisting of wooden boxes with a camouflaged hinged lid on the outer end. Sniping from buildings and behind walls was encouraged. Upstairs rooms were particularly effective, and snipers were taught to stand well back in the room taking an oblique angle through the window. Higher up again, possible hides were identified in the rafters or behind the chimneys of shelled buildings, which were both 'advantageous and difficult to detect'. Bricks could be removed from walls, creating loopholes to be used kneeling or prone. Walls were best fired around or through, unless the top of the wall had a very uneven profile.

The number of British snipers increased with time. By mid 1942 common practice was two sniper-observers per company headquarters, and one sniper per section. These were expected 'to locate and kill enemy commanders, reconnaissance parties, and snipers. By intelligent fieldcraft they should never have to shoot at more than 300 to 400 yards.' An *Army Training Memorandum* of January 1944 gave additional detail:

> Those who have been in close contact with either the Germans or Japanese realize the menace of the enemy sniper, and, conversely, the value of first class snipers. Snipers, if carefully chosen and trained into really good shots, will pay ample dividend in the field for the effort put into training them. In the Mediterranean it has been found invaluable to train one 'section sniper' in each section, over and above the War Establishment scale of snipers equipped with snipers' rifles. The section sniper cannot be so equipped, but is the best shot in the section – if possible a marksman. In attack

US RIFLE PLATOON IN DEFENCE; ARDENNES, 1944–45

A US infantry platoon deployed in frontline defence. The men are entrenched in hasty one- and two-man foxholes, the spoil concealed as well as possible with snow. Typically a platoon frontage in broken terrain could extend up to 250 yards, while open country (and thus more open fields of fire) allowed greater dispersal. The squads are disposed to provide interlocking zones of fire, while also covering the gaps between adjoining platoons. The outer pair of broken red lines indicate the edges of the central squad's field of fire; the inner lines show the overlaps from the flanking squads. (1) Browning Automatic Rifles reinforce the squad positions, and can fire across the fronts of adjacent squads. (2) Riflemen form the bulk of the line, being assigned main 'sectors of fire' by their squad leaders. (3) The platoon sergeant is positioned just behind the main line, where he can supervise a broad sector, and can keep in visual and voice contact with the platoon leader. (4) An observer from the 60mm mortar team, attached from the company's weapons platoon, is positioned so that he has a good view, close to the platoon leader and within hand signal distance of his crew. (5) The lieutenant platoon leader is centrally located for the best observation and control; his radio allows him to maintain communication with his company commander. (6) Within the platoon, a messenger relays information and orders from the platoon leader by word of mouth. (7) The attached 60mm mortar crew is located in a suitable defilade position no further than 100 yards from its observer. (8) The cache of small arms ammunition, and bearers for machine gun ammunition, concealed but handy for the weapon pits. A second cache would hold mortar ammunition and carriers. (9) Attached .30-cal machine gun team. (10) Flank rifleman from the adjacent platoon. (Brian Delf © Osprey Publishing Ltd)

he is employed to pick off, from a suitable position to a flank, individual enemy in the post which the remainder of the section is assaulting.

By D-Day British sniping had advanced considerably, with greater numbers of men receiving training. In the 5th Seaforths it is recorded that, following a slow start, schools were established during the Italian campaign and the establishment of snipers was doubled, resulting in a 'good team' in Normandy. In Commando and Airborne battalions, over and above ordinary 'section' snipers, the official complement was anything from 30 to 38. A piece of airborne clothing generally adopted by snipers was the camouflaged Denison smock, which had the additional advantages of a crotch piece that prevented it riding up while crawling, and ample pockets for ammunition and grenades for close defence. A typical issue of equipment to a sniper in the latter stages of the war comprised the Denison, camouflage net face veil, binoculars (or a 'Telescope, Scout, Regiment'), compass, two grenades, emergency ration and water bottle. The ammunition carried was commonly 50 rounds of ordinary 'ball', five of tracer and five of armour-piercing.

One should not deduce from these guidelines that British snipers were anything like 'uniform', since an unimaginative outlook would soon have alerted the enemy. Scrim (hessian strips – 'burlap' in US terms), nets, painted canvas and captured camouflage clothing were all used to advantage. The impressive *Home Guard Fieldcraft Manual* by Langdon-Davies even contained stage by stage instructions for making what is now called a 'ghillie suit'. This consisted of a loose hessian smock and hood on to which camouflage patterns could be painted, in schemes suited to specific localities; three main types were illustrated. Irregular patches of dark, 'almost black' olive green and mid-green were suitable for 'agricultural, hedge, field and parkland'. Dark brown with big areas of warm grey or light earth was deemed best for backgrounds of rock, stone or sandbags. A striking geometric camouflage of dark brown with stone or brick red was shown for built-up areas. In all instances greater or lesser amounts of unpainted hessian were also allowed to form part of the designs.

British snipers achieved some notable successes, particularly in the final stages of the war. Alastair Borthwick records that in the Netherlands the 5th Seaforths' snipers – a thoroughly independent-minded and slightly piratical gang – went so far as to keep a 'game book' of kills:

We did not lose a single man by sniping, and by the end of the campaign our total bag was 38. So great was our ascendancy at Olland that the redoubtable Fraser was seen one evening disappearing into No Man's Land on a bicycle. It was also a time when the snipers, never a particularly self-effacing crew outside working hours, developed an even more than usually vivid turn of phrase in describing their exploits. Fraser's best contribution was: 'I got him through the head. How did I know? Och, he just curled up and twitched his toes like a rabbit.'

How unnerving sniping could be is recorded by German machine gunner Günter Koschorrek, pinned down under Russian fire:

> Somewhere, in front of us, a sniper has dug himself in, so well camouflaged that I can't pick him out even with my telescopic sight. I am aware of his presence only because of the dangerous explosions all around our position which have a noticeably higher tone.

Koschorrek's assistant poked his head up from the gun pit, just at the moment when a fur cap was spotted. Both men dived to the bottom of the foxhole and were unable to move, while the battle continued around them. After a while Koschorrek risked lowering the tripod a little:

> Then there is another sharp crack, right in my eardrum. Quick as a flash, I duck down and then freeze. With his eyes wide open, as if struck by lightning, Paul slumps in a heap at the bottom of the foxhole... I stare aghast at the fist-sized hole in Paul's head just above his left eye, from which blood is leaking in dark red streams on to his steel helmet and from there right over his face and into his mouth, which is moving up and down. I am in total panic and try to turn his body ... the blood is now streaming out ... so fast that I can hear a light 'clucking' sound.

Koschorrek shouted for a medic, only to get the sensible reply that 'No one can get the bugger out' while the sniper was active. Eventually the dead man was pulled from the pit, and the gunner's assistant was replaced, but the replacement did not last long either.

Sniping was the prime motivation for experienced officers wishing to appear as much like other ranks as possible. In the US Army, with the connivance of officers, saluting almost disappeared in the frontline. Maps and binoculars were concealed inside jackets, and the tell-tale white bar on the back of an officer's helmet was often painted over or camouflaged with mud. The US 29th Division history records that both officers' bars and sergeants' stripes were commonly removed from field clothing, despite official orders to the contrary. Many British line officers adopted other ranks' webbing equipment, and some carried rifles.

PART 2
COMPANY & BATTALION

ORGANIZATION & DOCTRINE

Opposite:
British Army training photograph taken just before the war showing the firing of the 3in mortar, the standard battalion-level weapon throughout the war. The man on the right has the slung leather case in which the removable sights were carried, and holds the muzzle cap: replacing this after a shoot prevented any accidental discharge. A rate of ten rounds per minute was perfectly feasible for short periods. The total weight of the equipment in action was 112lb. (Stephen Bull)

According to the US manual *Infantry Battalion* of 1944:

> The battalion is the basic tactical unit of Infantry. It usually operates as an element of the infantry regiment. Its mission is assigned by the regimental commander, and its actions are coordinated with those of other units of the regiment. Exceptionally the battalion may be detached from the regiment to perform an independent mission.

In this, US and German practice were essentially similar. In the British system, single battalions of different regiments were mixed together to form brigades; even so, regimental tradition was strong, and as Lt Alistair Borthwick of the 5th Seaforths put it: 'The individuality of battalions is not, as might be imagined, a sentimental fiction: in war they can consume twice their weight in recruits and remain unmistakably themselves.'

The battalion required a huge amount of organization. Merely to document the equipment of a 1941 British battalion needed a booklet of 49 pages. Such a list was bewildering in its detail and complexity, including everything from

France, 1939: men of the Royal Warwickshires are posed manning a camouflaged frontline trench, bayonets fixed, while the company commander prepares a message. The continuous trench line, reminiscent of World War I, is a textbook example of the defences recommended in *Infantry Training* (1937); such elaboration would be unusual later in the war. (War Office Official)

'Cellular drawers, short (summer only)', 31 pairs of which were in the safekeeping of the headquarters, through to the seven 'Kettles, camp, oval 12-quart' which were usually 'left at base'. The cobblers' materials alone filled a page, and in addition to 14lb of hobnails listed over a thousand individual pieces, tools and spares. Actually doing anything required a further flood of paper. The assault crossing of a single dyke in Holland – Operation *Guy Fawkes* in November 1944 – required five closely typed pages of 'Battalion Operation Order'. Such brevity was only achieved by means of so many abbreviations and codewords as to make the whole virtually unintelligible to the uninitiated.

GERMAN TACTICAL DOCTRINE

After early successes, it was the Germans who set the tactical agenda. This being the case, it is remarkable how incompletely German methods have been described for the English-speaking readership. Contemporary translations such as *German Infantry in Action: Minor Tactics*, and the *1940 Handbook*, give only partial summaries. Farrer-Hockley's ground-breaking work omitted crucial elements, while Gajkowski looks primarily at the squad, working back from an incomplete US wartime translation.

In all branches of the Wehrmacht or armed forces, traditionally the 'school of the nation', theory and staff work were strong. The foundation of the German approach to infantry tactics was the pre-war service regulation HDV 300/1, the *Truppenführung* or 'troop leading'. Punningly referred to as the *Tante Frieda* ('Aunt Frieda'), this was primarily the work of Generaloberst Ludwig Beck. The thinking outlined in its introduction underpinned all other tactical doctrine. Warfare, so it said, was 'an art', but one that rested on science and made the very highest demands upon individual character. Warfare was under constant development, and its changes had to be predicted and evaluated, its variety being limitless. Perhaps most importantly, it was a subject impossible to 'exhaustively summarize'; therefore it was the 'principles' of regulations that were important, applied according to circumstance. Also stressed was the role of the individual and the human factor:

> Despite technology, the value of the man is the deciding factor; scattered fighting has made it more significant. The emptiness of the battlefield demands those fighters who can think and act for themselves, those who exploit every situation in a considered, decisive, bold manner, those full of conviction that success is the responsibility of every man. Inurement to physical effort, to self regard, willpower, self confidence and daring enable the man to become master of the most serious situations.

German cycle troops on the march, 1939. Bicycles remained in infantry establishments until the end of the war, when Volksgrenadier divisions had complete cycle regiments. Note the wagon at the end of the column: steel-bodied Hf7 infantry wagons could weigh over 2 tons laden, and were colloquially known as 'horse-murderers'. (Stephen Bull)

German field positions.
(1) 'Tobruk turret' (Ringstand).
This standard machine gun position
was used in many German defensive
schemes in the second half of the
war. Ammunition was stored in
the 6ft 4in high compartment at
the bottom of the steps, inside
a subterranean entrance.
(2) Reinforced squad position.
An outer defence of barbed wire
and anti-tank mines would typically
ring the position about 50 yards out
from the trenches. Dug off the zigzag
trenches are bunkers with overhead
protection, sandbagged machine gun
positions, and an advanced listening
or sniping post at the end of a tunnel
from an underground bunker.
The red dots are randomly
scattered anti-personnel mines.
(3) 8cm mortar pit. This is the
regulation 'winged' pit that was dug
whenever time allowed, with a central
weapon pit and separate ammunition
and crew shelters at the ends of
short trenches. (Peter Dennis ©
Osprey Publishing Ltd)

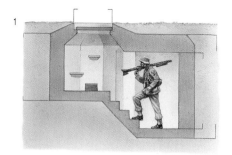
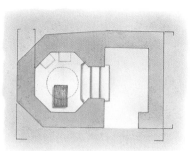
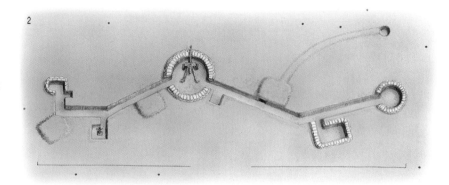

In hindsight, another inspirational document was Erwin Rommel's *Infanterie Greift* ('The Infantry Attacks'), a digest of tactical observations on battle in World War I that was first published in 1937. According to one source it was Hitler's reading of this volume which first prompted him to appoint Rommel to his headquarters the following year.

Great stress was put on tactical training: as trainee infantry officer Armin Scheiderbauer put it, the army service regulation HDV 130/2a *Schützenkompanie* ('Rifle Company') 'was the bible'. It covered not only sections, but also platoons and companies:

All that was contained in 670 points. Infantry officer training, however, not only required the knowledge necessary to command a section, a platoon or company, but also knowledge of the heavy weapons, i.e. the heavy machine gun, the heavy mortar, the light and heavy infantry guns, and the AT gun. It covered training in horse riding and driving, the latter including both horse-drawn and motorized vehicles.

Yet, in Scheiderbauer's opinion, even better than the official regulations was 'Reibert':

It was named after its author Dr W. Reibert, Hauptmann and company commander. A 300-page compendium, it was entitled *Der Dienstunterricht im Heere* ['Service Instructions in the Army']. We used the green-bound edition for men of the *Schützenkompanie*. The Reibert was an excellent systematic compendium of all the training material...

The highly regarded Reibert was therefore unofficial, but drew extensively on official literature; yet it was not always the latest word. Comparison of the 1940 and 1942 editions shows relatively little updating, and many of the illustrations were lifted directly from publications of the 1930s.

GERMAN BATTALION ATTACKS

These were frequently made on a narrow frontage of 400 to 1,100 yards, with a specific 'point of main effort' or Schwerpunkt as chief objective. Assaults could be frontal, *Frontaler Angriff*, or preferably, *Flankenangriff*, flank attacks. Enveloping attacks with the front pinned were dubbed *Umfassener Angriff* – interestingly, this German term also contains the ideas of 'putting one's arm around' or encirclement. A *Flügelangriff* or 'wing attack' was also recognized; in this, though unable to attack the opposition flank at right angles, the German infantry would drive obliquely into the enemy wing. Flanks were obvious points to attack, and even where none existed at the start they could be created by manoeuvre, or by picking out a weak point from an otherwise continuous enemy line. Attacks could be made directly from the line of march, 'shaking out' into aggressive formations from the columns of advance.

Although battalion commanders were encouraged to set up their command post in sight of the action, and company commanders were to 'arrange for constant close reconnaissance', time was vital; preparations were expected to take no more than 40 minutes from striking an obstruction to the assault. The common model was a threefold development, as Reibert explained:

Heranarbeiten, or working forward until within range for the 'break in'.

Einbruch, or breaking into the enemy position.

Kampf in der Tiefenzone, or 'fighting in the deep zone', within the enemy position.

Winning the *Feuerkampf* or firefight was an integral part of both attacking and defensive action, which demanded use of terrain and fieldcraft. The firefight could itself be divided into three major phases:

Niederhalten, or pinning down the enemy with the lead elements, up to a company in strength, with support from machine guns and mortars, while reconnaissance was completed and assault units were deployed.

Blenden, or 'dazzling' the defenders with shooting and smoke, denying them observation, and hampering their firing.

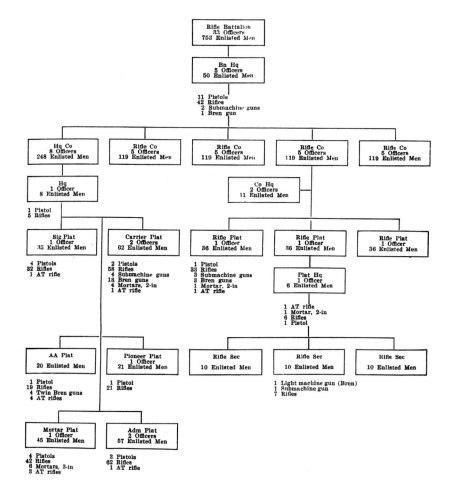

British infantry battalion organization, from the US *Handbook of the British Army* (1943). Note that the anti-tank rifle is still listed as a platoon weapon. By 1944 the HQ Co had lost the carrier, pioneer and mortar platoons to a new Support Co, which also had an AT platoon with 6 x 6-pdr guns; the anti-aircraft platoon had been disbanded. (Stephen Bull)

Niederkampfen, or winning the firefight and beating down the enemy, culminating in the actual assault into the enemy position.

As *Handbook on the German Army* observed, German methods stressed boldness and skill in infiltration by:

> … small detachments [that] penetrate between enemy posts which they engage from the flanks and rear. They often attempt to create the impression of large numbers by a liberal expenditure of ammunition… Reliance on prompt and efficient fire support of considerable volume from their heavier weapons which are handled with great skill and dash, and are brought into action well forward. Units are lavishly supported by infantry guns as well as AT guns, mortars and machine guns, and the co-operation between these weapons and infantry is excellent. Where necessary, support is given by dive bomber aircraft.

Where resistance rested on fortifications, different types of troops including infantry and engineers, with various weapons, could be brought together in ad hoc groups to achieve the task in hand. The idea of using *Stosstruppe* (assault detachments) for special tasks was not new; the concept was indeed familiar enough to become the subject of jokes. As the British publication *War*, the fortnightly journal of the Army Bureau of Current Affairs, explained:

> Assault parties, creeping forward with explosives and perhaps flame throwers, are a normal feature of infantry technique: so normal indeed, that a humorous article in a German paper gives the following advice to troops on leave … they must be careful to respect civilian habits almost forgotten at the front. If the front door is shut, the proper thing is not to blow it open with a charge in the normal way; for the custom of the country is to ring the bell.

A typical assault detachment was outlined in *German Infantry in Action: Minor Tactics* of 1941. This consisted of several sub-sections: 'wire-cutting parties' of three or four men for each gap to be made; similarly strong 'embrasure destroying parties'; two or three 'support parties', and a 'smoke party' of two or three. Under cover of heavy support fire and smoke, the wire parties were to advance and clear the wire by means of explosives and wire cutters, making use of grenades as required. Once this was achieved the embrasure parties would dash through the gaps, making use of dead ground to approach the weapon embrasures in the enemy position and destroy them with charges. Added refinements included

The German 7.5cm leichtes Infanteriegeschütz 18 or 'light infantry gun', a short howitzer capable of firing high explosive or hollow charge shells to just over 4,000 yards. Six light and two heavy 15cm guns (or alternatively, eight light guns) formed the infantry gun company which was an integral part of each German three-battalion regiment in 1939. A similar complement of close support 'infantry artillery' was retained as an independent 'regimental company' in the 1944-type infantry divisions. The US infantry regiment had a similar Cannon Company with 6 x short 105mm howitzers; the equivalent British three-battalion infantry brigade had no integral artillery. (Stephen Bull)

attached flamethrowers, the use of cans of petrol which could be ignited by a round from a flare pistol, and grenades dropped through loopholes.

The key to larger-scale battalion tactics was co-operation between the various elements: as Vol 2 of *Ausbildungsvorschrift für die Infanterie* put it: 'Only the tightly combined efforts of all the weapons of the company, working with the heavy weapons, brings success. The rifleman therefore needs to learn how to co-ordinate his efforts in order to achieve mutual effectiveness… He must accustom himself to other weapons firing past him or overhead.' Terrain was also central to success; in the words of *Schützenkompanie*: 'Terrain and use of cover either facilitate battle action or make it more difficult, and it influences the determination of the soldier. Skilful use of the terrain is the most efficacious means towards weakening the effect of enemy fire.'

Out of the *Stosstruppe* and close working with supporting arms evolved the *Kampfgruppe* or 'battle group', an amalgam of different troop types brought together for a combat task. There was seldom a 'standard' *Kampfgruppe*, but the *Regimental Officer's Handbook of the German Army* (1943) outlines a model in which a Panzergrenadier battalion is combined with two squadrons of a tank regiment, an AT company, an engineer platoon and a troop of light anti-aircraft weapons. As the US *Handbook* of 1945 observed, 'Coordination between the combined arms under a strong unified command is, the Germans emphasise, an absolute requisite' to shock tactics. This close working became more rather than less crucial as Allied forces learned better methods and introduced more effective AT weapons.

BRITISH TACTICS

Although British tactics of 1939 and 1940, as outlined in the manuals *Infantry Tactics* and *Infantry Section Leading*, were more similar to their German counterparts than many sources would lead us to believe, there was an undeniable

BRITISH COMPANY ATTACK, 1942

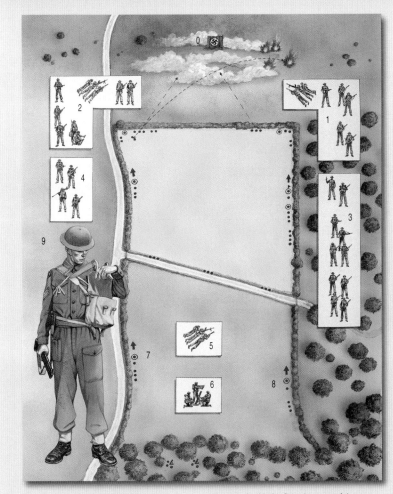

area of this plate. The sections advance most of the way to their final assault positions in single file on narrow fronts, allowing the LMGs to fire for as long as possible.
(0) German objective, under fire from Bren guns and mortars. (1) No.1 Section of lead platoon; at this date the recommended section strength was eight men – NCO section leader, three-man Bren group, four riflemen/bombers. (2) No.2 Section of lead platoon; as No.1, but plus 2in mortar crew. (3) Platoon commander and his runner, leading No.3 Section of lead platoon. (4) Remainder of platoon HQ element – platoon sergeant, Boys AT rifleman, two riflemen. (5) Bren groups from reserve platoon, which have given covering fire during advance. Now, before the final assault, they will move forward again to the last hedgerow, their movement covered by smoke and the final 3in mortar barrage. (6) 3in mortars from battalion Support Company. (7 & 8) Remainder of sections from reserve platoon coming up to reinforce or exploit the assault. (9) 'Brooksbank' equipment method, 1943. Taken from *Army Training Memorandum* No.45 of May 1943, this shows the so-called 'Brooksbank method' of lightening 37 Pattern infantry equipment. This corporal has only his gas mask satchel, slung behind his shoulders with its sling round his neck and secured by a tape; and his haversack or 'small pack' containing ammunition. (Peter Dennis © Osprey Publishing Ltd)

Based on a scheme diagram from the *Instructor's Handbook on Fieldcraft and Battle Drill* (1942), this illustrates the 'lane' method for a company attack. The lead platoon is illustrated, with the first elements of the reserve platoon coming up behind; a flanking platoon would simultaneously be carrying out a similar attack off to one flank, outside the assimilation of enemy ideas in the wake of Dunkirk. The key tactical concepts listed in the 1942 *Operations* manual were: fire, to dominate the battlefield and overcome the enemy's fire; concentration, of both fire and 'will power', at a point of decision; security; surprise; and co-operation. The same year the provisional *Instructors' Handbook on Fieldcraft and Battle Drill* stressed such matters as infiltration, use of smoke and platoons being reorganized into sections with pioneers for attack on fortifications – all elements represented in the German literature. It also outlined the theory of the 'Main Effort' on a narrow frontage, another significant parallel with German battalion and company tactical schemes. Detailed plans for attack were usually developed at brigade level as a result of reconnaissance and planning by 'R groups', and transmitted down to the unit through the meeting of 'O' or 'orders groups' comprising officers (and sometimes senior NCOs) of the units involved, near to the place where action was expected.

In terms of company attack drills for frontal assaults, British instructions of 1942 offer three basic methods:

Attack by sections in extended order. The sections move forward taking advantage of the ground in the familiar manner.

The 'pepperpot' method. The sections advance in extended order, but when they are held up by effective fire they each break down into three sub-groups, which advance independently, running about 20 yards before dropping down again. This was intended to present the enemy with only fleeting and dispersed targets, and was thought particularly effective for attacks through standing crops and hayfields.

The 'lane' method. The infantry advance in single files or 'snakes', using dead ground to form up. This leaves clear lanes down which the Bren guns can maintain continuous fire until the last possible moment, aiding the attack.

The 'lane' method has been criticized, particularly by Harrison-Place, on the grounds that it was too complex for impromptu action. Though it may have had some validity in the set piece attack, it was not stressed in *Infantry Training* (1944), in favour of more fluid action, and a general instruction that attack from the flanks was preferable, so allowing 'covering fire to continue right up to the moment the assault goes in'. 'Pepperpots' were no longer known as such in 1944, but appear to have survived as just one of several forms of fire and movement. The maxim 'Down; Crawl; Observe; Fire' was still taught – probably because it was easy to remember and practical to apply.

Though never developed to the extent of the German model, the idea of ad hoc combat groups became more accepted. Manpack flamethrowers, for example, could be part of the battalion. By the end of the war the *Tactical Handling of Flame Throwers* (1945) was recommending that 'Lifebuoy' and 'Ackpack' types be held in readiness for specific tasks, to 'form an integral part of the attack', preferably as part of a surprise action. Although the chief impact was 'moral' it was noted that the flame was highly lethal both through burning its victims and by asphyxiation. It was also observed that flame jets had the useful characteristics of 'ricocheting into apertures', and forming sticky blobs that were very difficult to extinguish. Unignited 'wet' shots could also be delivered, then ignited by the next blast of flame. Nearby infantry would co-operate by giving cover as the flamethrowers advanced, then attack as soon as the flame ceased.

As time progressed different attacking methods, using more or less of the battalion forward, were tried out. Anecdotal evidence suggests that cumulative experience in North Africa, Italy and eventually the close country of Normandy led to smaller elements being used as 'opening bids'. Terrain and economy of resources doubtless played significant parts, but it has also been observed that advancing troops were often in ignorance of the opposition. Under such circumstances a single section of a platoon, or a single platoon of a company, would be sufficient to test the situation. If the enemy opened fire the British commander would then

A column of German *Gebirgsjäger* (mountain rifles) prepare to move off, c.1940. Although some motor transport is visible at left, most of the kit – including the medical equipment, centre – is loaded on pack horses. The men carry rucksacks, and display the Edelweiss right sleeve badge of this branch. (Stephen Bull)

have the bulk of his force in hand ready to deploy the main firepower against the revealed locations. Frequently there was an understandable tendency to lean too heavily on the barrage, and a good deal of the infantry officer's task was directed at getting his men to shoot, and to act independently and intelligently under fire. As might be imagined, this was not necessarily easy when faced with a determined enemy that had the benefit of good cover.

It is interesting that by 1943 much of the terminology used for British battalion attack plans was identical to that used by the US Army, and that in both cases the underlying concepts were similar to those of the Germans.

US BATTALION COMMAND

The US battalion methods were also shaped by learning from the enemy, and the result was some particularly thorough tactical manuals. In the US appreciation, the battalion commander's role was particularly demanding. As the *Staff Officer's Field Manual* of 1940 put it: 'the commander alone is responsible to his superior for all that his unit does or fails to do. He cannot shift that responsibility to his staff or to subordinate commanders.' *Infantry Battalion* (1944) gave a full profile of the ideal:

> Aggressiveness and the ability to take prompt and decisive actions are prime requisites for a successful battalion commander. By these qualities he inspires confidence. By his boldness, energy, and initiative he influences both individual and collective conduct and performance… The battalion commander is responsible to the regimental commander for the condition and operations of the battalion. He meets this responsibility by anticipation; by timely decisions, plans and orders; and by supervision of execution… In preparation for combat, the mission of the battalion commander is to bring his unit to a high state of combat proficiency. He subordinates administration to training. He encourages initiative, ingenuity, and aggressiveness amongst his company officers. Having indicated his policies and given his orders, he allows his subordinates maximum freedom of action.

Given the complexity of the job, it was obvious that key tasks would have to be delegated. In the US system the 'battalion staff' comprised five officers: the executive officer, 'XO', or second-in-command; the adjutant or 'S1'; the intelligence officer or 'S2'; the operations & training officer, 'S3'; and the supply officer, 'S4'. Additionally, officers of sub-units also assumed specialist staff duties within the battalion, and liaison officers could also be appointed from adjacent units. Under combat conditions the battalion headquarters was so arranged that it could function continuously throughout an operation, night and day, with officers able to substitute for one another.

In US doctrine, the combat tasks of the battalion commander were termed 'troop leading' – a direct translation of the German equivalent. Time and thinking ahead were pivotal factors, since 'combat usually consists of a series of connected incidents most of which must be acted upon immediately.' Reconnaissance and planning with the aid of maps and his S3 would be followed by the issue of 'battalion field orders'. These were preferably relayed in advance in the form of 'warning orders', but could also be given in what we might now term real time, as 'fragmentary orders'. Where the battalion commander gathered his subordinates and spoke to them directly 'oral orders' were given, but the commander had to be sure that what he said was in 'simple, clear, and concise language'. Best results were achieved when this was done in good time, and at a location which was not under fire but which gave them as good a view of the field of operations as possible.

Battalion commanders worked from the command post in combat. This was to be located so as to 'facilitate control', but to avoid entrances to villages, crossroads and other places likely to attract enemy fire. In the attack the post was to be well forward, so that it did not have to move immediately the advance commenced. In defence it could be to the rear of the battalion area, so as to avoid the danger of being overrun. Ideally an alternative position was also prepared. The general location of the post was picked by the commander, but the detail was sorted out by the battalion S1. Nevertheless, the battalion commander was encouraged to go wherever he could 'obtain the fullest and most direct information regarding the operations and situations' of his companies, and 'exert the greatest influence'.

US Army battalion organization, and HQ Company organization, from the manual *Infantry Battalion* (1944). (Stephen Bull)

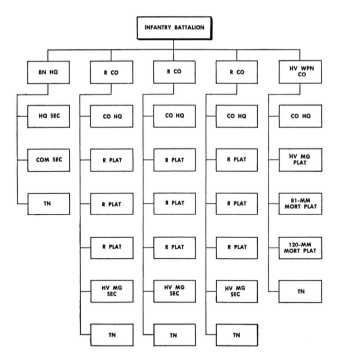

German infantry battalion organization, as used in 1944-type divisions, from the US manual *Handbook on German Military Forces* (1945). (Stephen Bull)

In addition to staff officers, the command post, and any associated observation posts, would be manned by the 'battalion headquarters section'. The key NCOs were the sergeant-major, the intelligence sergeant and the clerk with his typewriter. The 'operations sergeant' assisted the S2 and S3 officers. The main maps used in combat were the 'operation map' and the 'situation map'. This last was a 'graphic record of the tactical situation at any time', and was kept by the operations sergeant. Although the commander's tactical decisions and dispositions in battle were to be based on the 'immediate situation', any routine features could be covered by 'standing operating procedure'.

Communications were vital, to bring down artillery fire where and when it was wanted, and make possible changes of plan that would have been unthinkable in earlier conflicts. Most armies had radio communication down to company level, an important factor in making companies significant tactical units. The US Army had the most sophisticated communications network. The SCR300, weighing about 32lb, was a backpack model Signal Corps Radio giving a voice range of up to 5 miles, and was used for communication between companies and battalion. Shorter range SCR536 'handie-talkie' radios were eventually issued down to platoon level. In Europe the elements of US battalions used their sets for rapid communication, commonly voice to voice, without codes or scrambling. It was assumed, often correctly, that in fast-moving local tactical circumstances the enemy would be hard pressed to intercept, understand and act on any information which the system might let slip. Nevertheless, even American accounts suggest that US officers could be 'notoriously talkative'.

US OFFENSIVE TACTICS

Infantry Battalion (1944) gave considerable detail for combat. It recommended that the 'approach march' commence as soon as the unit was forced off roads by either shelling, strafing or the threat of these, and should end when the leading echelon crossed the 'departure line' or came under effective small arms fire.

The approach march formation was in small columns by section, squad or platoon, distributed in some depth and over a broad front – effectively, a partial deployment. The approach march would normally be ordered by the regimental commander, but could also be initiated by battalion commanders to reduce loss to their own units. In any case the battalion commander would soon issue his own orders, making sure to include details of enemy and friendly dispositions,

US BATTALION ATTACK, 1944–45

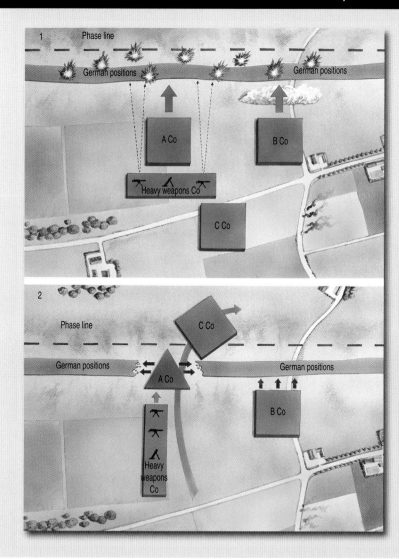

This diagram represents a US infantry battalion attack on a line of German positions.

Diagram 1: Phase line – this represents the battalion's objective for this phase of its operation. German positions – Separate company, platoon and squad defensive positions are placed along a line of low hills, sited for mutual support. They are under heavy bombardment by the US divisional artillery, perhaps supported by corps assets; their rear area is also brought under fire, to hamper any reinforcement of the line and to cut communications. A Co – The main assault company approaches the German defensive zone, supported by the fire of the Heavy Weapons Company past its flanks and overhead if elevation allows. B Co – Masked by smoke, this company prepares to put in a secondary 'holding' attack to pin down the defenders by fire. C Co – The battalion's third rifle company waits in support.

Diagram 2: A Co has broken into the enemy positions and is assaulting the vulnerable flanks this has created. B Co fights its holding action, laying down fire to pin down the defenders opposite its line, preventing them from attacking the flank of the assault companies.

C Co has come forward and passed through A Co, wheeling right to outflank the enemy line. Hvy Wpns Co – This now 'displaces' to follow the assault companies, and will take up new fire positions to continue supporting them. (Peter Dennis © Osprey Publishing Ltd)

the mission, 'phase lines', frontages and special orders for subordinate units. Frontage instructions regulated movement and helped determine the boundaries between sub-units, while phase lines – to be crossed at a certain time or in the event of a specific circumstance – gave the battalion commander control in battle. Under normal visibility phase lines were commonly 1,000–2,000 yards apart. Objectives could be expressed in terms of specific locations, or directions, and were commonly allotted to individual companies.

Formations were to be dictated by terrain, width of the zone of advance, and whether flanks were protected. A pointed triangular formation of one company forward and one echeloned either side to its rear was deemed particularly suitable when neither flank was secure, or when 'prompt enveloping action' might be required toward either flank. Advancing with two companies forward in line was more suitable in restricted visibility or where the zone of advance was wide. Three companies in line was best avoided, though drawing out 'flank patrols' from a rear company might be required. Machine gun sections and platoons and a mortar section could be detailed to follow the leading companies, or might be directly attached. According to the textbook a battalion was capable of delivering 'a powerful attack' on a frontage of 500–1,000 yards.

The battalion AT gun platoon's ideal position was between the leading and second echelons, the distance between echelons being commonly 100 to 200 yards. Reconnaissance was vital, being planned, continuous and progressive, taking full advantage of concealment, defilade and whatever maps and photographs were available. When covering forces were 'sufficiently strong', the battalion commander could come forward in person so as to obtain 'early information'. The approach march was made 'aggressively' from one phase line to the next, with junior commanders using their own initiative to take advantage of terrain, avoiding or hurrying past crossroads or features likely to be registered by hostile artillery or under observation.

In the event of a 'meeting engagement' or collision with a moving enemy force, the US appreciation was that the time element was vital, and that it was the party which attacked 'first in a decisive direction' that would win the advantage. In such an eventuality battalion commanders already engaged would remain commanding their units, sending a staff officer to receive orders from the regiment; unengaged battalion commanders would report in person.

'At the outset, a meeting engagement is a piecemeal attack, units being given missions and committed to action as they become available. Speed in launching the attack and rapidity of action are more vital at this stage than thoroughly coordinated and powerful fire support.' In practice, however, meeting engagements were rare, and powerful fire support was usual in what the manual described as attack against organized positions. In such an eventuality:

> … the battalion attacks by combining fire and manoeuvre to close with the enemy and then by employing shock action completes his destruction or capture. Fire weakens the enemy by inflicting casualties and neutralises his elements by forcing them to take cover; in the presence of the enemy, fire must be used to protect all movement not masked by cover, or fog, smoke or other conditions of reduced visibility. Through manoeuvre, the battalion

increases its fire effect by decreasing range and by placing elements in positions on the hostile flank from which they can develop convergent fires; by manoeuvre, also, the battalion advances its attacking echelon close enough to the hostile position to permit their assault to be made with hand grenades and the bayonet.

Two types of battalion 'attack manoeuvre' were recognized: 'envelopment' and 'penetration'. It was seldom possible to envelop the enemy immediately so as to attack his flanks and rear, but often an initial frontal attack could be so developed as to create a penetration, into which machine guns and other weapons could be inserted so as to create a flank attack. Since terrain was unlikely to be uniform it was desirable that the commander concentrate his efforts at a selected point, usually the weakest in the enemy dispositions. This concentrated point was the 'main attack'; but he was cautioned against using this term, presumably because men committed to the 'secondary' attacks would be less willing to hazard their lives.

'Secondary attacks' were important mainly as a means of holding or pinning the enemy, confusing him as to where the main blow would fall. In any event, it was desirable to hold back a reserve to exploit enemy weakness, or to strike the final blow. Depending on the information available, this could vary from a single platoon up to two whole companies. Perhaps the most common arrangement was to commit one company each to the main and secondary attacks, keeping the third back to reinforce the main thrust or turn a flank. The battalion commander was to remain flexible, carrying out his plan 'vigorously but not blindly', remaining ready to exploit opportunities as they arose, and if need be moving his main attack to a better point. In these particulars battalion level attacks had much in common with higher strategy.

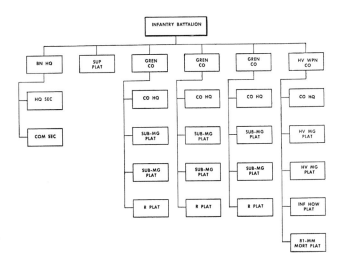

German infantry ('grenadier') battalion organization used in the new Volksgrenadier divisions, from late 1944. Despite the shrinking of this establishment due to Germany's massive manpower losses, the proportion of automatic weapons for close combat was much increased by replacing two rifle platoons in each company with 'submachine gun platoons'. By 1945 these were gradually being re-equipped with the Sturmgewehr 44 assault rifle. Battalion strength then totalled 642 all ranks, with 309 x bolt-action rifles but 253 x StG44, and 30 x LMG; 8 x HMG, 6 x 8cm mortars, 4 x 7.5cm infantry guns; 3 x motorcyles and only 2 x motor vehicles, but 70 horse-drawn. Only a company's 1st Platoon was now led by an officer, the others by NCOs. From *Handbook on German Military Forces* (1945). (Stephen Bull)

101

MACHINE GUN SUPPORT

The machine gun was frequently the key support weapon of the infantry battle. It aided the attack, but was probably at its most dramatically effective in defence. Machine gun fire alone was perfectly capable of halting an advance, as B Co, 4th Bn Somerset Light Infantry would discover near Mont Pincon in Normandy. Lt Sydney Jary recalled:

> The forward platoon… had barely crossed the stream when concentrated Spandau [MG34/42] fire came from the front and both flanks. There must have been about twelve machine guns firing at one time. This devastating firepower stopped the battalion dead in its tracks. There was no way forward or around it and no way to retire.

Pte W. Evans of 1st Royal Norfolks was also on the receiving end in Normandy:

> So far we had covered two or three miles and were doing well until we came to a cornfield. Then Jerry machine guns in a small pill box opened up. The lads were soon cut to pieces as the machine guns, with their tremendous rate of fire, scythed through the three-foot high golden corn. I remember one of the company cooks behind me getting a bullet in his neck.

At longer ranges machine gun fire was no longer 'flat trajectory', covering all the space between the firer and the target, but rose and fell, creating more limited 'beaten zones' that varied in size according not only to the type of weapon but the relative elevations of the gun and target. As distance increased, corrections for wind, temperature and the elevation of the firer became more important, making supporting machine gun fire a much more complex subject than simply 'pointing and shooting'. This technical subject matter filled whole manuals, of which the German H.Dv.73 *Scheißvorschrift für das Schwere Maschinengewehr* (1937; 'Target Regulations for the Heavy Machine Gun') was just one of the most significant.

In the US system, support weapons were grouped at both company and battalion level. The direct support element of the US rifle company was the 'weapons platoon' of two .30in LMGs, three 60mm mortars and three bazookas (2.36in rocket launchers). Each weapon team was accounted as a 'squad'. A heavy .50in machine gun was sometimes included, primarily for air defence. The two LMGs formed a 'section', where possible acting in concert – but not in such a way as to prevent the engagement of targets of opportunity. As the 1944 *Rifle Company* manual put it:

> As a general rule, most effective results are obtained by the simultaneous concentration of the fire of both guns on the same target. The section leader, in conformity with the platoon leader's orders, designates the targets, specifies the rate of fire, and gives the command or signal for opening fire… When squads have been assigned sectors of fire, each squad leader takes, as his primary mission, fire on targets developing in his own

Pre-war photograph showing the MG34 used in the sustained fire role on its tripod mount, here angled close to the ground to allow the crew to fire prone. The No.1 is looking through the x3 power prismatic telescopic sight while the gun commander observes with binoculars. (Stephen Bull)

sector, and as a secondary mission, fire on those targets developing in the adjacent sector. When the squad leader acts entirely on his own initiative, he decides how he can best support the general plan of the company and leads his squad accordingly.

Commonly the section leader would establish his own observation post, from which he could watch a given sector or targets and control his squads.

Where possible, the US weapons platoon was moved forward in carriers, crossing open ground 'by bounds' in the rear of the foot elements. Halts were to be in cover, ideally in gullies where there was protection from shell fragments. The platoon commander, or his NCOs, were to conduct their own reconnaissance. The positions chosen for the LMGs were to allow direct fire on the targets, taking account of likely locations where hostile MGs might lie in wait. The teams would move into their final locations on foot, making use of whatever cover was available, with ammunition bearers remaining in cover until needed. Ideally there would be shelter for the teams to the rear of the firing positions, and guns were separated by 'a sufficient interval, ordinarily 50 yards, to safeguard against both guns being hit by the burst of the same projectile.' Where tactical circumstance required, weapons could be attached directly to rifle platoons, or detached to the direct control of the company commander.

Light machine gunner from the US 44th Division in a camouflaged emplacement in eastern France, 1944; his .30-cal Browning M1919A6 is fitted with a bipod, carrying handle and shoulder stock for this light role with the infantry company. The M1919A4, on its tripod mount, served in the sustained-fire or 'heavy' role with battalion heavy weapons companies. (Stephen Bull)

In the attack the LMGs could fulfil a number of possible missions. These included supporting their own or adjacent companies, protection of flanks, breaking up counterattacks and covering reorganizations. When the mission could no longer be accomplished from the existing position the platoon commander would effect a 'displacement' to a new location – either moving forward as a section during a lull in fighting, or by moving one squad at a time while the other continued to fire. During the actual assault the LMGs were to concentrate on the point being attacked, thereby neutralizing enemy defensive fire.

The US battalion support element was the 'heavy weapons company'. Under the organization of 1944 this comprised two .30in tripod-mounted 'heavy' machine gun platoons and an 81mm mortar platoon. As the 1942 *Heavy Weapons Company* manual observed:

> The caliber .30 heavy machine gun is a crew served weapon capable of delivering a large volume of continuous fire. Medium rate of fire (125 rounds per minute) can be sustained indefinitely. Rapid fire (250 rounds per minute) can be fired for several minutes, but steaming will occur within two to three minutes. Because of its fixed mount, the heavy machine gun is capable of delivering overhead fires and of firing accurately at night from predetermined data. Due to the length of the beaten zone (horizontal pattern of dispersion) enfilade fire is the most effective type of fire delivered by this weapon. When overhead fires are not possible or desirable, fires are directed through gaps between riflemen or groups of riflemen. Gaps may be created and maintained for such fire.

According to US doctrine, the use of the HMG was limited mainly by observation in the direct-fire mode, and by both the maximum range and by the availability of accurate fire data in the indirect mode. It could be fired effectively against exposed personnel, or for the neutralization of entrenched troops, guns or observers, whose movement or action could be so hampered as to reduce or destroy the 'combat efficiency' of the target unit. Best use of the heavy weapons company concentrated its fire on a vital spot. In the attack this might mean putting the heavy weapons behind a specific rifle company, and assisting it by overhead fire. Weapons carriers were used wherever circumstance allowed, with displacements due to masked fire or friendly manoeuvre predicted as far as possible in advance. In set piece attacks the heavy weapons companies of the reserve battalions could be detached and moved up to increase the volume of fire supporting forward units. According to the *Infantry Battalion* manual, the heavy weapons company was ideally to be kept toward the front in any order of march, so as to compensate for the time taken to deploy, and to ensure that its firepower was immediately available. Normally the heavy weapons company was controlled by the battalion commander through orders issued to the company commander, thus co-ordinating their fire with the general plan of attack or defence. Initial deployment and target areas were thus designated at battalion level.

British machine gun tactics were shaped by the fact that the Bren gun, an ideal squad weapon, was not well suited to sustained fire missions (see Part 1). According to *Light Machine Gun* (1939), the best that could be expected, with changes of barrels and magazines taken into account, was 120 rounds per minute in short bursts. Nevertheless, the Bren could be tripod-mounted, and at 1,000 yards created an effective 100-yard long beaten zone 3 yards wide. Range courses instructions of 1939 specified that carrier platoons be trained to use tripod-mounted Brens at ranges up to 1,500 yards. Drum magazines with a 200-round capacity were also produced, mainly for anti-aircraft use. In defensive positions where friendly troops were likely to be forward of the firing point, LMGs would be set up to fire on 'fixed lines' through gaps, and the legs of the tripods weighted with sand bags to ensure they did not move. Firing from such predetermined positions was also possible at night.

Vickers team from a divisional machine gun battalion delivering supporting fire from within a house during the Italian campaign. Note how almost all of the weapon is within the room, and the tripod is weighted with sandbags, which steady the gun and give some protection to the crew. (Queen's Lancashire Regiment)

Given the strengths and weaknesses of the Bren, water-cooled machine guns were used predominantly for sustained-fire tasks. Under the 1944 organization, British infantry divisions included a specialist 'machine gun battalion', with one heavy mortar company of 16 x 4.2in mortars, and three machine gun companies, each of three platoons with 12 Vickers 'medium machine guns' (MMGs). Though a veteran of World War I, the .303in Vickers was a reliable weapon, capable of laying down potent streams of bullets for very long periods at an effective range of 2,000 yards. Area targets could be engaged at much greater distances, though beyond 2,700 yards accuracy decreased due to the minor differences in the velocity of individual bullets. At long range the enemy had the uncomfortable perception that bullets were almost falling out of the sky, searching behind ridge lines and hitting points far from the frontline. British theory acknowledged that machine gun support fire could be either direct or indirect. As the manual *Fire Control* explained:

The normal method of engaging a target will be by direct fire, i.e., by laying on the target over the sights. The main asset of direct fire is extreme flexibility, which enables

German street fighting in defence, 1943. This is based on positions held by German paratroops in the Italian city of Ortona in December 1943, but it is representative of German tactics for urban defence on all fronts. (B) Barricades of rubble formed by blowing down houses on each side of streets; height varied from 4 to 6ft. (AT) 7.5cm PaK 40 AT gun hidden to cover barricade. (MG1) Automatic weapon covering barricade from third floor of house in next street, with field of fire over demolished buildings between. (MG2) MG42 dug into actual barricade. (MG3) Automatic weapons – MG42s, FG42s and MP40s – in second and third floors of houses, to cover barricades, the whole square, and all roads leading into it. (Peter Dennis © Osprey Publishing Ltd)

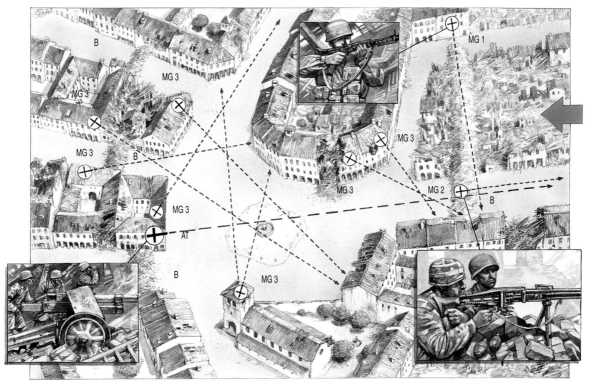

DIRECTION OF CANADIAN ADVANCE

Diagram showing the MG34 on its sustained fire tripod, Lafette 34; its spring-loaded cradle absorbed much of the recoil. Note the sling, and (bottom) the extension piece for use when the weapon was mounted for anti-aircraft fire. Below the shoulder stock note the precision traversing and elevation mechanism, allowing highly accurate pre-registered fire; there is also a remote trigger at this level. From Weber's *Unterrichtsbuch Für Soldaten* (1938). (Stephen Bull)

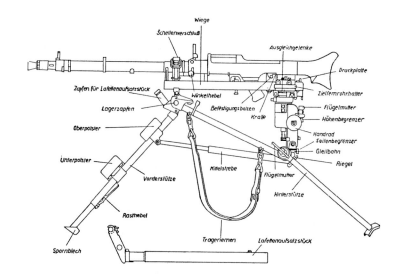

a succession of targets over a wide arc to be engaged quickly… The machine gun is capable of firing indirect, i.e. the gun is laid on an auxiliary aiming mark, with the elevation required to hit the target obtained and placed on the gun by instruments. Indirect fire is employed when it is impossible or inadvisable to occupy a direct fire position, or when shooting from a map. The main technical advantage of indirect fire is that the necessity for indicating the target to a number of individuals is removed. The laying of the gun is mechanical and is not affected by light or distance.

To this could well be added the significant point that machine gun teams using indirect methods would not usually be subject to direct enemy fire. On the down side, indirect firing entailed calculation and allowance for intervening 'crest clearance', and could not readily be corrected.

Firing orders to the gun teams were ideally in rigid sequence, to 'ensure that errors and omissions are detected immediately' and that personnel, knowing what to expect, would act more quickly. The best fire order was that 'which gets bullets on to the target in the shortest possible time'. Fire controllers were to give the following, 'loudly and clearly': range; indication of target; method of fire; side wind allowance; rate of fire; and then the actual order to open fire. Ranges were given to the nearest 50 yards, and when correction was needed it would be given by commands such as 'Up 400' or 'Left three taps'; the traverse was partially clamped, and was made by tapping either side of the rear 'traversing handles' with the heel of a hand. When several guns were under command the instruction would be prefaced with the number of the gun in question or the word 'All'. Wide targets could be engaged by 'tapping across' the target, while moving targets could be hit either by creating a fire zone through which the enemy would have to pass, or by use of the 'swinging traverse'. Contrary to war films and thus popular belief, swinging traverse was relatively infrequent, but was suitable at close range when other methods were too slow, or against lines of infantry caught in the open.

Support fire being acknowledged as the 'main tactical role of the machine gun', it was inevitable that friendly troops were likely to be in the vicinity of the target. Gun commanders were to give their safety 'first consideration', but fire was permitted to within three degrees of the known location of own troops, and fire over their heads and flanking fire in front was actively encouraged. Where friendly troops were defending nearby trenches, 'rules may be relaxed'; moreover, tanks were considered 'immune', so that supporting machine guns could 'put down close fire ahead of, or even among, friendly tanks'. The ultimate support was the 'machine gun barrage', normally delivered on a large scale as part of a set piece fire plan that might include artillery and mortars. To achieve sufficient density of fire it was recommended that at least one machine gun per 30 yards of front be used. Machine gun barrages could be delivered frontally, obliquely or from a flank, and could be 'standing' or 'creeping', but a safety margin of 400 yards in front of advancing troops was stipulated.

As we have seen, both main types of German machine gun, the MG34 and the MG42, were excellent 'general purpose' weapons. This made for ease of training, and their lack of water jackets made them relatively light. Under the 1944 divisional organization, a heavy weapons company was included in all infantry battalions; the machine gun platoon of the company numbered six guns, usually with horsed transport. Although most of the weapons with frontline units were MG34 and MG42 types, many other models were retained or pressed into service, and the old MG08 water-cooled gun still bulks large in the instruction manuals of 1940. The Dreyse MG13, theoretically discarded before the war, was also seen in small numbers, and interestingly turns up as the main support weapon of such second-line formations as the army postal service. Additionally, many foreign guns were pressed into service, especially with SS formations, which were at first relatively poorly supplied by the normal Wehrmacht sources.

As Weber's *Unterrichtsbuch* makes clear, the ideal machine gun detachment for the sustained-fire role was six men, including a *Gewehrführer* or gun commander, and a No.1 or *Richtschütze* who actually carried and fired the piece. The No.2 *Schütze* had the Lafette 34 tripod, which could be carried folded up on the back if moved any distance on foot. Gun Nos 3, 4 and 5 were essentially ammunition carriers, with a mixture of belt boxes, small ammunition drums or *Trommelträger*, and spare barrels. Other equipment including cleaning kit, entrenching tools and binoculars, was spread out among the team. In addition to the machine gun, the leader and Nos 1 and 2 two carried pistols, the remainder rifles. The Lafette 34 could be erected for prone, sitting or kneeling fire, and when making ready the gun commander would order 'Anschlag!', qualified accordingly by 'liegend', 'sitzend' or 'kniend'. The swiftest method was for two men to set up the tripod, one working on either side. The gun was then located on the sprung cradle of the tripod by the *Richtschütze*.

On the command 'Laden!' or 'Stellung!', the gun was loaded by feeding in a belt, which could be done with the top cover open or shut, and the gun was then cocked using the side handle. (Although strictly speaking *Laden* translates as 'load', *Stellung* – a word with many meanings – was still probably the safer option, being less easy to confuse in the heat of battle with *Entladen*, which was an order to 'discharge'.) Whatever the rate of fire employed, it was forbidden to use more than 250 rounds without pause, to avoid overheating and barrel wear. The 1940 *Handbook of the German Army* suggests that a common rate of fire was about 300 to 350 rounds per minute.

MORTARS

The mortar, a relatively low-velocity weapon with a high angle of fire, had been invented as long ago as the 15th century, yet it was only during World War I that its full potential as a battlefield weapon was fulfilled. By the 1930s many armies used 8cm or 3in calibre mortars, often based upon the simple Wilfred Stokes design, as support weapons at battalion level. Perhaps the most difficult operation was getting the piece and ammunition to the right place and locating a target. Thereafter firing was straightforward: manipulation of elevation and traversing screws brought the barrel to the right angle, and then a bomb was dropped into the muzzle. Most mortars in this category needed no separate firing mechanism, having a 'fixed striker' at the bottom of the barrel onto which the cartridge cap of the bomb fell, launching the round immediately. The German manual D147 for the Granatwerfer 34 gave typical instructions for action. Having set up and taken aim, the mortar commander gave the order 'Fire!' Mortarman No.2 then allowed the bomb, which he was 'holding firmly', to slide fins first into the barrel, and immediately removed both hands. All three of the immediate team then bent forward, with the Nos 1 and 2 ducking their heads and grasping either side of the mortar bipod.

Simplification and increased range were two areas of improvement pursued during the war. The German 5cm and British 2in platoon mortars were both simplified by the deletion of the over-complex sights originally provided, and in 1943 the German platoon mortar was actually deleted from frontline combat infantry companies altogether, being relegated to second-line and defensive roles. Toward the end of the war the Granatwerfer 34 was supplemented with a 34/1 model with a circular base plate, simplified bipod and a longer range.

The British 3in battalion mortar, which had a relatively modest 1,600-yard range on introduction, was uprated to 2,750 yards in the Mk 2 type. This particular change had a positive tactical impact in that fewer moves of the mortar were necessary in combat. On the minus side, greater range meant greater dispersal of the bombs, so where one 3in tube had previously been considered a viable 'fire unit', by 1944 it was desirable that the 'fire unit consist of two mortars or more'.

At the receiving end, mortar fire was a highly distinctive and terrifying experience. If one were close enough there was a hollow 'tonk–pause–tonk–pause–tonk' sound, followed by another longer hesitation before a deluge of

US troops firing the 81mm mortar. One man adjusts the aim by means of the traversing screw, which allowed alteration of direction five degrees to left or right without moving the weapon. When the crewman to the left drops the bomb down the barrel it will be fired immediately on hitting the fixed striker. To protect the eardrums mortar crews should – ideally – keep their heads below the level of the muzzle, and clamp both hands over their ears; under battle conditions such precautions were usually ignored. These soldiers are Nisei, Americans of Japanese extraction, who were gathered in units and posted to Europe, avoiding potential retribution by the Japanese. They fought with distinction in Italy and France; the Nisei 442nd Regimental Combat Team, which served with the 34th and 36th Divisions, became the most highly decorated regiment in the US Army.

bombs landed, exploding on impact. The projectiles could detonate on contact with pretty well anything, roofs and trees included. According to one British account, this was a handicap in street fighting; so some crews purposely fired their bombs with the sturdy iron safety cap still in place over the crushable percussion cap, hoping that the rounds would penetrate cover before exploding on the second, harder impact with the ground. The 'stonk' or sustained barrage was justly feared, but full effectiveness depended on observation. As Alistair Borthwick of 5th Seaforths remembered:

> We were watching from the Battalion Observation Post, which was an attic in D Company's area beside the road; and as we watched, a mortar bomb landed without any kind of warning right between the forward sections and wounded Sergeant Tommy Downs. It was a perfect shot, and could mean only one thing – without any more time being wasted on ranging, another dozen bombs would follow immediately. Everyone dived for cover. But no bombs came. Instead we heard the crack of a rifle. There was a slight pause, and then from the roof of one of Frazer's houses a German rolled slowly over and fell two storeys to the ground. There were no more bombs after that. The man had been invisible so long as he remained motionless, but Frazer had seen him when he signalled the first bomb.

Although sometimes overlooked, the mortar had its own peculiar tactical niche. As a British *Army Training Memorandum* of October 1942 explained:

> It is nearly always difficult to accurately locate an enemy; but, when he has been located, the 2in and 3in mortars can be relied upon to reach him in any square yard of ground in a given radius, no matter how enclosed the country. They are, moreover, relatively easy to handle and to maintain, and they have a high rate of fire and a considerable moral effect upon the enemy and (but inversely) upon our own troops. The 25-pdr gun is able to put down a total of 125lb of projectiles in one minute at 'intense' rate, while one 3in mortar can put down 200lb at rapid rate in the same period.
>
> It is obvious, therefore, that the mortar, with its disregard for cover, crests or undulations, is a very potent weapon: familiarity and skill in its use will repay a hundred fold the effort required in gaining it. A battalion commander has under his control, and ready to hand, weapons capable of blasting a concealed enemy in any normal cover. For short periods of time the six 3in mortars of a battalion can bring down a greater weight of fire than an eight-gun field battery; and yet they are flexible, easily controlled, and easily concealed.

According to another *Training Memorandum* of January 1944, there were different ways of using the 3in mortar during the attack. Sited to the rear of the 'start line' in such a way as to cover the entire battalion front, they could be directed by the platoon commander from a static observation post, following orders from the battalion commander. Alternatively they could make use of a 'mobile fire controller' going forward with one of the rifle companies, thus providing close support and fire on targets that were out of view at the start of the attack. Wherever the ground was suitable they could be pushed up with, and under command of, the forward infantry.

Ideally, 3in/81mm mortars were fired from pits, but achieving this during a rapid redeployment was problematic. One solution was to blast out a pit using six No.75 grenades placed in three 2ft deep holes; the result was a pit roughly 12ft long and 6ft wide. Outlining the task, digging out the small holes, laying the grenades and tidying the pit took about half an hour – but this saved more than four hours' laborious spadework. Those detonating the explosives were cautioned to be 30 or more yards away, wearing steel helmets.

Although sound ranging, flash spotting and eventually radar location were all used to find enemy mortars on the battlefield, given practice even the ordinary soldier could tell quite a lot from the evidence of his own eyes. Probably few infantrymen became really skilled in this obscure art, but as the British document *Mortar Location by Examination of Bomb Craters* (March 1944) observed, the shape of the hole could give away both the direction of flight and angle of descent. Using a stick, a map and a protractor – a handy example of which was printed on the back of the manual – a practised man could often narrow down the mortar position to a small probable area. The most obvious giveaway was whether the crater was round or oval, since circular craters were the result of bombs descending vertically from nearby locations.

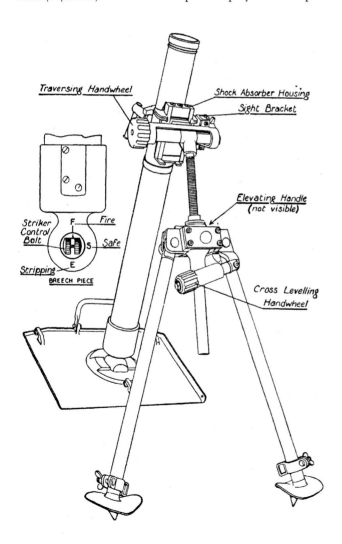

The German 8cm Granatwerfer 34, as depicted in *Enemy Weapons, Part V* (1943). The function and performance of this class of mortar in all its national variations were very similar. (Stephen Bull)

The US 81mm mortar deployed as part of the infantry battalion's heavy weapons company had a range of about 3,300 yards. The mortar itself was reckoned to have 'approximately the same mobility as the heavy machine gun'. Each mortar was capable of 'firing and effective concentration' in an area 100 yards by 100 yards, making the six-tube mortar platoon a potent force. Nevertheless, as the *Heavy Weapons Company* manual pointed out, there were significant tactical limitations to what could be achieved. Perhaps the biggest drawback was the high rate of ammunition expenditure. Depending on bomb type, each round weighed between 7lb and 10lb, and with a claimed maximum rate of fire of up to 18 rounds per mortar per minute, some hundreds of pounds of bombs could be fired in the first minute.

To husband ammunition, target selection was vital. Suitable targets were identified as including 'located, or approximately located, hostile machine guns, mortars and AT guns', plus:

> ...observed point or small area targets protected from effect fire of rifles and machine
> guns, such as personnel or weapons in road cuts, embankments or entrenchments.
> Reverse slopes and woods, which afford approaches defiladed from the fire of rifles
> and machine guns, are suitable targets in defensive combat. In offensive combat,
> reverse slopes and woods are also suitable targets in harassing a retreating enemy or
> to disrupt known or suspected movement or assembly of reserves. However, priority
> is always given to observed targets.

Additionally, mortars could be fired on positions with overhead cover, or to lay smoke. The high-angle fire of the mortar was a distinct advantage when it came to positioning the weapon. Provided observation could be had, directly or via available means of communication, the mortar could be placed in deep defiles, gaps in woods or other places that made them difficult for the enemy to hit.

MINES

Perfected in the interwar period, the anti-personnel mine added a sinister new dimension to the infantryman's war. Although technically engineer equipments, mines had considerable and growing impact on infantry combat, and not merely by causing casualties. Non-standard 'booby traps' were even less predictable. As the 1941 British official pamphlet *Booby Traps* explained, the object of the employment of traps and anti-personnel mines was to 'create an atmosphere of uncertainty and impose a sense of caution in the minds of the enemy, thereby

Allied postcard giving warning of a likely S-Mine booby trap, buried under a jerrycan – a desirable piece of booty, but not so obvious as to arouse suspicion – with a wire to a pull igniter. The same illustration appeared in the US *Handbook on German Military Forces* of March 1945. (Stephen Bull)

lowering his morale and slowing up his offensive. The casualties and damage inflicted are merely a means towards this end.' So it was that all arms required a basic knowledge of mines, and 'pioneer platoons' of infantry battalions often acquired the duty of locating and breaching enemy mines.

Mines could be laid in defined fields, with a tactical objective such as blocking an enemy advance, channelling him into 'killing grounds', or defending a specific locality. Anti-personnel mines could also be laid among, or even attached to, AT mines, thus making the clearing of a passage for tanks highly dangerous. Otherwise they were scattered as 'nuisance' mining. Interestingly, the British manual *Anti-Tank Mines* of October 1940 observed that AT types could on occasion be set off by motorcycles, horses or even a man 'walking, running, or riding a pedal cycle over them'. For this reason, all types of mine were to be considered dangerous by the infantry.

The main German anti-personnel mine at the outbreak of war was the small cylindrical S-Mine 35. This contained about 360 steel balls, and could be set off by means of a pressure igniter, a pull igniter used with a trip wire or an electrical command firing system. When the mine was activated, the inner casing was projected a yard or more into the air before the mine exploded into a cloud of fast-moving shrapnel – hence the American nickname 'Bouncing Betty'. In the absence of specialist detection teams the infantryman was supposed to avoid the S-mine by 'visual inspection and alertness'. He could also locate the mine by 'prodding' with a dedicated tool or ordinary bayonet: not jabbing, but 'pushing firmly into the ground at an angle of 45 degrees'. It took some time for the troops to learn how to react, as a sobering report in a British *Infantry Training Memorandum* of May 1944 records:

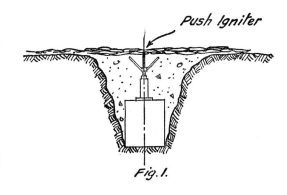

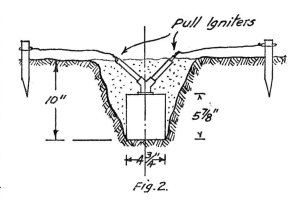

British illustration from 1941, showing how the German S-Mine could be used with either a multi-pronged 'push' igniter, or 'pull' igniters linked to trip wires. (Stephen Bull)

> I had been given to understand that if you stepped on an anti-personnel mine, the only thing to do was to hold the foot down, lean well back, accept that the foot might be blown off, but hope that the mine would not explode above ground level. Eighth Army engineers who had a good deal of experience with S-mines told me that though this idea had been current for some time it was quite erroneous. The anti-personnel mine has a delay of three or four seconds. When you step on it there is a muffled click in the

ground. Between three and four seconds after this click – that is, after the cap has fired – the cylinder blows four feet or five feet into the air. The cylinder seldom rises vertically on its axis, but generally takes a tilt one side or another. The splinters from the underside of the cylinder strike the ground about three yards from the position of the mine; those from the upper side fly in the air three or four feet clear of the ground. The base is usually blown downwards close to the original position of the mine...

It is probably best to move three or four yards away from the mine and lie down. Even though three seconds is quite a long delay, and a man lying flat on the ground twenty yards away is not likely to be hit either by the splinters or the steel balls that fly out of the cylinder, running any distance is not to be recommended. The enemy has a habit of laying mines in clusters, and a man running from one mine is quite likely to step on another without knowing it, and may drop down beside it or even on top of it. He may, of course, do the same even if he moves away only a short distance from the first click, but the risk is preferable to leaving the foot on the mine. Sometimes, too, the Germans put down mines that have no delay action. These jump straight out of the ground and allow no time for any action to be taken.

Nevertheless, there were extraordinary escapes. The chaplain of the 5th Seaforths trod on one that bounced up and knocked his glasses off: perhaps divine intervention prevented the main charge from exploding. Pfc Larry Treff of the US 26th Division was lucky enough to have one bounce up and hit him in the groin without exploding; he was thrown several feet but survived with minor injuries, though his groin area was so 'purple and swollen' that he was temporarily immobile. As Montgomery admitted in 1943, facing such a device needed 'a very robust mentality'.

By D-Day the S-mine was but one of a lethal family. Some German devices were made with the absolute minimum of metal so as to make detection by electronic means difficult. In the Schü-Mine, Types 1942 & 1943, the body of the mine was a wooden box, the pivoting lid of which depressed under the weight of the foot to activate a striker. An additional advantage was that the simple wooden boxes could be manufactured in schools and small workshops, thus saving on industrial capacity. In the 1943 Glas-Mine the body was of thick glass, with a thinner shear plate that set off the mine when broken by downward pressure. British soldiers eventually encountered so many types of enemy mine that it was impossible to teach all arms about every sort. From late 1943 policy was therefore to divide British troops into three training categories: the 'skilled' Royal Engineers; 'semi-skilled' trained detachments from most units; and the remainder, who were 'unskilled' in mines.

By the latter part of the war German mine warfare theory was highly developed, as the March 1945 US manual *Handbook on German Military Forces* explained. Major AT minefields would be laid out in uniform patterns, with anti-personnel mines sprinkled around the forward fringes – often with anti-lifting devices or trip wires. In all instances minefields were at their most useful when covered by fire. German mine layers would keep track of the layout with a *Minenmessdraht* or mine measuring cord, made from old telephone wire. This was usually 26 yards long, with marks for measurements and mine positions

GERMAN MINEFIELDS

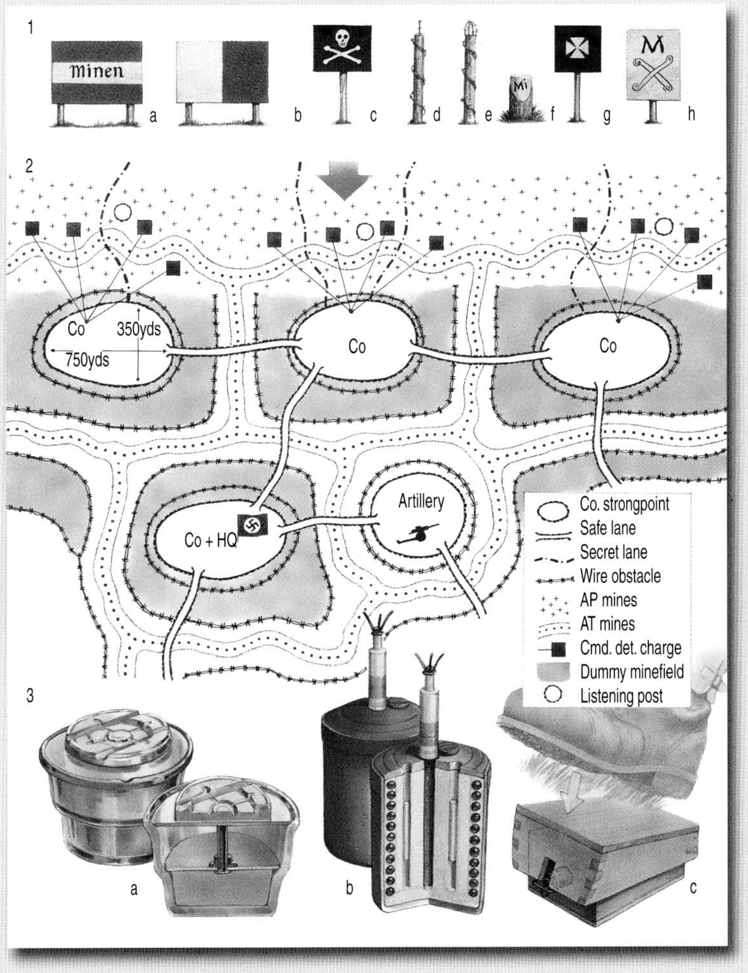

Diagram 1: Minefield signs.
(a) Actual minefield; (b) Minefield gap sign – gap on the white side, mines on the red; (c), (g) & (h) Alternative painted signs for actual minefields; (d) & (e) 'Subtle' signs made with barbed wire and stakes: (d) = anti-personnel mines, (e) = anti-tank; (f) Hastily painted sign on shaved tree stump. Diagram 2: Reinforced battalion position. Three company strongpoints forward, in line; headquarters co-located with fourth company, level with the artillery area; these areas, the open lanes linking them, and narrow parallel corridors flanking the anti-tank minefields, are free of mines. Command-detonated charges and listening posts are placed in the forward field of scattered anti-personnel mines; secret lanes through the latter allow the passage of patrols. Each of the company locations is surrounded by anti-tank mines. Inside these are large areas of dummy minefield bordered with wire. Diagram 3: Anti-personnel mine types. (a) The Glas-Mine; (b) The S-Mine or 'Bouncing Betty'; (c) The Schu-Mine. (Peter Dennis © Osprey Publishing Ltd)

on its length. Commonly, alternate rows would be staggered; optimum spacing for the S-mine was 2–4 yards apart, while Schü mines could be laid as closely as every 20in. Belts of anti-personnel mines were anything up to 12 rows deep, producing densities of perhaps four per metre of front. Forward of the main fields would be scattered unmarked mines denying avenues of approach, covering supply dumps or disused defences.

Standard mines were often supplemented by booby traps using igniters, blocks of explosive and grenades. The British *Army Training Memorandum* of January 1944 outlined four examples of such 'Nazi tricks'. In one instance booby traps were attached to British mines, so as to cause mayhem when they were eventually lifted. In another, grenades were left lying around rigged to explode as soon as touched; and in a third, attractive booty was fastened to explosives. The fourth subtle variation was not to booby-trap the 'bait' at all, but to mine a nearby hole or ditch from which men might attempt to observe or disarm any

Mine-clearing, Trier, Germany, March 1945: engineers from the 10th Armored Division pay the price for getting it wrong. The nearer casualty has a chance, and the medics are dressing his badly injured face, left arm and left leg (note that the left-hand medic has his own serial number stencilled on top of his helmet). The casualty lying ignored in the background seems to be dead already from massive head injuries.

traps. In one such instance an unwary NCO was said to have been transformed into portions too tiny 'to make even a small dog's breakfast'. A golden rule, therefore, was 'Don't fiddle about with any wires you may see lying around until you know what's at each end.'

US practice was exhaustively addressed in *Land Mines and Booby Traps* of November 1943. The main value of mines, according to American theory, was their AT potential. Minefields were best covered by fire, and intermingled with anti-personnel devices to discourage lifting or crossing, as 'minefields not covered by fire usually do not delay the enemy sufficiently to warrant the labor or materials expended on them'. It was recommended that defensive posts should be located within the minefield itself, and 'whenever possible in front of it', so preventing enemy patrols from finding the boundaries and lifting mines. Marked lanes and paths, visible from the friendly side, would allow the passage of troops – though these were not to become well-trodden paths that could be spotted by the enemy and additional wire, mines and covering fire were to be reserved to block the lanes in the event of attack. Where mines were needed but time was lacking for a formal field, 'hasty' fields were to be laid in a set pattern to make for rapid location, and not booby-trapped so as to be easy for friendly troops to locate and lift, or to be rearranged and improved into a properly prepared field.

The Tellermine TMi 42, one of five variants of a German mine that was manufactured in millions from 1929 until the end of the war, fitted with a range of fuse/igniter sets, and used on all fronts. All were about 11.8in in diameter and 2.75–4in deep, with a charge of about 12lb of TNT, carrying handles, and wells in the side and/or bottom for 'pull'-activated anti-lifting booby traps. It was usually employed as an anti-tank mine, but different pressure igniters were fitted, including a 99lb anti-personnel type. (Stephen Bull)

In the event, and with the major exception of the Ardennes, US troops were usually on the offensive, and so finding and lifting or avoiding enemy mines was the order of the day. Not using roads that had yet to be examined or cleared was important, but:

> To investigate every yard of ground with a mine detector or by probing would slow the advance too much. Risks must be taken, but losses will be lessened considerably if all personnel are alert, and are trained to search visually for mines at all times… Disturbed soil, piles of stones, mine boxes or traces of mine material, and unnecessary pickets all are likely indications of mined areas. Low wires of all types must be approached with caution. Anything unusual is worth suspecting, and any investigation must be made with care.

Five anti-tank TMi 35s fitted with a pressure bar, for simultaneous detonation. Note the cable for pulling it across the road when needed. (Stephen Bull)

Aerial reconnaissance, questioning civilians and looking at patterns of disturbance and tracks with no obvious purpose, might all lead to the discovery of enemy mines. Reconnaissance of enemy minefields was started as soon as possible, though preferably at night, with the objective of discovering boundaries, cross section and suitability for traversing with vehicles. With preliminary knowledge established, the 'minefield reconnaissance party', comprising an officer or NCO and six men, could start detailed work. Such parties could be either specially trained infantry, or engineers: in the infantry it was likely to be the battalion 'ammunition and pioneer platoon' that carried the burden.

It was recommended that two of the reconnaissance party carry submachine guns or carbines, while the remainder were armed only with hand grenades. The leader, who decided the direction of advance, was to go equipped with map, compass, nails, 200 yards of cord, flashlight and pliers. The No.1 and No.2 actually walked ahead of the leader, with the No.1 operating a 'short arm' electrical mine detector, or prodding, on a 4ft wide path. The No.2 carried white tape and markers to indicate mines, and cut any trip wires. The tape and cord were unreeled in parallel as the party advanced. The leader examined each find. His decision regarding the suspect object was recorded by knots in the tape as follows: trip wire – 1 knot; anti-personnel mine – 2 knots; AT mine – 3 knots; new type of mine – 4 knots.

'Local security' was provided by the armed Nos 3 and 4 moving about 25 yards behind the forward element, though these were to hold their fire 'unless absolutely necessary'. Further back still came the No.5, who was the relief detector man, carrying extra supplies, though his most critical duty was disarming the marked mines. If encountered, new types of mine were not tackled at this stage, the leader dealing with them on the return trip. The No.6 was a reserve man who remained at the point where the party entered the field, with any additional supplies including a spare detector. It was important that everything with the exception of the cord be removed as the party retired. The tape was reeled up again on the way back, and examination of it, compared with other tapes made by other parties, would allow important deductions about the nature and depth of the field.

What methods of breaching the field might be applied varied according to circumstance. Electrical detection and hand removal was judged the 'most reliable and quickest method', though slow prodding by hand was necessary for non-metallic mines. Flail tanks and rollers had the advantage that they could work under small arms fire, but were surprisingly slow, and in late 1943 still imperfect. Explosive or blast methods included the 'snake' type bangalore torpedo; the 'carrot' charge, which was dangled in front of a tank; the primacord net; and small charges placed on individual mines. Whatever was chosen, infantry were still likely to have a key role:

> Breaching a minefield in preparation resembles the opposed crossing of a river and requires the establishment of an infantry bridgehead force to cover the troops clearing vehicle lanes through the minefield. Since the enemy maintains a close watch over his minefields with observers and patrols, and frequently covers them with fire, it will seldom be possible to clear lanes without opposition, therefore full use is made of darkness, and heavy artillery concentrations and barrages.

In breaching the field there were several tactical considerations to be borne in mind. Speed was particularly important to allow the 'infantry bridgehead' to be reinforced with tanks and other weapons. Climatic conditions such as moonlight, fog and the possibility of the use of smoke could be turned in the attackers' favour. Rehearsal behind the lines took precious time, but could pay dividends in improved co-ordination and timing. Good communications and traffic control would make the best use of whatever lanes were cleared. (For more on AT mine warfare, see p. 170.)

MOTORIZED INFANTRY

Although there had been experiments with vehicles capable of transporting troops in battle as early as World War I, the evolution of 'motorized infantry' was essentially a phenomenon of the interwar period and World War II. The concept of troops keeping pace with tanks and acting in concert with armoured assault was a significant breakthrough. Tanks acting alone were relatively swift and powerful, but largely incapable of holding ground, and vulnerable to artillery and infantry if left exposed. The answer was a new type of formation that was a mixture of all arms using motorized transport. Arguably the consequences of this went far beyond the tactical; it made possible what we now know as *Blitzkrieg* warfare and made a significant contribution at the strategic level.

GERMANY: THE *PANZERGRENADIERE*

German exercises with infantry borne in requisitioned civilian lorries commenced in the Harz Mountains as early as 1921, and these were combined with aircraft by 1923. Britain established an experimental mechanized brigade in 1927. One of those 'deeply impressed' was the then captain Heinz Guderian, who built upon the ideas of the British Gen Fuller and Liddell Hart's 'Expanding Torrent' theory, and was instrumental in the formation of the first Panzer divisions in October 1935. Despite this relationship, British and German methods would be very different in the execution. As Guderian put it in his *Achtung Panzer!* (1937):

The main tasks of motorized supporting infantry are to follow up at speed behind the tank attacks, and exploit and complete their success without delay. They need to put down a heavy volume of fire, and require a correspondingly large complement of machine guns and ammunition. It is debatable whether the striking power of infantry really resides in the bayonet, and more questionable still in the case of motorized troops, since the shock power of tank formations is invested in the tanks and their firepower… Combat is not a question of storming ahead with the bayonet, but of engaging the enemy with our firepower and concentrating it on the decisive point.

So it was that German efforts centred on mechanizing supporting elements within the Panzer division and more lightly equipped 'motorized' formations, capitalizing on mobile firepower. As of 1938, motorized infantry and cavalry were all designated *Schnelltruppe* or 'fast troops' and came under General Guderian's command. In addition to the motorized infantry elements of the Panzer divisions there were four separate motorized divisions by 1939. Thereafter many more were added, and in 1943 the motorized infantry were renamed *Panzergrenadiere*.

Russia, summer 1941: Panzergrenadiers deploy from their armoured carriers in a blazing village. The half-track in the background is the SdKfz 251/10 platoon commander's vehicle, mounting a 3.7cm gun for fire support.

The manual for the *Schnelltruppe*, current as of January 1943, stated that motorized soldiers were capable of performing every infantry combat task. Moreover, they were to be able to fight from their vehicles, 'quickly alternating' between fighting mounted and dismounted. As Gen Farrar-Hockley has observed, they were thereby expected 'to mount a strong attack directly off the line of march'. The Panzergrenadier company generally fought with its battalion, but due to its generous allowance of support weapons was also suitable for independent missions. Armoured transport in some of the battalions made close co-operation with tanks a realistic option, and the Panzergrenadiers were often tasked with capitalizing on armoured attacks, mopping up and occupying territory won by tanks, supporting the tanks by destroying enemy nests or eliminating obstacles, and occupying bridgeheads.

In each 12-man squad three soldiers were expected to be fully trained drivers. These were taught to drive tactically, and by taking advantage of terrain to keep out of sight and enemy fire. Other tactics included rapid reversing to get out of fire, and driving with hatches closed and gas mask on. The squad was to use all its weapons, including grenades and machine guns, from the vehicle itself, when both stationary and in motion. In some instances targets were to be identified while in motion, with a brief halt to allow mortars or other weapons to be fired accurately. While on the move action might be expected anywhere, and the team was to travel in a state of 'combat readiness' – with weapons loaded, safety catches on, and all-round observation maintained by three of the squad. Particular care was to be taken for defence against close-in enemy who might attempt to lob grenades or Molotov cocktails into the vehicles. In the event of coming under fire the order to shut hatches would be given: halting under fire was not recommended, the preferred tactic being to drive around artillery fire zones, or through them if this was not practical. AT gunfire was a particular threat, which the leader would attempt to obscure by throwing out smoke grenades.

The squad was ordered to remain with its half-track as long as possible, fighting from the moving vehicle with the driver running down any enemy in their path. The half-track could also operate 'fire and movement', dashing from cover to cover while engaging with its machine guns. Some of this firing would be deliberately aimed for effect from the halt, but sometimes the shooting would be more general; short bursts fired on the move were intended to force the enemy under cover and suppress his return fire. Using a 'clock face' system, the commander could designate sectors around the vehicle to be put under fire – particularly useful when crops or other cover concealed potential enemy positions.

On the command 'Abspringen!' ('Bale out!'), the fighting team were to jump out of the half-track, over the sides as well as through the rear door, and immediately seek cover in the vicinity of the squad leader. They were to take two of the team's three machine guns with them; the driver and his assistant, who then secured the door, were to remain with the half-track and man the remaining gun. This manoeuvre could be executed at slow speeds as well as at

GERMAN PANZERGRENADIER PLATOON ASSAULT, 1943–44

The platoon are going into action directly from their SdKfz 251 personnel carriers, against a Soviet infantry position which brings them under fire during their advance. The vehicle formation is the *Zugbreite* or staggered line. The different infantry squads are shown at different stages of deploying from their half-tracks – in reality they would all be acting more or less simultaneously. (S) Soviet position.

(A) Platoon commander's half-track. On coming under fire, it speeds forward toward the objective, with the machine gunner putting down fire on the target; while another man throws smoke grenades ahead. (B) The vehicle slows to a crawl, the MG gunner keeping up suppressive fire on the target the infantry disembark swiftly, over the sides as well as through the rear door. As soon as they hit the

ground they begin to deploy forwards. (C) The vehicle has halted and its section has deployed forward in a loose linear formation, with their two MG42s and small arms.
(D) This half-track is still advancing at speed.
(MC) Motorcycle outrider, keeping back out of danger from the firefight but available to maintain communication within the formation.
(Peter Dennis © Osprey Publishing Ltd)

the halt. Once outside, the fighting tactics of the ten dismounted men were similar to those of the ordinary infantry squad, but the presence of two machine guns allowed heavy firepower to be placed at either end of the *Schützenkette* or firing line, or brought together either side of the leader in the centre of the squad.

A Panzergrenadier platoon comprised four half-track vehicles, three mounting squads and the fourth for the *Zugtruppführer* or platoon leader and his headquarters. This HQ team was to include messengers and a medic, and ideally this vehicle also carried a heavier weapon such as a 3.7cm gun or rocket launchers. A motorcycle outrider was intended to act as a messenger. Although the platoon could drive in close order columns and lines, the essential fighting formations were the *Zugkeil* and *Zugbreite*, with a minimum 50-yard dispersal between vehicles. In the *Zugkeil* the three squad vehicles formed a triangle with the platoon leader out to the front, while the *Zugbreite* was a loose line. The Panzergrenadier company had four rifle platoons, and additionally two heavy machine gun squads and a mortar squad; an infantry gun squad towed a 7.5cm gun. As of the late 1943 establishments, a tank destroyer squad packed a 2cm gun and rocket launchers. Total company strength was three officers, 52 NCOs and 165 other ranks. Light vehicles and trucks were added to the company column for supply, maintenance and other auxiliary duties.

Innovative, aggressive and frequently successful as German Panzergrenadier tactics were, they could come dangerously unstuck when confronted with an enemy who was determined and prepared. One instance was reported by Pte Len Stokes of the 7th Somerset Light Infantry, during a night assault in Normandy:

> Two enemy half-tracks drove right into our midst firing their machine guns like mad… Most of us were scurrying round looking for non-existent cover in the dark. Major Whitehead took immediate action. He snatched the loaded PIAT gun out of my hands, thrust his rifle at me. He then fired one shot at the first half-track which exploded and burst into flame. He then took up his rifle and fired at a German. The man fell back into the flames with his arms outspread. No.10 Platoon had not got their PIAT ready so the second half-track escaped.

Perhaps the most graphic illustration of the misapplication of armoured infantry assault tactics occurred on 18 September 1944, when SS-Panzer Aufklärungs Abteilung 9 – the armoured reconnaissance battalion of 9. SS-Panzer Division 'Hohenstaufen' – attempted to storm the road bridge at Arnhem. This unit of lightly armoured cars, half-tracks and 'soft skin' lorries was sent into the attack along a narrow ramp against British Airborne opposition equipped with AT guns

and PIATs. The defenders were swiftly alerted as the first armoured cars swept across the bridge, and lack of surprise and an inability to deploy under a hail of bullets and grenades led to the deaths of Hauptsturmführer Gräbner and many of his men. Photographs show upwards of 20 wrecked vehicles that had made repeated attempts to batter their way through.

According to one account, the main rush was '16 half-track vehicles and armoured cars'. As the German vehicles went by, 'Corporal Simpson and Sapper Perry, whose conduct that day was outstanding, stood up and fired straight into the half-tracks with Sten and Bren guns. The range was about 20 yards.' From an upstairs window Pte James Sims had a grandstand view of attacks from more than one direction:

> They made straight for us but obviously did not realise that some of the houses on
> their right flank were occupied by paratroopers. They were lorried infantry and made
> a bold attack, but many of the Germans died in their trucks and those that tried to

German motorcycle combinations were used to transport machine guns, 5cm mortars, ammunition and headquarters personnel at platoon and squadron levels. The strapped bundles contain the crews' packs and bedrolls.

escape were shot down before they could reach cover. One terribly wounded soldier, shot through both legs, pulled himself hand over hand towards his own lines… A rifle barked out next to me and I watched in disbelief as the wounded German fell back shot through the head. To me it was little short of murder but to my companion, a Welshman, one of our best snipers, the German was a legitimate target. When I protested he looked at me as though I was simple… They attacked with great spirit but we were lucky enough to have two 6pdr AT guns… The German AFVs were knocked out one after another as they tried desperately to disengage or negotiate the flaming metal coffins.

Another factor of limitation was simply Germany's inability to equip all Panzergrenadier units with armoured transport. Half-tracks were normally limited to the first battalion of a regiment; the rest had to make do with trucks. US intelligence documents of early 1945 state that at that date only one in four of the battalions attached to a Panzer division was designated as *Gepanzert* – 'armoured' – and able to fight directly from the vehicles.

US ARMORED INFANTRY

On the Allied side it was the US 'armored infantry' that most successfully emulated the aggressive motorized methods pioneered by the Germans. Huge-scale production of a suitable vehicle, in the shape of the M3/M5 half-

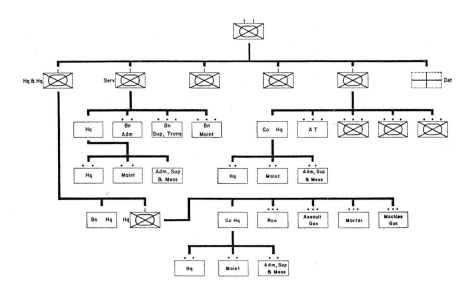

The organization of the US Armored Infantry Battalion, from the manual *Armored Division* (1944). The main combat components are three rifle companies, each with an AT platoon (3 x 57mm towed by M3 half-tracks) and three rifle platoons; each platoon has three rifle, one mortar and one LMG squad, each squad in one half-track. The Bn HQ Co includes a reconnaissance platoon (5 x jeeps, 1 x half-track); 81mm mortar platoon (4 x half-tracks); assault gun platoon (2 x half-tracks, 3 x SP howitzers), and machine gun platoon (3 x half-tracks). (Stephen Bull)

track series, was a major factor in the equation, but carefully formulated tactical literature and training reminiscent of that of the enemy was also important. US instructions of 1944 described the armored infantry as 'powerful, mobile, and lightly armored'. Generally it was to move forward, 'in vehicles until forced by enemy fire, or unfavourable terrain to dismount. Its primary role is support of the tank elements.' Twelve possible tasks were foreseen:

The 8.7-ton, six-wheel drive US M8 could reach 20mph cross-country and 55mph on a good road surface, and had 19mm turret and frontal armour. Its turret gun was a 37mm cannon, and it carried 80 rounds of high-explosive, armour-piercing and canister ammunition. Secondary armament was a .30-cal co-axial machine gun, and either another .30-cal or a .50-cal machine gun on a turret-top mounting.

    a. Follow a tank attack to wipe out remaining enemy resistance.

    b. Seize and hold terrain gained by the tanks.

    c. Attack to seize terrain favorable for a tank attack.

    d. Form, in conjunction with artillery and tank destroyers, a base of fire for a tank attack.

    e. Attack in conjunction with tanks.

    f. Clear lanes through minefields in conjunction with engineers.

    g. Protect tank units in bivouac, on the march, in assembly areas, and at rallying points.

    h. Force a river crossing.

    i. Seize a bridgehead.

    j. Establish and reduce obstacles.

    k. Occupy a defensive position.

    l. Perform reconnaissance and counter-reconnaissance.

Under the US organization described in *Armored Division* (1944), armoured infantry battalions consisted of a headquarters and headquarters company, a 'service' company, and three rifle companies. The headquarters company included not only command and communications elements but also a reconnaissance platoon, three mortar vehicles, three 75mm self-propelled guns and a HMG platoon. The service company carried out many of the administrative functions, with platoons for supply and maintenance. Each rifle company consisted of a headquarters, three rifle platoons and an AT platoon with three towed 57mm AT guns. The rifle platoons were three squads strong, plus a 60mm mortar squad and an LMG squad.

BRITAIN: MOTOR BATTALIONS, CARRIER PLATOONS AND KANGAROOS

The carrier platoon of 1st Bn, The Loyal Regt, 2 Bde, British 1st Infantry Division on the move under air cover from a P-47 in Italy, 1944. The versatile 'Bren' or 'Universal' carrier, first tested long before the war, was an ingenious concept, and proved extremely useful to the infantry battalion in a variety of roles. However, with a capacity of only five men plus the driver it was too small for fully fledged armoured infantry attack, and it was too lightly protected to confront armour. (Queen's Lancashire Regiment)

In 1939 the British approach was to motorize as widely as possible. Even though troops often marched, the supporting transport of infantry divisions was entirely motorized, and each infantry battalion also had a fast-moving 'carrier' element. Lorried infantry were also included in armoured formations, with two motorized battalions in the armoured divisional establishments of 1939–41. Subsequently this was increased to three, and by 1943 there were four motorized battalions per armoured division.

Where the British methods differed from the German was that vehicles were regarded as transport rather than fighting platforms, and it was usual practice to 'debus' prior to close engagement. This stance was at least in part due to the lack of armoured transport. Until supplies of M3 half-tracks were made available from the US in the last two years of the war, the British Army had nothing offering sufficient protection to make close combat from vehicles viable. The little fully tracked 'Bren' and 'Universal' carriers, adequate for moving scouts, machine gun or mortar teams, were much too small to accommodate complete infantry sections. Nevertheless, the 1944 establishment would see the 'motor battalions' – i.e. the integral infantry battalion of the armoured brigade within the armoured division, though not the division's separate infantry brigade – equipped with half-tracks on the scale of four per platoon. (Traditionally such units were provided by the Rifle regiments.)

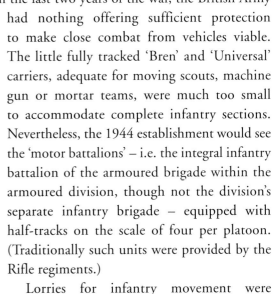

Lorries for infantry movement were frequently referred to as TCVs ('troop carrying vehicles'). These were widely used by the ordinary infantry battalions, especially later in the war. The cost of not leaving soft-skinned transport in good time could be catastrophic, as Lt Peter White of 4th King's Own Scottish Borderers discovered when facing an 8.8cm gun in Germany:

A short time later the lopsided shattered remains of my TCV was towed in by the last of my Platoon trucks… At the wheel, in the wreckage, but astonishingly apparently unharmed, I was pleased to see my pal, Walrus Whiskers. He was grey in the face and shaking. Seven large chunks of shrapnel had been splashed through the front of the truck's metal. All seven had passed in a compact pattern of gaping fist sized holes through the back of the seat I had so recently evacuated, and then into the Jocks in the body of the truck. There I was sad to find it had killed Jones, the paratroop chap, and seriously wounded five more, one of whom died later, and slightly wounded two others… shrapnel had hit and embedded five of Cutter's own .303 inch rounds of ammunition from his bandolier into his back. Yet another of our radio sets had been written off in the process. The back of the truck was in a chaotic mess of tattered equipment, torn metal, glass, blood, and broken eggs by the score.

Unique to British and certain Empire establishments was the 'carrier platoon', an integral part of the infantry battalion. Under the organization outlined in the 1943 *Handbook on the British Army*, the platoon comprised two officers and 62 men mounted on 13 Universal Carriers, 12 motorcycles and motorcycle combinations and a 15cwt truck. The firepower was considerable. The platoon was subdivided into four 'carrier sections' and a headquarters, each carrier section being nine men armed with three Bren guns, an AT rifle, a 2in mortar, a submachine gun and nine rifles. The main combat tasks of the platoon were close co-operation with infantry and tanks, flank protection and consolidation. Subsidiary activities included reconnaissance, intercommunication, raids and transporting weapons, stores and personnel. The carriers formed a handy reserve of mobile firepower, and for short periods could hold a front of anything up to 1,000 yards while the battalion advanced or retired.

It is interesting to note that during the 1940 campaign new uses for the carriers were found. As the June 1940 *Army Training Memorandum* explained, they could be used to infiltrate, or rush forward, parties of 'bombers' to neutralize enemy strongpoints. On night patrols they had the unexpected benefit that they could be mistaken for tanks. On the downside, the open-topped carriers were vulnerable to small arms fire from above, as well as to most types of heavier weapon. Although reasonably agile across country they had little trench-crossing ability, and were apt to be stopped 'by any obstacle which is a tank obstacle, and by many which are not'. The platoon would therefore advance near to the point of deployment, the Bren teams would dismount and take position, and the carriers were withdrawn under cover. As *Carrier Platoon* (1943) put it, 'if in doubt, dismount.'

Another tactical use of carrier platoons that appears in memoirs of the 1944 Normandy campaign was the establishment of 'joint posts' or JPs. These occupied the interstices of brigade positions, using carrier elements found from all the brigade's units. Being well armed and highly mobile, they formed a 'cement' to hold the front together, and at the same time allowed rapid transmission of information between the battalion headquarters.

Only in the last year of the war were the possibilities of fully tracked armoured carriers for the infantry section investigated. The first were a Canadian innovation, so-called 'unfrocked Priests' – the hulls of American 105mm self-propelled howitzers of that name, with the guns removed and the openings plated over. These were used during the breakout south of Caen in early August 1944. From October more were converted in Italy, and used alongside turretless Shermans. The 'Ram Kangaroo', which appeared at the end of 1944, was based on a Canadian Ram tank chassis, and was probably the best of the breed, although it still lacked overhead protection. The appearance of the fully tracked carrier promised more adventurous tactics, but it is clear from the account circulated in *Current Reports From Overseas* in April 1945 that 'debussing' before entering combat was the norm. Indeed, Kangaroo drivers were taught to halt completely, with one man on the Browning machine gun, while the infantry clambered out as swiftly as possible from all sides of the vehicle. The Kangaroo then remained stationary while they scrambled clear; the reasoning was that a vehicle that moved off instantly was apt to detonate mines, which would injure the now vulnerable troops.

One episode where daring and luck triumphed over doctrine was the celebrated battle fought at Medicina in northern Italy on 16 April 1945. Prior to this action the 14th/20th King's Hussars had undergone conversion, so that while B and C Sqns retained Sherman tanks, A Sqn received converted Priest carriers. As the regimental history records:

> The regiment was not best pleased at being 'mucked about' in this manner, but everyone cheered up considerably on learning that the infantry which they were to escort round the battlefield were their old friends of the 43rd Lorried Gurkha Brigade, with whom they practised such tactics ad nauseam, and who were just as anxious to try them out on the Germans as themselves.

The crossing of the Scolo Sillaro being contested, it took until almost last light to reach Medicina. There were still water obstacles to be crossed, and with some of C Sqn now firing into the town Col Tilney of the 14th/20th decided to dismount the 2nd/6th Gurkhas to enter on foot. At this moment Brig Barker drove up and told Tilney to direct the tanks straight into the built-up area. Aware that it was infested with rocket launcher teams and AT guns, Tilney is said to have resorted to prayer before relaying the order. Radio operator Isaac Freedman was one of those giving the message to the crews of Maj 'Bodge' Browne's C Sqn:

BRITISH PLATOON ATTACK ON STRONGPOINT, 1944

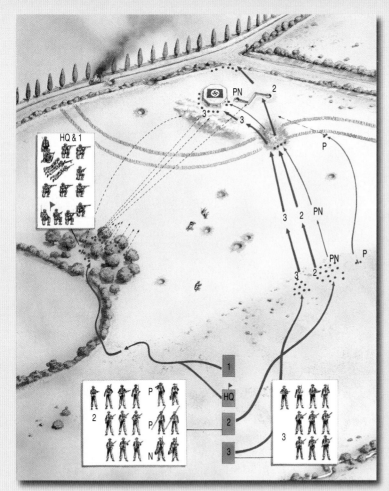

platoon sergeant, 2in mortar crew. The attack begins when this group brings the target under heavy and sustained fire. It will remain in these positions throughout the attack, firing until the assault sections are just short of the objective. (2) No.2 – the 'cut-off section' – are reinforced with the PIAT crew from platoon HQ (P), and by attached assault pioneers (PN) from the battalion's Support Company equipped with Bangalore torpedoes and demolition charges. They deploy under cover on the right, with the PIAT on the outer flank, and await covering fire from No.1 Section. When it is provided, they advance to the outer wire defences, led by the pioneers. While the PIAT crew take up a flank position and bring the pillbox under fire, the pioneers throw smoke grenades and then breach the wire and minefield with the Bangalores. When the breach is achieved, No.2 Section assaults through it, to clear any enemy trenches supporting the pillbox. When these have been silenced it hooks behind the pillbox to prevent any retreat from it, and takes up a temporary fire position. The pioneers follow, and place charges against the embrasures and entrances of the pillbox. (3) No.3 – the 'clearing section' – advances on the flank of No.2. When the pioneers breach the wire, No.3 Section assaults through the gap and attacks the pillbox, entering it through the blown doors and clearing it with grenades and small arms. (Peter Dennis © Osprey Publishing Ltd)

Advancing from the bottom of the page – in the order of march No.1 Section, HQ, No.2 Section (reinforced), No.3 Section – the platoon deploys forward. (HQ & 1) No.1 Section – the 'fire section' – takes up positions in the edge of woodland on the left flank. Behind them is the HQ element: platoon commander, signaller or runner,

> The order that the tanks were to lead the attack into Medicina came from Brigade and seemed a most astonishing decision. Tanks, to say the least, were not at their most effective in close quarters action such as confronted C Squadron. They were to attack down the narrow main street, with houses on each side in which there were desperate defenders armed with bazookas amongst other things… I was on the radio at the time that Major Browne urged his tanks into the attack calling out 'Yoicks Tally Ho!'

When C Sqn made their 'cavalry charge' down the street they were met with Panzerfausts and 8.8cm gunfire. Browne's tank succeeded in knocking out a self-propelled gun and two 8.8cm guns, but was then disabled by infantry AT weapons. Those of his crew who were still able dismounted, and attacked their attackers with revolvers, killing some and driving others away. Squadron SgtMaj Long was killed while engaging the enemy with his Thompson gun from his open turret. Fortunately the remainder of the regiment now arrived, and the carriers deposited the Gurkhas nearby: 'The first blood was drawn by the Subedar who chased the man with the bazooka, responsible for blowing up Plumley's tank, and chopped him up round a corner. The Gurkhas then went off in full cry, hunting Germans through the houses and killing them in cellars, lofts and on the roof tops.'

Freedman described their attitude as 'enthusiastic', and as far as he could tell they were taking no prisoners. This was all very effective, but not, as Col Tilney later admitted, the way he would have preferred to have done it.

TANK CO-OPERATION

As the power balance between armour, infantry and AT weapons shifted, so did the tactics for infantry and armour co-operation. Classic *Blitzkrieg* theory envisaged armour as the spearhead of attack. As Necker put it in *The German Army of Today*, tanks, in conjunction with aircraft and motorized supports, made the breakthrough on a narrow front, leaving 'the mopping up operations to the infantry proper, who were following up.' Use of such tactics on a large scale came as a considerable shock to the Allies, who naturally sought either to frustrate or to emulate them. Yet as AT defence gradually improved, and surprise became more difficult to achieve, closer tank-infantry co-operation became the order of the day.

By 1941 the standard British practice, as outlined in *The Infantry Division in the Attack*, was to place the forward infantry 'with the second echelon of tanks'. 'Cruiser' tank tactics, with armour-only formations, proved largely ineffective as they were vulnerable to dug-in AT guns, and could not hold the ground that they succeeded in occupying. In the wide open spaces of Russia attacking German formations formed large armoured arrowheads, or boxes, within or behind which motorized infantry would advance. The infantry were thus difficult to separate from the tanks, and could penetrate the enemy front in their wake, fanning out once through the gaps to take the enemy in the flanks and rear. In 1942, *Periodical Notes on the German Army* observed that where tanks could not go, or tank obstacles hampered armoured effectiveness, the 'lorried infantry brigade' would make the main effort of the Panzer division. Intelligence in the *Regimental Officer's Handbook* of August 1943 showed that whether infantry or tanks were to the fore of the German attack now depended entirely on the situation, and that larger formations would be screened by a mixture of both. 'All arms columns' or *Kampfgruppe* – battlegroups – were a common feature. Both tank-riders and troop carriers would be used.

By the latter part of the war infantry preceding tanks had become commonplace. The British pamphlet *Notes From Theatres of War* (1945) explained that the 'introduction of close range AT weapons on a large scale has increased the responsibility of co-operation that rests on the infantry.' The scheme described in the *Handbook on German Forces* saw complete integration, with Panzers advancing:

> … by bounds from cover to cover, reconnoitring the terrain ahead and providing protective fire for the dismounted Panzergrenadiers. The tanks do not slow their advance to enable the infantry to keep continuous pace with them, but advance alone and wait under cover until the infantry catches up with the advance… The tank's machine guns usually engage infantry targets at about 1,000 yards range and under, while the tank guns engage targets at 2,000 to 2,500 yards.

Where self-propelled assault guns were used to support an infantry attack these were invariably with or behind the attacking troops. Deployed en masse whenever possible, they were not to betray their presence before the start of the attack, but were to be used primarily 'to neutralize enemy support weapons at short ranges over open sights.'

Russia, autumn 1941: a whole squad – *Gruppe* – of infantry riding on a PzKw III tank, along with the turret crew. The infantrymen wear their *Zeltbahn* camouflaged tent sections as ponchos against the rain. Judiciously handled, 'tank-riders' could give close protection to armour while receiving valuable support themselves. (Stephen Bull)

US tactics of 1944 envisaged circumstances under which a tank battalion could be attached to an infantry regiment, with tank sub-units attached directly to the infantry battalions, or 'directed to support an attack'. When tanks were

GERMAN *KAMPFGRUPPE* TANK/INFANTRY ATTACK, 1944/45

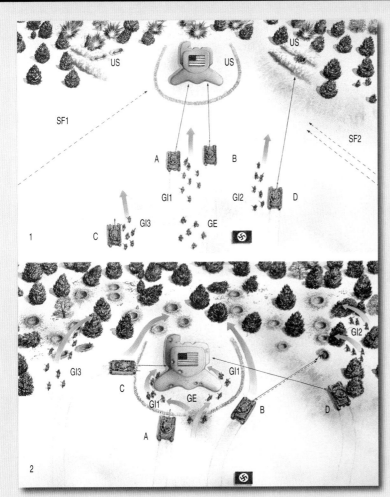

(GI1) Under cover of this fire, one or two German infantry squads have dismounted from the tanks and advance for the frontal assault. (GE) A squad of German assault engineers accompany the main infantry sections. (C) The third Panzer halts to dismount its infantry – (GI3) – who begin to deploy toward the US right flank positions. (D) The fourth Panzer has dismounted its 'riders' – (GI2) – and shells the US left flank machine gun nest while they deploy toward it. Diagram 2: (GI3) German infantry clear the US right flank trenches and hook forward behind the pillbox. (A & C) Two tanks close up to the outer US defences – which they do not attempt to cross, for fear of mines – and give direct supporting fire. The Panzer on the flank will shortly advance to help cut off any retreat by the defenders. (GE) The German engineers have blown a breach in the outer defensive wire and minefield. Some of them now accompany the assault infantry up to the pillbox. (GI1) Once through the wire the assault infantry sections divide for close-in attacks on the embrasures and entrances of the pillbox with grenades and small arms fire, supported by the engineers with charges. (B) The third tank fires on the US left flank position with its main gun and machine guns. (D) The fourth tank fires on the pillbox before advancing to outflank it. (GI2) Timing their advance to avoid friendly fire from the tank, the German right flank section clear the woodland before hooking round behind the US positions. (Peter Dennis © Osprey Publishing Ltd)

This represents a fully integrated attack on a US-held position in the Ardennes, 1944/45, by a German tank platoon, an infantry platoon and attached engineers.
Diagram 1: US platoon holding old Belgian pillbox, with flank parties entrenched in edge of woods. German artillery is laying down smoke and high explosive on and behind them. (SF1 & SF2) From the flanks, German 2cm cannon and machine guns fire on the US positions. (A & B) Two German PzKw IV tanks fire on the pillbox with their 7.5cm main guns.

attached to infantry the senior tank officer became a 'special staff officer' to the battalion commander, and his role was to 'advise the infantry commander of his tanks' capabilities' and make appropriate tactical recommendations: 'Tanks assist the attack of infantry by destroying or neutralising hostile automatic weapons, reserves, counter attacking troops, artillery, communication and supply installations, barbed wire and similar obstacles, and by dominating objectives.'

In the Normandy bocage the assistance was closer still. According to the US 90th Infantry Division history, the motto became 'one field, one section, one tank': the tank broke through the hedged boundary under cover of the infantry weapons, then took position to allow the foot soldiers to advance along the field edges. On occasion the relationship could be reversed, so that part of an infantry battalion was attached to a tank battalion for local security and ground-holding purposes:

> Infantry assists tanks by destroying or neutralizing hostile anti tank weapons and tank hunting teams, locating and removing mines and other tank obstacles, seizing ground from which tanks may attack, locating defiladed routes of advance for tanks, or taking over an objective which the tanks have captured or are dominating. Tanks are capable of capturing and briefly dominating an objective, but not of holding it for a considerable time.

Where possible, attached infantry moved in trucks, but:

> ... it may be necessary for them to travel on the tanks. A tank company can carry 75 to 100 infantrymen; six can ride on the rear deck of a medium tank, and four on a light tank. In rear areas more men can ride, when rope hand holds are provided. The infantry dismount prior to the launching of the tank attack.

As demonstrated by photographs showing dozens of men clinging precariously to tanks, this instruction was as often honoured in the breach as in the observance. Moreover, the question of 'tank riding' was never satisfactorily resolved. Having infantry actually on the tanks ensured that they were there when needed to protect the armour from AT infantry, and also that tank support was as close as possible to the infantry. But armour was a magnet for enemy fire; and there were grisly episodes when armour reversed or accelerated blindly over their own disembarked passengers.

* * *

Perhaps surprisingly, the basic tactics of rifle, LMG and grenade fighting changed less between 1939 and 1945 than they had done between 1914 and 1918. Moreover, while World War II is widely assumed to have been a war of technology, characterized by tanks, submarines, radar, encryption and the atomic bomb, it would be a serious mistake to assume either that infantry was no longer important, or that it failed to adapt to changing circumstance. Confusion and luck were always liable to be governing factors in infantry combat, but tactics – sometimes new tactics – were decisive in battle. Self-reliance by the small unit of infantry became ever more important as the war progressed.

The old themes of exploitation of terrain and integration of different types of personal and support weapon remained central to infantry combat. Tactical training improved, and the thorough learning of battle drills and skills to fall back on in times of trouble helped to maintain morale and prevent panic. Important advances were made in many areas. Over time the invention of effective hand-held AT weapons and new tactics for their use significantly reduced the dominance of armour. Increasing numbers of machine guns and the birth of the 'assault rifle' multiplied infantry firepower, and there was a growing tendency to replace numbers of men with fewer but more effective weapons.

US Seventh Army infantry riding an M10 tank destroyer into Bourg, France, 1944. This dangerous degree of overcrowding was about three times the capacity recommended by instructions.

Waffen-SS *Sturmpioniere* blowing a gap through barbed wire defences using a 'Bangalore torpedo'. In most of the combatant armies assault engineers were attached to the attacking infantry companies for demolitions.

'Armoured infantry' tactics evolved rapidly, though not uniformly, among the combatant powers. Germany achieved the most spectacular results early on, but not without cost. The British adopted a 'safety first' approach, not least because they lacked equipment, but they later experimented successfully with the fully tracked carrier. The Americans with their M3 half-tracks were more able to emulate the German methods, but changing circumstances led to less dramatic outcomes by the time that they were fielded in large numbers. The new AT weapons – plus mines, which were widespread and difficult to detect – ensured that the campaigns of 1944 and 1945 were quite unlike the *Blitzkrieg* of 1939 and 1940. Another US contribution was the increased use of battlefield radio communication by very small infantry units.

Obviously, not all soldiers were familiar with all of the tactics, and some of the less well trained were woefully ignorant; yet the amount of information printed and circulated on every aspect of military activity was truly astonishing. Learning to obey orders, to drill, to master fieldcraft and new weapons, and to maintain health were just parts of the infantry story – there were manuals on virtually everything. From *Handbook on Clothing and Equipment in Cold Climates*, compiled for the British War Office in 1941 by Drs Roberts and Bertram of the

Scott Polar Research Institute, one learns how to urinate in sub-zero winds without freezing the genitalia. In the official Nazi party publication *Landser lachen* ('Squaddies' Laughs') of 1944, the German soldier was taught that fighting on the Eastern Front had its funny side after all. Yet if any printed words pointed to the core motivation of the infantryman, they were to be found in the *British Soldier's Welfare: Notes for Officers*. Soldiers were more upset by unfairness than hardship; good officers made good troops; and boredom was the worst enemy of morale. More revolutionary, and perhaps a key reason why the infantrymen of the Western democracies ultimately triumphed, was principle 'No.7':

> Every man is entitled to be treated as a reasonable human being, unless he has shown himself unworthy of such treatment. Whenever possible, therefore, the reason for irksome orders or restrictions should be explained to him, and in most matters affecting his own welfare the man's point of view should be considered. Such action strengthens discipline and is not a sign of weakness.

PART 3
ANTI-TANK TACTICS

INFANTRY & TANKS

Infantry are inseparable from tanks, both in the assault and in an integrated AT defence. This concept was understood almost immediately upon the first fielding of tanks, and became a basic precept of tank and AT warfare:

> Tanks unaccompanied by infantry cannot achieve decisive success; they must be supported by infantry, who alone can clear and hold ground gained... If [enemy] tanks succeed in penetrating the line, the [friendly] infantry must hold out and concentrate all their efforts on stopping the advance of the enemy's infantry, while the hostile tanks are dealt with by our artillery. The defeat of the enemy's infantry must therefore be the first consideration in all plans for anti-tank defence.

These statements are found in the US Army's *Instructions for Anti-tank Defense* (Provisional – February 1918). Other than the fielding of dedicated AT weapons, these concepts remained unchanged throughout World War II.

At the beginning of World War II most countries had a basically sound AT doctrine. The fatal flaw was that the effect of employing the tank in large combined

Opposite:
Regardless of the armour, tankers were quick to add additional protection from AT fire. Here a US Stuart M5A1 light tank has track links, a road wheel and sandbags fastened on the hull front; even filled 5gal water cans gave a little extra protection, and more track links are fastened to the turret sides. The toothed attachment on the bow was a locally fabricated blade to cut through Normandy hedgerow banks. Note too the 'grousers' added to the outer edge of the tracks, to increase track width and reduce ground pressure.

Tank design and capabilities varied greatly during World War II; this German PzKw IV Ausf F of 1941 may be considered a typical medium tank of its day. The thickest armour (50mm) is on the hull and turret fronts and the gun mantlet; turret sides and rear are 30mm, upper glacis 25mm, hull sides and rear 20mm, hull roof 15mm, turret roof 10mm. Early in the war the main gun was optimized for infantry support – here a short-barrelled 7.5cm for knocking out field fortifications. By 1943 the role of the tank had evolved; long-barrelled high-velocity guns were being mounted, to fight a new generation of enemy tanks led by the Soviet T-34.

arms formations was not fully understood. France had placed complete faith in its underpowered AT guns, deployed in depth. In spring 1940 the Germans massed seven Panzer divisions on the weak Ardennes front, attacking through an unexpected sector and overwhelming French defences. Once they broke through they thrust deep into the rear, completely dislocating French attempts to respond. The French still viewed tanks as infantry support weapons; they never massed their armour, supported by other arms, to manoeuvre against breakthroughs.

The 1940 *Blitzkrieg* sent other armies into near panic, and a rush to find a means of countering it ensued on both sides of the Atlantic. The fear was often exaggerated, convincing some that infantry units were helpless against tanks. Often the planning committees looked only at the tank itself, and did not consider the combined arms aspects of German doctrine; but effective AT defence would also have to be a combined arms effort.

Anti-tank tactics and weapons were in a constant state of evolution throughout the war. Improved models of tanks, evolving armour tactics, new field innovations and the overall development of combined arms tactics all contributed to this process. Anti-tank weapons changed drastically: there was a constant search for more lethal, more accurate, longer-ranged, more compact and lighter weapons. While improved tank designs and increased armour protection greatly influenced the development of AT weapons, those other factors were equally important.

TANK VULNERABILITIES

Except to the tank's immediate front and the direction in which the turret was oriented, the crew were for all practical purposes blind. Many of the means of vision were mounted high to maximize their fields, and stealthy and courageous infantry could easily move into the tank's blind zone or 'dead space' (*Toter-Raum*). This might extend out as far as 20 yards (inset, B), within which a prone or crouching infantryman was invulnerable to the main gun (1) and co-axial machine gun (2). Within perhaps a 10-yard inner zone (inset, A)

he could not be seen or engaged from pistol/submachine gun ports (3) or by hand grenades tossed from a hatch such as the turret side escape hatch (4). Of course, the width and configuration of these zones varied from tank to tank and changed as the turret rotated. The driver (5) and bow machine gunner (6) could only see directly ahead and a few degrees to either side. The turret gunner had a very narrow field of vision through the gun sight, and only in the direction the main gun was pointing. The commander had the

best field of vision through vision blocks or slits in the low cupola (7), and possibly a periscope set in or beside the hatch. This tank is fitted with three-tube smoke grenade projectors (8) on either cheek of the turret. Here, in North-West Europe, an American infantryman rushes a PzKw IV Ausf H tank with a 20lb M1 satchel charge. The most favourable direction from which to attack was the quarter behind whichever direction the turret was oriented (inset, C), unless it was facing to the tank's rear. (Steve Noon © Osprey Publishing Ltd)

THE TANK THREAT

From the first use of tanks by the British Army on the Western Front in September 1916, infantry has perceived them as a 'terror' weapon capable of routing troops, piercing defensive lines and driving deep into rear areas. Considering the limitations of period AT weapons, there was considerable justification for this fear.

To understand the capabilities and limitations of AT weapons and tactics, one must be familiar with the capabilities and limitations of tanks themselves. Tank design evolved so rapidly during World War II, and the characteristics of individual models differed so markedly, that generalizations are difficult. In any discussion of general strengths and weaknesses it must be borne in mind that these do not necessarily apply, in specifics or in comparable degree, to all tanks.

At the beginning of World War II the light tank was the most common class. Light tanks weighed some 6–15 tons, with comparatively thin armour usually vulnerable to the modest AT guns of 1939–41. They had a crew of two to four men, and were generally armed with a 37mm main gun, though often only with machine guns. Their principal role was scouting, and acting as 'light cavalry outriders' for heavier tanks. In less affluent armies, however, the light model was sometimes the principal combat tank. As the war progressed light tanks fell from favour because of their vulnerability; lightly armoured scout cars, with a high degree of mobility and speed, better served the reconnaissance role. Some light tanks were retained in secondary roles, and some new 'light' models were fielded with almost the capabilities of early-war medium tanks.

Medium tanks were more heavily armoured; they were usually capable of withstanding light AT gunfire, and to some extent medium calibre AT guns, at least from the front. They were generally in the weight range 15–30+ tons, had crews of four or five, and mounted main armament of between 47mm and 76mm calibre. Mediums were often viewed as supporting tanks, providing heavier calibre, longer-ranged guns to support their light counterparts. Initially their speed was comparatively slow.

As it was realized that medium tanks provided the best overall capabilities to withstand improving AT weapons, to manoeuvre, provide fire support and fight other tanks, so their capabilities were steadily upgraded. Armour and speed were improved, and while the gun calibre was seldom increased beyond 76mm, weapons were upgraded to offer longer range and more penetration. In the second half of the war mediums, in the character of 'general purpose' tanks, appeared in overwhelmingly greater numbers than other classes.

A sub-category of mediums was the 'infantry tank', a product of two opposing schools of thought. Some planners believed that two separate tank types should be provided, one to fight other tanks (in the British term, 'cruiser tanks'), and the other to support the advance of infantry. The latter were generally more heavily armoured, and mounted a gun intended to knock out enemy positions; they could be slow, since they had only to keep pace with the infantry.

While some examples of what could be termed heavy tanks existed at the beginning of the war, their tactical purpose was not carefully thought through;

Any tank that could be seen could be hit and knocked out with the appropriate weapon. This German PzKw V Ausf A Panther was holed through the 45mm hull side armour by an AP round from a 75mm gun, which probably killed the entire turret crew. Note the track links on the turret side, and skirt plates hung along a rail on the hull side, intended to detonate bazooka rounds before they struck the hull.

they were multi-gun, heavily armoured and very slow. More effective heavy tanks began to appear midway through the war. Designers strove to provide a mount for a heavy high-velocity gun of between 88mm and 122mm, capable of killing any tank at long range, under armour sufficient to defeat medium tank guns and infantry AT weapons. They were generally slow and very heavy (55–70 tons), which limited cross-country and even road mobility, as many bridges could not support them. They were present on the battlefield in only small numbers, but when skilfully employed they might have a definite, and occasionally a decisive, effect.

While other types of armoured fighting vehicles (AFVs) were encountered by the infantry, most were relatively vulnerable to light AT weapons. These included scout cars, reconnaissance vehicles, half-track personnel carriers and self-propelled assault and AT guns. Only two of these types presented a threat comparable to that of tanks: the assault gun and the tank destroyer. Both were built on tank chassis, giving them the same mobility as tanks. Assault guns lacked a revolving turret, having the main gun mounted with limited traverse in a heavily armoured hull superstructure. These were mainly infantry support weapons, but some mounted longer guns capable of AT fire (though the lack of a rotating turret greatly limited this ability). Tank destroyers – self-propelled AT guns – sometimes had a rotating turret, but this often had an open top, and the vehicles' armour was lighter than that of the tanks they fought; they relied on speed or concealment for survival.

Tanks were shock weapons, intended to be used en masse, capitalizing on their armour protection, firepower and mobility. At the very least a tank was intended to protect its crew from machine gun and small arms fire, shell fragments and anti-personnel mines. They also offered varying degrees of protection from AT fire, other tanks' guns, mortars and artillery. They could travel cross-country over uneven ground and through dense vegetation, and surmount anti-personnel and light anti-vehicle obstacles, as well as rubble in built-up areas. All these advantages had their limitations, however, depending on the specific tank model.

PROTECTION & VULNERABILITIES

Despite their psychological impact on infantrymen in the open, tanks were far from being the undefeatable, unstoppable, fire-breathing monsters so often portrayed. Vulnerabilities abounded – if conditions were favourable to those fighting against them; if leaders made the right series of assessments and decisions; if the troops possessed the necessary cunning and determination; and if the situation permitted them to take advantage of varied terrain and of the constantly changing tactical situation. Tanks are large and extremely noisy, and thus difficult to conceal. No matter how effective a camouflage pattern a tank may be painted with, or how thoroughly it is covered with vegetation, its every movement (and on dry ground, the dust it raises) signals its presence. It is difficult to conceal from the air in all but the densest woodland, and the tracks gouged out by its passing are easily detected.

It is difficult to concentrate or relocate tanks in a combat zone, because of the considerable effort required to transport them long distances by heavy road transporter or rail wagons. Long-distance travel on their own tracks over even improved roads renders a significant percentage mechanically disabled before they see combat. Tanks require a considerable support 'tail' in the form of specialized maintenance personnel, spare parts, field repair facilities, recovery vehicles, and fuel and ammunition transport.

Tanks originated to provide a means of conveying protected weapons and their crews over obstacles and while under fire, so their armour is one of their defining advantages.

The armour on a tank was not consistently thick; typically, the thickest was found on the gun mantlet (the shield protecting the opening where the gun

A tank destroyer was not a tank; while built on tank chassis, their armour was generally lighter and they often had open-topped turrets. They were designed to kill tanks and not to support infantry, although they often had to perform that task – a role in which they were made vulnerable (like this US M10) by the lack of a tank's co-axial and bow machine guns. In urban fighting all AFVs suffered from the limited elevation of their guns, which restricted their ability to engage targets on the higher floors and roofs of buildings.

emerges from the turret) and other frontal parts of the turret, and on the front of the hull. This too varied: the upper glacis – the down-sloping portion of the hull front – was thicker than the lower glacis on the bottom of the nose. Next in thickness were the turret sides, followed by the forward and central portions of the hull sides, especially above the tracks. The lower hull 'inside' or 'behind' the tracks was thinner: being lower, it was difficult to hit, and was also protected to some extent by the tracks, road wheels and return rollers. The rear portions of the hull sides, the back of the hull and the top surfaces of both hull and turret were relatively thin; so was the turret rear, though this was thicker than much of the hull side armour. The belly, except for the most forward portion, was relatively thin. Heavy armoured gratings protected the top of the engine compartment, but were vulnerable to demolition charges and incendiaries.

The construction of a tank's armour was also a factor in its level of protection. Homogeneous armour maintained a constant degree of hardness through its entire thickness, while hard-faced armour had a harder exterior than interior. Hulls and turrets might be manufactured by riveting or welding armour plates together, or might be cast in single pieces. Bolting and riveting was the least effective, as a hit could buckle the plates and break them loose, while simultaneously turning 'popped' rivets into projectiles. Welded armour was more effective, but cast armour was even better. The use of sloped armour increased during the war in order to deflect the strikes of AT projectiles; this greatly increased armour effectiveness, allowing thinner armour and thus reducing weight. More attention was given to external design to reduce the number of 'shot traps' – i.e. turret overhangs and right angles in armour that allowed projectiles a purchase.

Besides a tank's integral armour, tankers often took measures to provide additional protection. Spare track sections and road wheels were attached to turret and hull, sandbags were wired to the hull, wire mesh screen or sheet metal skirts were fastened to the hull sides to lessen the effect of shaped-charge ordnance, or wooden planks were affixed to ward off magnetic hand mines.

Regardless of the thickness, type and slope of armour, a tank requires openings for crew entry, weapons, sights, vision, ventilation, external fittings and access to the engine and other automotive components. At the very least there was a hatch over the driver's position and one or two hatches for the turret crew. There might also be escape hatches, in the turret side or rear, hull side above or behind the tracks, and sometimes in the belly; late in the war this latter feature was often deleted, as it made tanks more vulnerable to mines. (Contrary to popular perception, hatches could be locked from the inside.) Sometimes a small hatch was provided in the turret rear or side through which to load ammunition or eject spent shell cases. Smaller pistol/submachine gun ports were sometimes provided in turret sides, and flare pistol ports in the turret roof. Early tanks had vision slits around the commander's cupola, in the turret sides and other positions, and a shuttered driver's view port. All these were vulnerable to concentrated small arms fire. Flare pistols could also be fired at vision ports to blind crews at night. Periscopes and bulletproof glass vision blocks came into wider use with time, but these too could be damaged by gunfire.

Early tanks possessed enough small openings that air could enter. These were very susceptible to flames, smoke and tear gas – all commonly recommended as early infantry AT measures. Later tanks were better protected from these effects; protected ventilation ports were provided, often with forced air ventilation, both intake and exhaust.

LIMITATIONS TO MOBILITY

While tanks possessed a high degree of cross-country mobility over rough terrain and obstacles, they were limited to some degree. Among a tank's weakest points was exactly what made it a tank: its tracks, formed of separate plates linked and

A Sherman of 6th South African Armoured Division crossing an Italian river. A tank's fording depth was limited, and seldom exceeded 3ft. This could be extended by waterproofing and fording kits, as here, but these required time-consuming preparations; once prepared for deep fording the turret often could not be turned, the guns elevated or certain hatches and ports opened without breaking waterproof seals. Water obstacles provided more of a barrier than just their depth; steep banks on either side, muddy or rocky bottoms, and marshland on adjacent banks could easily prevent a tank from crossing even a shallow water barrier.

pinned together in a flexible belt. Mines, gunfire or obstacles could break tracks; and exceedingly rough terrain and violent manoeuvres could 'throw' a track off its guiding sprocket.

Many tanks were relatively underpowered, which affected their speed, manoeuvrability and ability to negotiate obstacles and rough terrain. The maximum speed obtained by most tanks was 12–25mph. Moving such a heavy vehicle often caused the engine to overheat, whether it was air- or water-cooled. The ravages of abrasive, clogging dust were a constant problem; engine life was short, the powerplant requiring frequent maintenance and replacement. Fuel consumption limited operating range, and was measured in gallons per mile rather than miles per gallon. Tanks might be powered by petrol/gasoline or diesel; petrol engines required more frequent refuelling and were more prone to catch fire, but required less maintenance. Diesel engines were more expensive to produce, but provided better power-to-weight ratios; the fuel was less combustible, gave greater range for its volume, and was cheaper.

Rough terrain and obstacles caused more difficulty than is often appreciated. Sinking into deep mud, swampy ground or soft sand could 'belly' a tank; running the nose over tree stumps or boulders could break traction because of the low ground clearance. Tanks could easily lose their grip on ice, mud, gravel and steep inclines. Most early tanks had comparatively narrow tracks, limiting their ability to cross soft ground due to the relatively high ground pressure per square inch. Wider tracks, or 'grousers', added to the outside edge, were often provided to reduce ground pressure; but wider, heavier tracks further reduced speed, increased fuel consumption and caused more wear on the running gear.

The height of the man-made or natural obstacles that a tank could negotiate depended on the design and angle of the front of its tracks and hull; most tanks could not mount a wall much over 3ft high. Trenches and ditches whose width was more than one-third the length of the track's 'ground footprint' could halt a tank; so could closely spaced trees of even moderate diameter. Extensive tangled barbed wire and other debris could jam running gear. Long-barrelled guns were restricted in woodland and built-up areas, where their traverse was sometimes blocked.

ARMAMENT

The main gun was mounted in a turret with a 360-degree traverse; elevation and depression were typically limited. Ideally the gun would be a long-barrelled high-velocity weapon capable of defeating other tanks, but short-barrelled low-velocity guns were often provided for the infantry support role; this was a mistake, as tanks so armed were mostly incapable of engaging enemy tanks. There was much resistance in many armies to providing improved or larger calibre guns. All sorts of tactical rationales were argued, but the real reason for using low-velocity guns was to reduce costs or conserve materials. In a very few instances tanks also mounted a smaller calibre secondary gun, but the complications outweighed the advantages. Gyro-stabilization was not always provided for the gun, and this greatly reduced the ability to engage targets while moving; a tank would have to halt to aim and fire, during which time it was vulnerable. Other weaknesses affecting weapon performance were hand-operated as opposed to powered turret traverse, and relatively inefficient sighting systems.

A tank's machine guns are often discounted, but in fact they proved to be extremely valuable for engaging enemy positions, troops and soft-skinned vehicles. They were even more important for protecting their own and other tanks from attacking infantry. Most tanks mounted a co-axial machine gun in the main gun mantlet. Frequently a bow machine gun was mounted in the right front hull, and another externally on the commander's cupola for air defence and ground targets. Occasionally a machine gun was mounted in the back of the turret or other unusual positions, mainly in some Russian and Japanese types. The British and

Germans employed smoke grenade dischargers on some AFVs. These were small tubes fitted outside the turret, capable of throwing phosphorus smoke grenades 20–100 yards, rapidly creating a dense smoke screen to conceal the tank while it withdrew or changed course. (The bursting phosphorus threw out burning particles that were dangerous to both the attacking and the supporting infantry.)

THE CREW ENVIRONMENT

St Vith, Belgium, December 1944: GIs from the 23rd Armoured Infantry, 7th Armoured Division take a watchful rest in the streets, covered by a white-washed M4 Sherman. The GIs are wearing field expedient white helmet covers and capes apparently made from bedsheets.

The greatest tactical weakness of a tank is the crew's very limited field of vision, and their complete inability to hear anything outside. Communications between tanks was critical in order to co-ordinate effective tactics. In the early days hand and flag signals were used, but these could not be employed once tanks came under fire, in forest, or in poor visibility due to night, rain, snow, fog, smoke or dust. Visual signals also required tank commanders to constantly observe unit commanders'

tanks for orders. Only radios provided effective intra-tank communications. Most countries provided only sub-unit commanders' tanks with two-way radios, and line tanks with receivers. Communication with infantry was even more difficult. In most armies infantry below company level lacked portable radios, and even if they were so equipped infantry and tank radios used different frequencies. Infantry–tank co-ordination was accomplished by hand signals, coloured smoke grenades, signal flares, tracer fire and limited verbal communication. The problem was compounded by the difficulty of simply attracting the tank commander's attention. Late in the war the Western Allies fitted some tanks with an external telephone set for communication between tank and infantry commanders, but this was never a complete solution.

The tank crew had to endure great heat, deafening noise from the engine and running gear, dizzying fumes from the engine and gun, cramped space hampered by awkward interior fittings, violent pitching and lurching during cross-country movement, poor visibility and the ever-present fire hazard. Driving with the unwieldy steering and clutch systems of the period was physically exhausting, and sometimes drivers and co-drivers had to be rotated at intervals. The loader had to cope with insufficient space, heavy ammunition and the dangerous recoil of the gun. The gunner was busy acquiring targets and operating the main gun and co-axial machine gun, and in smaller tanks he sometimes had to load for himself. The commander was the busiest, having to guide the tank, determine routes, search for targets and threats, watch his commander's tank, maintain formation and co-ordinate the crew. In some light tanks he additionally served as gunner and/or loader. Either the commander, loader or co-driver/hull machine gunner also had to man the radio.

For self protection if they were forced to abandon the tank (and were quick and lucky enough to do so, before exploding ammunition turned it into an oven), most crewmen were armed with pistols, and one or two submachine guns were often stowed in the tank; a supply of hand grenades was also carried to fend off infantry attacks. 'Baled out' crews were a legitimate target who routinely drew fire from enemy tanks and infantry.

*   *   *

Mines, other tanks, AT guns, infantry AT weapons, artillery, ground-attack aircraft and direct infantry attack were the main causes of tank losses. Natural obstacles halted more tanks than man-made, and banal mechanical breakdowns took a high toll. Regardless of all their limitations, however, tanks were formidable weapons; they could be decisive if handled and supported effectively, and were a serious threat to infantry. A brief note on tank unit organization is necessary.

Germany and the USSR employed tank regiments with two or three battalions. The US replaced its three-battalion regiments with separate battalions attached to regimental-sized 'combat commands', although two divisions retained regiments. British Commonwealth and Japanese tank 'regiments' were of single battalion size. Most tank battalions had three or four companies, either of the same type, or occasionally with three light or medium companies and one of the opposite type. A tank company typically had three or four platoons. A platoon consisted of between three and six tanks, but four or five were common; and one to three tanks were assigned to each company headquarters. Commonwealth armies referred to their company-size units as 'squadrons' and platoon-size units as 'troops', in the cavalry tradition; their squadrons each had four three-tank troops.

Regardless of the number of tanks assigned to a company/squadron, a company in combat would soon be reduced by combat losses and mechanical failure. Tankers preferred to operate in company formations for mutual support, firepower and shock effect. Platoons were considered the smallest practical element for combat; and the absolute minimum was for tanks to operate in pairs.

Equally important was for tanks to be accompanied by infantry – to reconnoitre and clear routes, warn of AT weapons and attacking infantry, direct tanks to bypass mines and obstacles, co-ordinate manoeuvres, identify targets and direct the tanks' fire. Accompanying infantry were essential to protect tanks from close-in attacks, especially in close terrain or built-up areas. Tanks committed without infantry, separated from infantry by enemy action or leaving their infantry behind were extremely vulnerable.

ANTI-TANK WEAPONS – AN OVERVIEW

At the beginning of the war most countries followed fairly similar AT doctrines, varying according to the terrain of their expected areas of operation, the numbers and types of allotted AT weapons and the expected enemy's tank capabilities. The main precepts of AT warfare included: separating tanks from their supporting infantry; channelling armour into 'kill zones'; positioning AT weapons in depth; causing tanks to 'button up' (close all hatches), thus increasing their vulnerability and hampering command and control; massing AT fires; exploiting tank-restrictive terrain, man-made and natural obstacles and minefields; and blinding and screening by means of smoke.

This discussion of AT weapons is limited to those found at battalion and lower levels of infantry units. Large-calibre towed and self-propelled AT guns operated by specialist units generally fall outside the remit of this book, though with isolated exceptions.

A wide variety of AT weapons existed in 1939, and during the war the search for more effective weapons arguably saw more variations of design and developmental effort than those for any other category of weapon, ranging from the mundane, to the innovative, to the frankly bizarre. Regardless of the weapon's design – be it a high-velocity gun, an advanced rocket launcher, or a bomb slapped on to a tank's surface by a desperate infantryman – the aim of any AT weapon was to deliver a projectile or explosive charge capable of penetrating a tank's armour or otherwise disabling the vehicle.

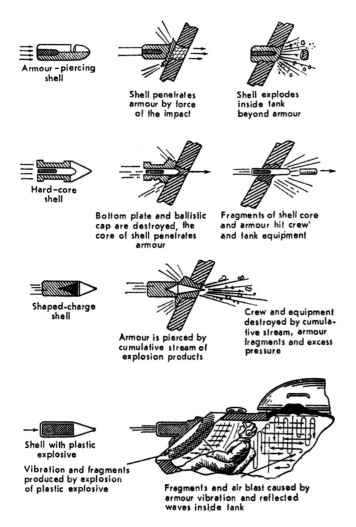

This diagram translated from a Soviet manual depicts the four most common types of AT projectiles used in 1943, and their capabilities when fired at 300 yards' range. Top to bottom: Armour-Piercing High Explosive (AP-HE); Armour-Piercing Capped, with a penetrating core (APC); Shaped- or hollow-charge – High-Explosive Anti-Tank (HEAT); High-Explosive Plastic or 'squash head' (HEP or HESH).

ARMOUR-PIERCING SHOT

Kinetic energy is the basic means of penetrating armour, and this must be delivered by a high-velocity gun. The simplest vehicle of kinetic energy is the armour-piercing (AP) shot: a solid projectile made of hardened steel with a comparatively blunt nose, though usually provided with a streamlined 'windshield' (the tip of a sharp-nosed projectile, like an arrow, will break off on impact and the mass will be deflected). AP shot relies on its speed and hardness to penetrate. All armies issued AP cartridges for their rifles and machine guns; these pre-dated tanks, having been developed in World War I to defeat snipers using steel plate shields for cover. They were ineffective against all but the lightest AFVs, since they typically penetrated only 6–10mm of armour when striking at right angles (i.e. 90 degrees) and within a 100-yard range.

Variations on the larger AP rounds include a small high-explosive (HE) or incendiary charge in the projectile's base; such AP-HE and AP-I rounds, fitted with base-detonating fuses, explode or ignite after penetrating, to cause fragmentation or scatter burning particles to ignite fuel or ammunition stored inside the tank. Armour-piercing capped (APC) is AP shot with a soft metal nose cap that 'turns' the projectile to roughly 90 degrees when it strikes armour. Another variation is a smaller calibre hardened penetrator sheathed in a larger soft metal projectile; when it strikes armour the softer material is stripped off and the penetrator punches through. Enhancements aside, the AP round itself causes little damage to the tank other than making a hole. Most crew casualties and internal damage are caused by fragmentation from the penetrated armour and the projectile, breaking up and ricocheting around the cramped interior with lethal effect. The least desired effect is for the projectile to pass entirely through the tank and out the other side, causing minimal damage.

A US 57mm M1 AT gun in 'full battery'. The M1 had an artillery-type hand-cranked traverse rather than the shoulder traverse of the British 6-pdr from which it was copied. The M1A2 was provided with the shoulder traverse, however – a panel beside the breech allowed the gun to be swung freely by the gun layer's weight. The wavy shield edge, retained from the British design, helped distort the shield's appearance for concealment; and note the gun's low profile.

'SQUASH HEAD' MUNITIONS

The high-explosive plastic or 'squash head' (HEP or HESH) round is a plastic explosive charge contained in a thin-walled projectile with a base-detonating fuse. It relies on brute force to smack into the tank, with the pliable explosive 'squashing' out and detonating, so that the explosion sheers off fragments from the inside of the armour. If the armour is sufficiently thin the HEP round may blow a hole through it or severely buckle it. This round has the advantage of low cost, and is also useful against soft-skin vehicles, and light fortifications and buildings, since it has the same effect on concrete and masonry as on steel.

'SHAPED-CHARGE' MUNITIONS

'Shaped-charge' or 'hollow-charge' munitions rely on the 'Monroe effect', employing an explosive charge with a cone-shaped cavity. When the open end of the cavity is placed against the target it focuses the blast on a single small point, cutting a hole. Early shaped charges had shallow cavities. During World War I a German designer improved the concept by lining the cavity with thin metal, and detonating the charge not directly against the surface but a short distance from it (a 'stand-off' of two to three times the diameter of the charge) to further focus the blast. In 1938 two Swiss engineers perfected the principle and demonstrated its use in demolition charges. A British ordnance engineer

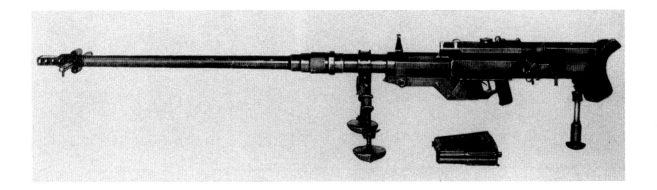

Anti-tank rifles were too heavy and awkward for infantrymen, but at the beginning of the war there were few other weapons available to them for AT defence. This is a Swedish-made Solothurn 20mm s18-1100; it weighed 103lb, and was 7ft long. It had semi-automatic feed from a 5-round magazine, and could penetrate 15mm of armour at 300 yards. This weapon was used by Italy, Hungary, Romania, the Netherlands and to some extent by Germany.

employed the concept in his design for the first shaped-charge AT rifle grenade; and the first use of the shaped charge by most countries was for such munitions.

During the war an entire range of weapons were provided with shaped-charge warheads; these 'high explosive anti-tank' (HEAT) munitions were fired in/from hand and rifle grenades, AT and tank guns, AT rocket launchers, light field artillery shells and hand-placed demolition charges and mines. While widely used by the US, Britain and Germany, shaped-charge rounds saw limited use by the USSR, Japan and Italy. One of the main benefits of shaped-charge projectiles is that they do not rely on velocity or mass to penetrate armour; such a round will achieve the same penetration at 500 yards as at 50 yards. It makes no difference if the projectile is hand-thrown or fired from a high-velocity gun: while the two entirely different types of projectiles will by necessity be of different designs, if they are of the same size and internal arrangement the penetration will be the same.

The projectile is comparatively light and inexpensive to make. Upon impact, the projectile is detonated by a base-detonating fuse, and the metal cavity lining is transformed into a molten 'hot solid slug', which punches through armour plate at approximately 33,000ft per second. This process is usually described as the liner being 'vaporized into a plasma jet that instantly burns through armour'. This molten metal slug carries with it fragments from both the projectile and the armour itself. The hot slug and fragments ignite ammunition and fuel and kill or seriously injure anyone in their path. The entry hole is surprisingly small, its outer diameter being larger than the hole on the inside. Besides armour, shaped charges penetrate any resistant surface such as concrete, masonry, timber or even sandbags.

Fin-stabilized shaped-charge rounds have more effective penetration than spin-stabilized projectiles; the former do not rotate, or do so at a very low rate. The high rate of spin imparted to spin-stabilized projectiles (achieved by rifling) dissipates up to three-quarters of the penetrating effect through centrifugal force.

This is why rocket and rifle grenade HEAT rounds are more effective than one fired from a rifled AT gun.

The effects of shaped-charge warheads can be reduced by placing heavy wire mesh or thin steel plates a short distance outside the armour plate. This causes the shaped charge to detonate short of the target and dissipates the effects of the plasma jet, resulting in little or no penetration.

SMOKE MUNITIONS

Various chemical munitions were also used against tanks. Smoke-producing projectiles and grenades are a double-edged sword. White phosphorus (WP) is the most effective of several smoke-generating agents; apart from creating a dense white smoke cloud, its burning particles, scattered by a small bursting change, burn on stubbornly at 5,000°F. They rain down on troops in open positions, to burn through flesh, and they stick to any surface they touch. Other types of smoke only burn upon impact and do not produce casualties. While WP does not inflict appreciable damage on tanks, smoke is a useful AT aid; dense smoke screens blind tanks, causing disorientation and breaking up formations, and

Bazookas – here an M1A1, still in service in August 1944 – were not used by specialist crews; riflemen were trained to operate them, and individuals within a US rifle platoon were designated to use them in combat. More often than not tank destroyers were assigned to support infantry units, a role far different from their mission as originally envisioned – note the M10 in the background.

Infantry anti-tank weapons, 1939–40. The first campaigns of the war found most infantry relying on a variety of comparatively simple weapons for AT defence, and those carried by this German tank-hunter team typify the range available. The AT rifle, here a 7.92mm PzB 39 Panzerbüsche (1) with the butt folded, was often the main platoon AT weapon. One rifleman (2) has Nebelhandgranate (NbHgr) 39 smoke hand grenades and smoke cylinders (Rauchrohr 39). Another (3) carries a *Doppel-Ladung* ('double charge'), a pair of 2.2lb TNT blocks fastened to the ends of a short length of wire, to destroy main gun or machine gun barrels by throwing them over the barrel like saddlebags. Another (4) has a concentrated charge (*Geballte-Ladung*) of six Stielhandgranate (Stg) 24 stick-grenade heads, with detonators and handles removed, wired around a complete central grenade. Another rifleman (5) is armed with a GG/P40 rifle grenade with a spigot-type discharger on his Kar98k rifle. Regardless of weapon, planning and rehearsals were critical to success. Here the squad leader (6) briefs his men before deploying for an exercise, even though they are in a combat zone. (Steve Noon © Osprey Publishing Ltd)

conceal the approach of close-in infantry attacks. Equally, smoke also screens the movement of tanks, conceals them and prevents enemy gunners from effectively engaging them. Hand-placed smoke pots, smoke candles and smoke grenades were also used by wartime armies.

ANTI-TANK GUNS

Among all the many weapons developed, AT guns remained the most widely used means of attacking tanks. At the beginning of the war most countries fielded a 37mm AT gun with fairly common characteristics. A great deal of development had taken place in the 1930s as improvements in tanks were noted. These guns were mounted on two-wheel carriages that were capable of towing by a light truck; most countries had recognized the necessity of providing AT guns with motorized mobility in order to get them into position, withdraw them and reposition them rapidly. Nevertheless, since most weighed only several hundred pounds they could be manhandled for short distances. Typically they had a protective shield, a split trail mounting and could be traversed rapidly.

These small guns were basically obsolescent in 1939, and obsolete by 1941. They sometimes remained in use until the war's end out of necessity, though mostly in supplementary roles; all were provided with HE rounds for use against other targets. Introducing improved ammunition sometimes extended their life, but the small-calibre guns were simply incapable of punching through the increasingly heavy tank armour encountered from the mid-war years.

The development of larger calibre AT guns had begun in most countries before the war, but few had been fielded. Medium-calibre weapons in the 45mm to 57mm range soon began to appear, and largely replaced the 37mm class, of which most were simply scaled-up versions. (Calibre alone can be misleading: e.g. the performance of underpowered Japanese and Italian 47mm guns did not compare with that of their contemporaries.) Although they too soon became obsolescent, medium-calibre guns generally remained in use by infantry units. The shortage of AT guns was so dire that many armies employed anything they could get their hands on, including captured weapons and obsolete light artillery pieces modified for the AT role.

Still larger calibre weapons in the 75mm range were developed; these were usually assigned to divisional and higher level AT units, but some found their way into infantry AT units. Anti-tank guns had their limitations. Even the light pieces were heavy, and while the crew could manhandle them into and out of position, this was by no means rapid. The 37mm guns were small enough and possessed a sufficiently low profile that they could be concealed easily, and existing cover was often employed. As the guns became larger they required a vehicle for positioning, and were more difficult to conceal – concealability was crucial to the effectiveness and survival of an AT gun. Considerable effort was

The British 2-pdr Mk I AT gun weighed 1,858lb, about twice as much as its US and German 37mm counterparts. It could be fired from its wheels, but they were normally removed for action and the gun set up on its integral three-legged mounting. Side shields were available, but seldom used.

required to dig in these larger pieces, and they were difficult to withdraw and reposition rapidly. The heavy behemoths fielded by Germany (8.8cm) and the USSR (100mm) were verging on impractical in the role: their size and weight had become a liability, negating their destructiveness. On the plus side, AT guns used well-proven artillery technology, they were reliable and they were accurate at comparatively long ranges.

Anti-tank guns organic to infantry units were manned by specially trained infantrymen rather than artillerymen or specialist AT troops. Typically an early infantry battalion had a platoon of three to six 37mm guns, while the multi-battalion infantry regiment/brigade had an AT company with six to 12 guns. Later in the war the battalion AT platoon was often deleted, having been replaced by other weapons at company level. In some armies it was retained with 37mm guns mainly in the infantry support role. The regimental/brigade AT company usually received larger calibre guns.

OTHER INFANTRY WEAPONS AND MUNITIONS

The AT rifle was in widespread use but essentially obsolete in 1939. The Germans had fielded a 13.2mm AT rifle late in World War I, and development had been rapid in the mid 1930s. Most countries employed an AT rifle when the war began, with the exception of America, which relied on its .50-cal HMG. The calibre range of AT rifles varied between 7.92mm and 20mm. These weapons were heavy, weighing from 30lb to over 100lb, and were very awkward to handle, requiring two or even three men to transport the weapon and its ammunition. The rifles measured from 5ft to 7ft in length, and were supported by a bipod; the longer ones sometimes had removable barrels. They were actually more awkward to move than many machine guns, and their weight and bulkiness were frequent causes of complaint.

For their weight and size their armour penetration was marginal, usually only about 0.5in at 200–300 yards. Some performed better, such as the 14.5mm and 20mm, but were still far from effective even against 1939 tanks. Because of their weight most did not have excessive recoil, but the muzzle blast could be uncomfortable. Their designs varied greatly, including magazine-fed or single-shot, semi-automatic or bolt-action. By 1941/42 they were largely withdrawn; only the Soviet Red Army kept them in widespread use.

The development of bazooka-type AT rocket launchers began in 1941, and they were to have a profound effect on close-quarters AT warfare. These man-portable, shoulder-fired weapons projected a HEAT warhead; most were reloadable, but the revolutionary German Panzerfaust was a single-shot disposable weapon. Their light weight made them easily portable by infantrymen on the battlefield, and they were quick and inexpensive to produce in large numbers. Since the HEAT warhead was more effective as a fin-stabilized projectile, this provided an ideal match between launcher and warhead. They were also effective in smashing through light fortifications.

The shoulder-fired AT rocket launcher was an answer to the infantryman's prayers, but early weapons did have their problems. Their range was short – less than 200 yards, and often under half that; the reliability of the rockets, both in launch ignition and detonation on the target, was sometimes wanting; and the design of early warheads was far from optimum. This class of weapons suffered (and still does) from tactical limitations. Rocket launchers needed an unobstructed area to the rear for their considerable back-blast; they generated a noticeable firing signature of smoke and dust (partly countered by their ease of relocating); and they could not be fired from within enclosed spaces – such as a room of a conventional house – because of the back-blast overpressure.

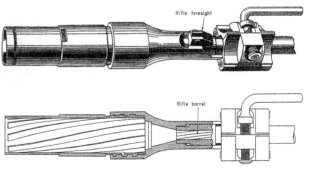

FIG. I   RIFLE DISCHARGER (CUP TYPE)

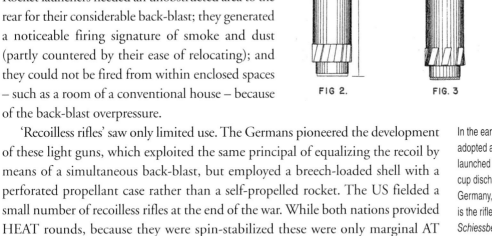

FIG 2.   FIG 3.   FIG. 4

'Recoilless rifles' saw only limited use. The Germans pioneered the development of these light guns, which exploited the same principal of equalizing the recoil by means of a simultaneous back-blast, but employed a breech-loaded shell with a perforated propellant case rather than a self-propelled rocket. The US fielded a small number of recoilless rifles at the end of the war. While both nations provided HEAT rounds, because they were spin-stabilized these were only marginal AT weapons; the German design was slightly more effective as it used standard artillery HEAT projectiles with a slower spin.

Most countries developed rifle-launched AT grenades to give any infantryman at least a halfway effective means of combating tanks. Being fin-stabilized they were somewhat effective for delivering a shaped charge, but the 1940 cone designs, light explosive charges and often inferior fusing gave them poor penetration and

In the early 1940s most countries adopted a shaped charge rifle-launched AT grenade of some type; cup dischargers were adopted by Germany, Britain and Japan. Fig.1 is the rifled German 30mm *Schiessbecher* adopted in 1942, capable of firing 30mm AT (Fig.2), over-calibre 40mm AT (Fig.3), and 30mm high explosive grenades (Fig.4).

reliability. Effective range was seldom over 100 yards, and that only against light armour. The use of rifle grenades required a special launching device fitted to the muzzle and special launching cartridges. One or more launchers were provided to rifle squads/sections; these could also launch anti-personnel, smoke and signal grenades.

There were three types of rifle grenade systems. The discharger cup type required a cup-like device attached to the rifle's muzzle in which the grenade was inserted. Their disadvantage was that the cup blocked the use of rifle sights for regular firing while it was fitted. The spigot type featured a tube attached to the muzzle; the grenade had a hollow tailboom that slid over the tube. The rod type grenade, dating from before World War I, was soon abandoned. The grenade was fitted to a long metal rod inserted into the muzzle; it required no special launcher, but would eventually damage the bore. Most grenades had to be fired with the rifle's butt on the ground and the barrel angled at the necessary range elevation. The grenades' heavy weight caused tremendous recoil that would damage a rifle after repeated use – to say nothing of the shoulder of any grenadier unwise enough to try firing it with the conventional grip. For the direct fire required by some AT grenades the rifle stock was placed under the arm and clamped tightly to the side of the torso with the elbow.

Anti-tank hand grenades were developed before the war, but were essentially weapons of last resort. Most relied on a simple HE charge to penetrate light armour or break a track. Because of their necessarily small size they were none too effective, especially against all but the lightest tanks after 1941. They were most effective against tracks, however, and upper surfaces such as turret tops and engine decks. Britain and the USSR were the main producers of AT hand grenades; the USA did not bother with their development, and Japan only fielded some inefficient designs late in the war. To be effective some stabilizing system was necessary to ensure the grenade struck the target in the right attitude to maximize the blast. They were larger and heavier than standard grenades, and so could be thrown only about 20–30 yards.

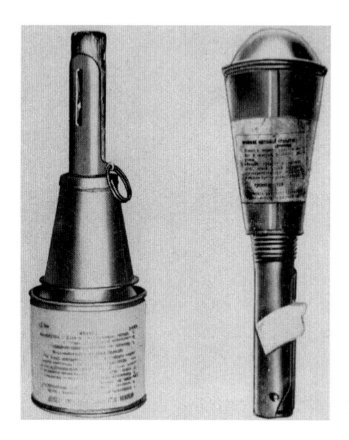

Anti-tank hand grenades were heavy, due to the necessarily large explosive charge, and this gave them a short range. These are the flat-nosed Soviet RPG-42 (left) and domed RPG-6 (right) of 1944, with shaped charges penetrating 75mm and 100mm of armour respectively. To ensure that they struck the target at the necessary angle, stabilizing tail streamers deployed when they were thrown.

A larger version of the AT hand grenade was the hand mine. These were larger explosive charges hand-placed by very bold infantrymen – in reality, virtual suicide weapons. Most had shaped charges and were attached to the tank by magnets; the mine was slapped on to the tank, with a delay fuse that left barely sufficient time for the attacker to dive for cover. Others were hand-thrown and impact-detonated, but because of their weight their range was as short as 10 to 15 yards. In the hands of determined men in close terrain they offered a considerable threat, however, forcing tank crews to take drastic protective measures.

Among chemical munitions, smoke grenades, smoke candles and smoke pots were employed by infantry in close-in attacks. Early in the war some store was also placed in tear gas grenades; the idea was to bombard a tank with irritant gas grenades so that the fumes sucked into the tank's ventilation system would blind or drive out the crew. The Japanese developed a toxic gas grenade to be employed

In North Africa, a British ordnance disposal engineer poses with a German Teller AT mine attached (for the photographer's benefit, unconvincingly, with a long white string from the handle) to an anti-personnel S-Mine ('Bouncing Betty') rigged to kill mine clearers. In reality they would be coupled by a short wire to a well in the underside of the AT mine. The TMi 35 held 11lb of TNT, and was set off by pressures of 420lb on the centre but only 175lb of pressure at the edges.

in the same manner. In reality smoke and gas grenades were relatively ineffective, as the tank merely drove out of the small area affected, often before a troublesome amount of gas entered the tank.

The first AT mines were buried artillery shells used in World War I. Extensive development of purpose-made AT mines was pursued in the late 1920s/early 1930s and continued throughout the war. During World War II all armies laid millions of mines on all fronts. All combatants in North Africa created vast minefields because of the lack of natural defences and obstacles, and the Japanese made increasing use of mines as the Pacific War progressed.

Typically, AT mines were pressure-activated by a tank's crushing weight. Most mines would blow off a track, but the heavier models could cause substantial damage. The layout, density and location of minefields varied greatly. Minefields were tied into natural obstacles, laid on likely avenues of approach and often in patterns that would lead tanks into the sights of AT guns; the use of dummy minefields alongside real ones multiplied these effects.

Like any obstacle, a minefield – whether a few mines buried at a road intersection, or multiple belts of thousands of mines – was worthless unless covered by observation and fire. If effectively sited, camouflaged and covered by fire, they could halt or at least slow a tank advance. Once the defenders were driven away it was a relatively straightforward matter (though seldom without bloody cost) to clear routes through minefields that had taken much time and effort to lay. As noted earlier, the harassing and delaying effect of a small number of mines laid at wisely chosen points could be more effective than large minefields.

A wide and imaginative variety of expedient AT weapons were employed. Regardless of how ingenious or effective these last-resort weapons may have appeared, and how thoroughly troops were trained in their use, any army forced to employ them was in desperate straits. Most required direct attack by a soldier or at least an attack delivered at very close range, demanding a high degree of exposure and a slim chance of escape. In order to succeed the attacker required great courage, a well-chosen position, a stealthy approach, effective covering fire, absence of enemy infantry and no small measure of luck; in the 'invasion scare' summer of 1940 a British Army manual on such tactics frankly compared the risks with 'tiger shooting on foot'. Nevertheless, training was widespread and serious; in 1940–41 such methods were often all that the British or Soviet infantryman had.

Examples of expedient weapons included:

Satchel charges. 10–20lb explosive charges packed in a haversack with a short time fuse, thrown on the engine deck, into the tracks, or jammed under a turret overhang. A variation

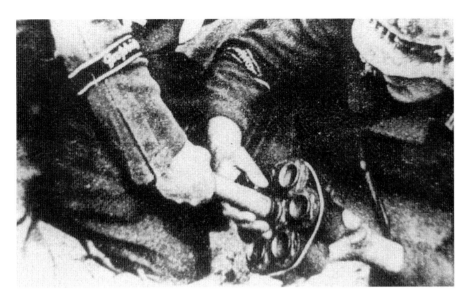

Soldiers of the 'Grossdeutschland' Division prepare a concentrated charge with seven stick grenades. Such a charge might break a track, damage an engine if thrown on the rear deck, or penetrate lighter armour over a hatch or if jammed under a turret overhang. The concussion was reportedly enough to temporarily stun a tank crew.

was the pole charge, a demolition charge on a 4–6ft pole, allowing it to be placed on a vulnerable spot.

Concentrated charges. Bundle of about six hand grenades or small demolition charges wired together with a central detonator, and usually a handle. Employed in the same way as satchel charges. A single grenade might also be shoved down a gun barrel.

Double charges. Two demolition charges linked by wire and thrown to tangle around a gun barrel. Smoke grenades were used similarly, in the hope of blinding gunners.

AT mines. Hand-delivered mines placed directly in front of a track.

Fire bombs. Large petrol/gasoline cans (5gal) with incendiary or smoke grenades attached for detonation, and thrown or dropped on to a tank's engine deck.

'Molotov cocktails'. Glass bottles filled with petrol/gasoline and often enhanced with oil, rubber, tar, phosphorus etc. to make it burn longer and hotter and adhere to the tank, or to cause more smoke to blind the crew. A rag stuffed in the bottle neck was lit and the bottle thrown at the tank, preferably at vision ports, hatches or engine compartments; some were provided with self-ignition devices. Results were often disappointing because of the small amount of fuel, and later tanks were better sealed.

'Daisy chains'. AT mines fastened together along a rope or plank, concealed beside a road and pulled across in front of a tank by a hidden soldier.

Various mechanical means of attacking tanks were suggested; some of these may have worked on early war light tanks, but against larger types they had little effect. It was recommended that a steel bar, pipe, wooden beam or even a rifle be wedged into the running gear to jam the tracks. Battering machine gun barrels with a bar, hammering on glass vision ports and periscopes, driving wedges into turret rings, forcing open hatches with crowbars, covering vision ports and periscopes with mud, burning blankets or overcoats, and similar acts of physical mayhem were measures of desperation. These, like some of the improvised munitions, were born of real experience in such conflicts as the Spanish Civil War (1936–39); but against the heavier tanks of later years they usually accomplished little, and were often fatal to those who tried them.

Field artillery and mortars are often said to be ineffective against armour. While it is true that long-range indirect fire had little effect on tanks (a direct hit being rare), it did have the benefit of separating the infantry from tanks and forcing the unit to deploy into dispersed formations early in an action. Near misses only caused superficial damage. (These limitations did not apply in some exceptional cases, such as the very heavy naval gunfire concentrations occasionally available to the Allied armies in Sicily and Normandy.) Concentrated artillery could destroy light tanks, however, and this was accomplished in several instances against Japanese and Italian armour. Artillery and mortars could lay smoke on tank formations, though this had the disadvantage of obscuring targets for friendly AT guns; often smoke was dropped only on the rear two-thirds of a tank formation, still allowing gunners to target the lead tanks.

This Soviet 76.2mm ZiS-3 was the standard divisional light field artillery piece from 1942. The Red Army required field artillery to be capable of engaging tanks effectively, and the ZiS-3 proved well adapted to this role; it is often considered as more an AT weapon than a field gun.

In an emergency, light field artillery of up to 105mm could engage tanks with direct fire, and AT or HEAT rounds were often available for field pieces. Most were marginally effective in this role because of inadequate sights and slow traverse. Infantry guns – i.e. light, simplified artillery pieces manned by infantrymen – were used by some armies as fire support weapons, and some were provided with HEAT rounds, but they were ill suited as AT weapons for the same reasons.

Most anti-aircraft guns were provided with anti-personnel ammunition, and possessed a high rate of fire and rapid traverse. They took time to emplace, though most could be fired at ground targets while still mounted on their travelling carriage. Most anti-aircraft guns were large and their high profile made them difficult to conceal and therefore vulnerable when engaging tanks. Some 20mm and 37/40mm anti-aircraft cannon could be effective against light tanks. The German use of 8.8cm Flak guns in the AT role is well known. The round was devastating to tanks and the weapon was extremely accurate and long-ranged, but the gun's large size and the time and labour it took to emplace was an impediment. Few other countries employed their large-calibre anti-aircraft guns in a similar manner, although the Soviets used their 85mm gun against armour at least as much as the Germans.

EVOLUTION OF ANTI-TANK TACTICS

1939–42

The broadly similar AT doctrines followed by all armies in 1939 were based on very little practical experience. The pre-war conflicts in which tanks were employed (Spanish Civil War, Italian conquest of Ethiopia) provided few viable lessons; only small numbers of light tanks were used, in relatively low-level conflicts against forces with few if any AT weapons. These episodes gave little warning of the imminent large-scale operations by mass formations of combined arms. Peacetime manoeuvres often failed either to validate or challenge doctrine, as they seldom accurately portrayed the actions of opposing armour forces.

As already mentioned, there were two schools of thought on the likely employment of armour: one foresaw massed armour plunging through the frontlines and deep into the enemy's rear, the other the parcelling out of the available tanks to support the advance of the infantry. In fact both concepts were valid, but money-strapped armies tried to skimp and tended to restrict themselves. The Germans, for example, while proponents of the deep armoured thrust by massed tanks supported by mobile infantry and aircraft, also specified that PzKw IV tanks were to advance no more than 100 yards beyond the infantry and were to support the foot troops with machine gun fire.

The infantry AT tactics taught in the different armies varied in detail because of local factors, but there were two broad forms of AT defence: *Passive defence* included patrols and outposts to warn of approaching armour, AT obstacles and minefields, incorporation of natural obstacles into the defence, selection of defensive sectors that hindered armour and reinforced the defence, and camouflage. *Active defence* combined the skilful selection of AT weapon positions and fire zones, deployment of AT weapons, tank-hunter teams and the use of AT reserves and counterattack forces.

Because of the mobility of tanks and the comparatively static nature of infantry AT tactics, these are normally thought of as defensive – 'Tanks conquer, infantry holds' (J. F. C. Fuller). This is largely true; however, some degree of offensive measures could be conducted against armoured forces by even the early self-propelled AT guns, typically mounted on obsolescent tank chassis or trucks. The infantry itself, especially if restricted to movement on foot, had very limited offensive capabilities against armour. Armoured or motorized infantry were not much better as their transport had little or no armour, possessed less cross-country mobility than tanks and had few weapons capable of engaging tanks at long ranges. Tank-hunter teams could not truly be considered offensive because they had limited mobility, could cover only short distances, and their small-scale operations were usually conducted in a unit's defensive sector; they were thus basically defensive.

The following discussion is generic; the reader should keep in mind that each country's tactics varied to some extent, and these differences are addressed in the next chapter.

Anti-tank defensive measures were incorporated into the routine establishment of a defence. The extent of armour employed by the enemy, known enemy armour tactics, the number and types of available AT weapons and terrain were the

Anti-tank obstacles took many forms, and to be effective it was necessary to keep them under observation and fire. This Soviet roadblock is excellently designed, being tied into the tank-proof terrain of dense forest. Raising it to turret height prevents the tank from climbing it or breaking through with the force of its hull. It prevents the tank from firing down the road, since it masks the main gun; allows the defenders to fire at the weaker lower hull; and denies cover to accompanying infantry.

determining factors. An infantry regiment (or British Commonwealth brigade), regardless of nationality, typically deployed defensively with two battalions forward and one in reserve. Each battalion had two rifle companies in the line and one in reserve; the same applied to each company's rifle platoons. This meant that one-third of any echelon's sub-units were in reserve positions, and this depth of defence was essential to AT defence. The deployment of AT weapons depended very much upon the actions and disposition of the infantry units they supported, and a high degree of co-ordination and co-operation were required.

BRITISH STREET FIGHTING AT TEAM, 1940

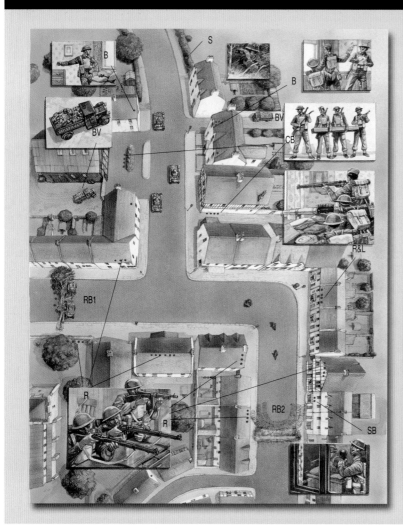

This diagram is based on theory of how British AT teams might have countered German armour in the case of an invasion of Britain. A troop of PzKw II tanks, led by motorcycle and motorcycle combination outriders, moves from top to bottom through the village. The British ambush party (blue spots) are dispersed in small groups behind cover, in the upper rooms or loopholed lofts of houses, and behind the crest of a roof: (S) Scout; (B) 'Bombers', with grenades and 'Molotov cocktails'; (BV) Blocking vehicles – commercial lorries, loaded with rubble etc. for extra weight. These will move forward to block the road behind the tanks when they have passed; (CB) Two crowbar teams with crowbar, wooden beam (e.g. a railway sleeper), small arms and grenades, who will run out and try to jam the tank tracks; (R&L) Riflemen and Lewis LMG in upper room facing the cross street; (RB1) Roadblock of felled tree, rubble-filled farm carts, etc; (R) Several parties with rifles and other small arms; (RB2) Second roadblock – U-shaped barbed wire 'concertinas' in front of a trench dug across the road; (SB) Covering the roadblock, a party with small arms and 'sticky bombs'. (Peter Dennis © Osprey Publishing Ltd)

When a division established a defence the divisional reconnaissance unit and elements detached from the reserve regiment were deployed forward as a screen to protect the units preparing defences. The screening force kept enemy patrols at a distance, observed enemy activity, prevented surprise attacks, warned of the enemy's approach, and engaged the enemy if he advanced. To prevent surprise attacks by armour, AT guns from the regimental or divisional AT unit might reinforce the screening force. Once the main defences were established part of the screening force was withdrawn, but some remained, along with some AT weapons depending on the tank threat. Each regiment and battalion in the main line of resistance placed its own screen forward in the form of outposts, observation and listening posts, and security patrols. Anti-tank guns might be deployed with these elements if there was a high armour threat, but early in the war there were few weapons available even to arm the main positions.

Ideally an 'anti-tank obstacle' fronted the main positions. This could be a minefield, tank ditch, natural obstacle (river, swamp, gully) or other tank-restrictive terrain, or simply point obstacles such as AT barricades or clusters of mines e.g. at intersections and chokepoints, or blown bridges. Shortage of time and resources often prevented the preparation of extensive obstacle systems.

Infantry battalions typically had two to six AT guns; these would be attached to rifle companies depending on tank avenues of approach, and not necessarily equally distributed between companies. As depth was important to AT defence – it was accepted that at least some tanks would invariably penetrate the main line – some of the guns might be attached to the reserve company. Anti-tank rifles, organic to battalions or companies, were usually allocated to rifle platoons. These were most effectively employed by multiple rifles engaging a single tank. Great store was placed in hand and rifle grenades, hand mines and expedient weapons, since little else was then available to rifle platoons.

Defensive positions were placed well inside any woods rather than on the edges, since this prevented direct fire from tank guns and artillery being brought to bear on positions; it also restricted tank movement, and provided concealment for AT weapons and tank-hunter teams. Fighting positions were dug deep to allow soldiers to crouch in the bottom with 2ft of overhead clearance to protect against a tank's crushing action. The same applied to crew-served weapon positions, with narrow slit trenches dug to the sides as crew refuges from overrunning tanks.

A key to a successful defence – or at least to preventing a rout – was for infantrymen to be trained in the vulnerabilities and limitations of tanks. Confidence-building training was essential: soldiers might be made to lie on the

The 30mm *Schiessbecher* cup-type grenade discharger introduced in 1942 for the Kar98k rifle could launch 30mm, 40mm, 46mm and 61mm AT rifle grenades (*Gewehr Panzergranate*), as well as anti-personnel and various pyrotechnic and special purpose rounds. Though generally superseded by the Panzerfaust, these grenades remained in use until the end of the war.

ground between its tracks, or squat in foxholes, as a tank was driven over them. They were instructed that when tanks approached they had to remain hidden until the last moment; the closer the tank was, the safer they were, and if they waited to move out of the way until they were inside the tank's blind zone they ran little risk of being machine gunned. They could then attack, if close-attack weapons were available, or remain concealed until the tank passed and engage the accompanying infantry.

Some of the regimental AT company's guns might reinforce the forward companies; more often they were held in reserve, either positioned to cover likely tank avenues into the rear, or ready to move into position to block a breakthrough. Early doctrine often called for tanks to be engaged at the weapons' maximum range. Artillery would take the enemy formation under fire at maximum range to inflict casualties on the accompanying infantry, and force tanks to assume a battle formation early, thus slowing their advance. Early in the war it was learned that it was more effective to wait until tanks were within a few hundred yards – in effect, springing an ambush – and this proved to be effective even in the North African desert. Rather than forewarning the advancing tanks with missed shots, which allowed them to take evasive manoeuvres, it was better to ensure hits at relatively close range. Mortars and machine guns would target the infantry and attempt to separate them from the tanks.

The AT guns positioned further back would engage tanks penetrating the forward positions, and if necessary the regimental reserve AT guns would go into action. Infantrymen in small teams were to take on scattered tanks with close-attack weapons, especially in forested, built-up and other close terrain. Some of the divisional AT battalion's guns might be attached to forward regiments, but most were held in reserve to block penetrations. Early in the war few if any tank units were available for attachment to divisions to serve as a counterattack force.

In the attack, AT sub-units would accompany attacking units, usually following somewhat to the rear. They were to go into action if enemy tanks attacked the column; they might be called forward for direct fire on pillboxes, and to cover tank approaches on the flanks.

The ultimate mobility for an infantry AT weapon was to be portable by an infantryman over any terrain. In this staged shot a US bazooka crew 'engage' a Panther PzKw V Ausf A with the 2.36in M1A1 rocket launcher, whose light weight and handy size made it easy to manoeuvre into a favourable firing position – unlike that chosen by this photographer for his reconstructed drama: facing the Panther's massive, sloped frontal armour and inviting fire from its co-axial and bow machine guns.

1943–45

By 1942/43 the nature of AT warfare had changed in many respects. Armour was employed in smaller scale as well as mass operations, and more frequently to support infantry, both in the attack and defence. Self-propelled assault guns were also more common on the battlefield.

Conventional AT guns were being upgraded to medium and large calibres, but improvements in tank design, armour, firepower and mobility outpaced the appearance on the field of adequate AT guns. 'Quick fixes' were common, with existing tank and anti-aircraft guns mounted on AT gun carriages. Anti-tank rifles were falling from use, and in the US and later the German armies they began to be replaced by shoulder-fired rocket launchers. (The British Commonwealth armies went down their own cul-de-sac, and the USSR and Japan fielded nothing comparable – see below.) These highly portable weapons provided the infantry with the protection they needed, and led to new small-unit AT tactics. They did not replace conventional AT guns, being considered supplementary weapons of opportunity; yet although their range and lethality were limited, they went a long way to transform the tank/infantry balance in the latter's favour, particularly in the West in 1944/45. The importance of close-attack weapons such as hand mines and AT rifle grenades did not diminish, with some countries fielding new designs.

It was realized that effective AT tactics required mobility equal to that of tanks, and more AT guns were mounted on full-tracked chassis; in a logical conclusion, it was also realized that the best tank-killers were other tanks.

The US 37mm M3A1 gun was the mainstay of American AT defence until 1943, when it began to be replaced by the 57mm M1. The 37mm often remained in use in infantry battalion AT platoons, especially in the Pacific; it was easily manhandled over rough terrain into positions allowing it to engage pillboxes and caves. This gun in Tunisia is protected by a rock sangar.

The necessity of making AT defences as deep as possible, maintaining mobile AT reserves, and utilizing tanks and dedicated tank destroyers was appreciated. While warfare had become more mobile, when time permitted an army in the defence prepared strong AT positions protected by extensive obstacle systems and minefields. The Red Army made extensive use of AT strongpoints, as did the Wehrmacht after the tide of success turned. More artillery was provided with AT ammunition, as were light anti-aircraft guns.

After 1943 large German tank offensives were seldom seen, and only occasionally possible after major efforts to mass forces; the Japanese never employed armour on a large scale. The Allies' ability to produce tanks and field large armour formations increased. Because Axis tank attacks largely ceased apart from small-scale operations and counterattacks, the importance of small-unit AT weapons and tactics increased. Because of the ability of tanks to penetrate deeply, even in local counterattacks, the need to provide artillery units and other rear elements with AT protection was realized.

TANK-HUNTER TEAMS

Most armies employed tank-hunter teams, and their use increased as the war progressed and more lethal portable AT weapons became available. Their organization was usually left up to individual units, though some experiments had been undertaken and recommendations were made. Units often developed their own tactics, and the terrain remained a governing factor. A hunter team might consist of anything between four and 12 men, with six to eight being typical, led by a junior NCO. A two- to four-man attack element was armed with a stand-off weapon such as an AT rifle or shoulder-fired rocket launcher, or close-attack weapons such as AT hand mines and grenades. Covering elements of two to four riflemen armed with hand, rifle and smoke grenades backed up the attack element, protecting them against accompanying enemy infantry. Often a two-man automatic rifle or LMG team was included for support.

Hunter teams were deployed forward of the main line of resistance, especially in close terrain, to ambush advancing tanks. Other teams were held in readiness by frontline and immediate reserve sub-units to attack penetrating tanks, and others could be held deeper in the rear to ambush or intercept tanks. They were especially useful in forests and built-up areas where good cover and concealment were available, and where tanks were restricted to predictable routes and forced to move slowly. Ideally teams would be co-ordinated with other friendly elements, but the nature of combat and the scarcity of tactical radios often precluded this. Hunter teams might also be used offensively, by infiltrating enemy lines and attacking tank 'laagers' and assembly areas.

US ARMY AT AMBUSH, 1944–45

Tank-hunter teams were built around a 12-man rifle squad, though these were typically understrength – as here. The weapon of choice was the M9A1 bazooka with M6A3 HEAT rocket (1); a grenadier armed with an M9A1 AT rifle grenade propelled from an M7 launcher on an M1 rifle (2) provides back-up; it was only effective for side or rear shots.

An M19 WP smoke rifle grenade (3) lies in readiness to blind the tank or accompanying infantry as the team withdraws. A rifleman crouches ready with a Mk IIA1 fragmentation grenade, and an M15 WP hand grenade (4). The squad's .30-cal M1918A2 Browning Automatic Rifle (5) would engage accompanying infantry to drive them away from

the tank; sometimes a .30-cal M1919A4 LMG crew was attached to the team for more firepower. One or two riflemen would always be deployed to give the team rear security (6). The squad leader (7) would give the signal to spring the ambush by opening fire himself and shouting 'Fire!' (Steve Noon © Osprey Publishing Ltd)

Ideally a hunter team would ambush a tank – let it come to them – but often they had to intercept or pursue their quarry. Poor visibility (night, fog, rain) was preferred, but conditions could not be waited upon. Smoke grenades might be used to blind the crew and/or screen the attack element's approach. The covering element might deliver the smoke, distract the tank with small arms fire, and engage enemy infantry, as would the machine gun crew. If using a stand-off weapon the attack element would move in as close as practical, to 100 yards or less; if using close-attack weapons they would have to attack the tank directly, at zero range.

Tanks were attacked from the rear quadrant if possible. Even with the more powerful portable AT weapons flank and rear shots were usually necessary to kill a tank. The use of hunter teams was hampered by normal tank tactics of seldom operating alone or without infantry support. Such an ambush was often an immediate action without specific organization or planning; small groups of infantry simply attacked tanks with whatever was available when the opportunity presented itself. This was particularly true of Japanese and Soviet troops, who might 'swarm' tanks, accepting heavy losses in the hope of destroying this high-value target.

SPECIFIC WEAPONS & TACTICS

Where AT guns are discussed under the national sections below, their theoretical maximum range is omitted. Under combat conditions the greatest effective range, regardless of calibre, was seldom beyond 1,000–1,400 yards, and often much less.

UNITED STATES

Before the war America was lean on infantry AT weapons, though its doctrine was basically sound. Besides infantry AT elements, the field artillery was responsible for AT defence; they put little effort into it, however, taking the view that their few AT guns were to protect the artillery and not the division as a whole. After testing in pre-war manoeuvres the Tank Destroyer (TD) Force was established in November 1941, and all existing divisional AT battalions were re-designated TD battalions. In a period of exaggerated fear of German armour, 220 battalions were ordered to be established. A more realistic judgement of the actual threat, and Germany's forced shift to a defensive posture, saw only 106 battalions organized, and 35 of these were never deployed overseas; some were converted into other types of unit. About half of the battalions used half-track mounted (later fully tracked) guns, and the others half-track towed guns.

The basic infantry AT weapon was the 37mm M3A1 AT gun first fielded in 1940; this was a copy of the German 3.7cm PaK 35/36. A good weapon when adopted, by 1941 it was outdated; production ceased in mid 1943 when the 57mm was adopted, though the 37mm often remained in use by battalion AT platoons, especially in the Pacific. It was provided with AP, APC HE, and canister ammunition, and fired 15 to 20 rounds per minute; AP shot could penetrate only 36mm at 500 yards with a right-angled impact, though APC achieved 73mm under the same conditions. The gun required a crew of six, and was towed by a ½-ton or 1-ton truck.

The 57mm M1 was a copy of the British 6-pdr Mk II modified for American production; the later M1A1 and M1A2 had improved traverse gear. It could fire AP and APC rounds at 12 to 15rpm, had a ten-man crew, and was towed by a 1-ton or 1½-ton truck. Even with AP penetration of 73mm at 1,000 yards and 20 degrees, it too was soon inadequate for European service; a replacement was sought, but none was fielded because of the abundance of tanks and tank destroyers. The 3in M5 AT gun, issued to some towed TD battalions, was a modified anti-aircraft gun on a 105mm howitzer carriage.

In the Army an AT platoon with three 37mm or 57mm guns was organic to the infantry battalion's HQ company. The regimental AT company had three three-gun platoons, usually 57mm. Unlike those of most contemporary armies, the US division did not possess an organic AT unit, but a TD battalion was habitually attached at this level (except in the Pacific), with 36 x 3in or 76mm gun self-propelled tank destroyers, organized in three companies each with three four-gun platoons.

The only other AT weapon in use was the M9A1 rifle grenade, a spigot type. The 1941 M9 had been copied from the German GG/P40 and lacked a nose

The M9A1, and other rifle-launched AT grenades, could be launched from the M1 rifle with an M7 launcher, the M1903 rifle with an M1 launcher, the M1917 rifle with an M2 launcher, and from an M1 carbine with an M8 launcher. More often than not this HEAT grenade was used against field fortifications, buildings or even personnel.

cone providing stand-off detonation; to make matters worse, the fuse was fitted to the nose rather than the base, further hampering the shaped-charge effect. It was withdrawn in favour of the 1942 M9A1 with a nose cone and base-detonating fuse, which penetrated 75–100mm of armour. Fired from the M1 rifle it had a range of about 285 yards, and from the M1 carbine, 185 yards. Range could be increased by 30–50 per cent by the use of a booster cartridge ('vitamin pill') inserted in the muzzle of the launcher tube; this was not used with the carbine, to avoid damage from the greater concussion. Until a grenade launcher became available for the semi-automatic M1 rifle in late 1943, squads used a bolt-action Springfield M1903 rifle for grenade launching. Initially there was one launcher per squad, but by 1944 the Army was issuing two or three, and the Marines one to every rifleman.

The mainstay infantry AT weapon was the 2.36in rocket launcher or 'bazooka'. The bazooka was light, simple to operate, and quick and inexpensive to produce. Most importantly, it was effective; and just as significant as its main role was its ability to knock out pillboxes. The Army allotted 112 bazookas to an infantry regiment, 558 to a division; infantry battalions were issued 29, but only five to each of their three rifle companies. The remainder were assigned to headquarters, artillery and support units throughout the division, to provide AT defence. Additional bazookas could be borrowed from the battalion HQ and heavy weapons companies.

The 2.36in M1A1 bazooka and earlier M1 (note the characteristic wooden shoulder stock) required the gunner to wear face and hand protection to prevent injury from the unconsumed propellant as the rocket left the muzzle. Rather than a gas mask, as here, gunners normally wore a pair of goggles with a small face mask, though protection was often dispensed with in combat. The later M9 bazooka did not require such protection because of its longer tube and improved propellant.

The US Marines added 132 bazookas to their divisional establishment in July 1942, with 44 per regiment. In April 1943 the numbers were increased to 243 in a division and 53 per regiment. Like the Army, the Marines at first provided bazookas to service units. In May 1944, however, this policy was reversed and bazookas were reduced to 172 per division, with 43 per regiment, owing to the limited Japanese armour threat.

The first bazookas were shipped to the British in North Africa, and to the Soviet Union. The 600 delivered to the British in September 1942 were tested and deemed unsuited for desert warfare; it was reasoned that attacking infantrymen could not approach German armour due to the lack of concealment in the desert. The bazooka's value as a defensive weapon was apparently ignored, and the British placed them in storage. By contrast, the Red Army saw their value immediately, and the first of theirs to be lost in combat provided the model for the German 8.8cm Raketenpanzerbüchse or *Panzerschreck* ('armour terror').

The M1 bazooka saw its first American use in November 1942 in North Africa and on Tarawa. Weighing 13.1lb, it is recognizable by its wooden shoulder stock and two pistol grips. The M1A1 was standardized in July 1943, though it was not fielded for some months; it eliminated the forward handgrip and had an improved electrical ignition system. Both models had a 250-yard maximum range, rate of fire of 4–5rpm, and were 54.5in long. The M9 was standardized in September 1943 at the request of the Airborne Command, and began to be fielded in mid 1944. This had a longer 61in tube, increasing its accuracy and range to 300 yards, and had more reliable rockets. The tube could be broken down into two sections for ease of transport. The M9A1 differed only in an improved barrel-coupling latch; both models weighed 15.87lb. Total production was 476,628, of which 277,819 were the M9A1 model.

The M6 HEAT rocket had a pointed nose, six long blade-like tailfins, and could penetrate 76mm of armour at 30 degrees impact angle and 119mm at 90 degrees. However, malfunctions were so frequent that its use was suspended in May 1943. The improved M6A1/A2 quickly arrived, and the M1A1 and M9 launchers could not fire M6 rockets. In August 1943 the M6A3 rocket was adopted; this had a round nose to lower the angle of effective impact, a short cylindrical fin assembly with four vanes for improved stability and an improved cone-liner in the shaped-charge warhead that increased penetration by 30 per cent. In 1944 the M10 WP rocket was approved.

* * *

US AT doctrine emphasized combat outposts with some battalion AT guns temporally attached. Most battalion guns were placed near the main line of

The half-track mounted 75mm Gun Motor Carriage M3, as used by the early US Tank Destroyer Force battalions. This example is in British service in Italy, firing in a supplementary field artillery role – it proved only marginally effective for its intended mission.

resistance with few if any provided to the reserve, and thus there was little depth of defence. Regimental AT guns were positioned to the rear of the forward battalions, or held in readiness to occupy alternate positions covering the main line or to support counterattacks. If non-regimental AT guns were attached, usually in the form of TD companies, they could be positioned to the rear to provide more depth, as well as being attached to the screening force.

The main tasks of an AT defence were the organization of the defence of the main line of resistance and the formation of counterattack units held in reserve. The latter was the primary function of TD units. Anti-tank weapons were not equally distributed across the front; reconnaissance was conducted to determine their deployment based on the following criteria of rising priority: (1) routes of advance that man-made and natural obstacles made impractical for tanks; (2) areas that could be interdicted by passive AT defence; and (3) zones that had to be covered by AT weapons and mines to block armour. Efforts were made to channel tanks into the third zone in order to engage them.

The major flaw in the employment of TD units was that more often than not no German tank threat was immediately present. To employ tank destroyers gainfully they were therefore allotted to support infantry units as assault guns, often with a company to each regiment, a platoon to each battalion and a two-gun section to each rifle company. If a major German tank attack did develop, the division's attached TD battalion was thus too widely dispersed to concentrate and conduct a counterattack. Lack of time, and often inadequate roads usually choked with support vehicle columns, prevented the unit from concentrating rapidly in the necessary area. Tanks were found to be more effective tank-killers; and the last TD unit was deactivated in May 1946.

In the Pacific the Japanese tank threat was minimal, and relatively light AT guns were adequate for dealing with the small number encountered. The Japanese frequently employed dug-in tanks as static pillboxes, or committed them piecemeal in small numbers. When large numbers were employed in counterattacks they were often accompanied by inadequate numbers of infantry, and were frequently committed to counterattack a landing force too late, by which time AT guns, half-track mounted guns and tanks were already ashore. The US units usually made short work of the obsolescent Japanese tanks with barrages from bazookas, AT guns and artillery; often few US tanks were even present on these occasions. The first Japanese tank attack on Guadalcanal was defeated by a few 37mm AT guns (eight tanks knocked out), a 75mm half-track mounted gun (one tank) and 75mm howitzers (three tanks); Marine light tanks only showed up in time to mop up the enemy infantry. The largest tank battle in the Pacific saw a few Marine tanks, AT guns, bazookas and artillery destroy 24 of 37 attacking Japanese tanks on Saipan.

US 57mm M1 AT gun partly protected by a building corner – a common means of hastily positioning a gun in a built-up area. Often rubble and debris would be piled around the exposed parts of the gun, more for concealment than cover.

There were instances when US troops were overrun by German tanks, in Tunisia in winter 1942/43 and early in the Battle of the Bulge in December 1944; but for the most part US forces possessed overwhelming numbers of bazookas, AT guns, tanks, tank destroyers, artillery and air support, defeating most armour assaults easily.

BRITISH COMMONWEALTH

Britain entered the war with the 2-pdr Mk I quick-firing gun adopted in 1938. Its design was unusual in that when it went into action its wheels were removed and three legs spread to provide a stable mount with a 360-degree traverse. It weighed twice as much as its German 37mm counterpart. The British envisioned it engaging tanks from well-concealed prepared positions, and mobility was not an issue. This soon proved an error; speed of emplacement and displacement was essential, and its high profile was difficult to conceal, especially in the North African desert. Its maximum effective range was 600 yards and it could penetrate 50mm of armour, which soon proved inadequate; its five-man crew could crack off 20 to 22rpm, but it was provided only with AP-tracer ammunition, thus limiting its role. It was normally transported on the back of a 1½-ton Morris truck or 'portee'. Ramps allowed it to be off-loaded for ground firing, the preferred method, but it could be fired from the truck bed. It could also be towed by a ½-ton truck or full-tracked Universal Carrier.

Large numbers of 2-pdrs were lost in France in 1940, and while the 6-pdr gun existed in prototype, production of the 2-pdr had to continue as a stopgap in view of the desperate need for AT weapons. A number of Swedish-made 37mm m/34 Bofors guns were intercepted en route to Sudan in 1940 and pressed into service in Africa as the Mk I. Provided with AP-tracer and HE ammunition, they were only effective up to 400 yards, but weighed less than half as much as the 2-pdr. German mountain units, Poland, Denmark and Finland also used the same gun.

The 6-pdr Mk I was delivered in late 1941, to be quickly followed by the shorter barrelled Mk II, and by the Mk IV with a 16in longer barrel. They could be porteed on a 1½-ton lorry or, more commonly, towed by a tracked carrier. The 6-pdr (see above under the basically identical US 57mm) was a well-designed, low-profile weapon.

In May 1942 a much larger 17-pdr AT gun was approved for service, the first reaching the Tunisian front ('jury rigged' on 25-pdr gun-howitzer carriages) late in 1942, just in time to greet the first PzKw VI Tiger tanks deployed there.

Weighing 1,822lb and with a 165.45in barrel, it fired an APC round which could penetrate 109mm of armour at 1,000 yards at 30 degrees, and an HE round with a range of 10,000 yards. An APDS ('disposable sabot') round with a tungsten carbide penetrator, which could pierce 231mm of armour at 1,000 yards and 30 degrees, reached the front in August 1944. (This excellent gun was also

BRITISH AT ROADBLOCK, 1943–44

Mountainous Italy was a challenge to tank troops. If the lead vehicle could be disabled it trapped those following, which were vulnerable to intense artillery fire – as will soon be experienced by this StuG III 7.5cm assault gun and SdKfz 251/1 halftrack. The

PIAT (1) is loaded with the 3.5in Mk IA HEAT bomb (2) and No.75 or 'Hawkins' AT grenades (3) are here strung together in a 'necklace' or 'daisy-chain' at 2ft intervals; they are being pulled across the approaching vehicle's path. Heavier conventional AT mines could be

linked in the same manner. One rifleman lies in wait with a No.77 WP smoke grenade (4), and a No.73 'thermos flask' AT grenade (5). A Bren LMG team (6) is placing suppressive fire on the personnel carrier. (Steve Noon © Osprey Publishing Ltd) modified for mounting in the British 'Firefly' Sherman tank variant, eventually giving each tank troop in North-West Europe one tank that had a chance against the Panther and Tiger.)

The Boys 0.55in Mk I bolt-action AT rifle was fed by a five-round magazine; it weighed 36lb and was 64in long. Adopted in 1936, by 1940 it was obsolete, being able to penetrate only 20mm of armour at 300 yards. Unpopular for its savage recoil, weight and awkwardness, it was replaced as the rifle platoon AT weapon in 1943 by the PIAT, but it remained in service on various light AFVs. A few hundred were employed by Finland, and they were also provided to China by the USA.

The Mk I Projector, Infantry, Anti-Tank (PIAT – pronounced 'pee-at') saw its first combat with Canadian troops in Sicily in July 1943. The PIAT was a spigot-type discharger; and while its round was effective, the launcher had some unique drawbacks. At 31.7lb it was heavy, but it was only 39in long. Its range against tanks was 100 yards; the 3.5in HEAT bomb could penetrate 100mm of armour, but it could hit building-size targets at 350 yards and became prized as a 'bunker-buster'.

The projectile was launched by a powerful spring driving a rod into its tail and igniting a propellant cartridge. Unlike bazooka-type weapons, the PIAT itself had no backblast; it could be fired from inside a building, and threw up no signature of smoke and dust. Mounted on a monopod, it was shoulder-fired, but there was a difficult knack to using it. Like the Boys, one PIAT was issued to each rifle platoon headquarters; some 115,000 were produced.

Mobility was essential for AT guns. The British made wide use of the 'portee' concept, transporting 2-pdr and 6-pdr guns aboard a truck. While the gun could be fired from the truck bed, steel ramps were provided to dismount the gun for ground fire. This is a 6-pdr Mk II on a 1½-ton lorry; the side shields could also be used when in a ground position, but seldom were.

The No.68 AT rifle grenade was the first British weapon to employ the shaped-charge principle. Fielded in the summer of 1940, at just under 2lb this was the heaviest rifle grenade employed in World War II. It was fired from a 2.5in cup discharger, and was fin-stabilized. The warhead had a poorly designed cavity, lacking any form of stand-off, and its flat nose degraded its accuracy. Regardless of its poor design, its ability to penetrate armour was considered remarkable in 1940. It was withdrawn from service when the PIAT was issued.

Early in the war an AT school was established and operated by ex-International Brigade members with combat experience from the Spanish Civil War. A pamphlet, *Tank Hunting and Destruction*, gave advice which was relevant to a desperate last-ditch guerrilla campaign, but hardly for more conventional scenarios. In the true summer 1940 spirit of 'You can always take one with you...', it described tank-hunting as a sport akin to big game hunting, and recommended it for 'men who have bravery, resource and determination'. While a few expedient weapons were recommended, the main tank-hunting weapons prescribed were hand grenades, of which the British employed a wide variety. In the absence of anything like enough AT guns, they had little else with which to face the expected German invasion. All relied on blast effect, and none possessed a shaped charge; they were ineffective against all but the lightest tanks after 1940, but were retained to blow off tank tracks or for demolition and wall-breaching:

No.73 or 'thermos flask grenade'. 3.75lb, 10–15 yards range; impact fuse armed by 'Allways' system – safety pin withdrawn in flight by unreeling of weighted tape. Used in 1940–41, withdrawn, then reissued in 1943 for demolitions.

No.74 ST or 'sticky bomb'. 2.75lb, glass sphere with handle, filled with nitrogelatin (often mistakenly called nitroglycerin) and thickly covered with adhesive-soaked cloth, carried in discardable metal cover. After safety pin removed, grenade thrown or placed by hand; release of hand grip initiated 5-second time fuse. Very unpopular, but saw limited use 1940–43; after 1940 most were passed on to the French Resistance.

No.75 'Hawkins grenade/mine'. 2.25lb, tin canister; initiated by various fuses, it could be used as grenade or (more commonly) landmine, as well as for wall-breaching. Reliable device, also used by US forces; in use 1942–55.

No.82 'Gammon grenade'. Elasticated cloth bag in which varied amounts of plastic explosive were placed as appropriate for the target; initiated by 'Allways' fuse (see No.73 above). In use 1943–54.

France, 1939–40: a British crew man a French 25mm Mle 1934, which the Tommies called the 'Hotchkiss'. Besides helping to meet the BEF's shortage of AT guns, this was a limited effort at weapons standardization with the French. Assigned to brigade AT companies, the 25mm was found to be a very poor weapon, only barely able to defeat the German PzKw I light tank; penetration and range were little better than those of an AT rifle, and it was too flimsy for truck towing (thus necessitating the British Army's 'portee' concept). These weapons were gratefully abandoned in France before Dunkirk.

The 2-pdr AT gun was first assigned to the divisional AT regiment, a battalion-size Royal Artillery unit; these had four batteries of 12 guns each. A battery was attached to each divisional brigade, consisting of three four-gun troops, one attached to each infantry battalion. The 2-pdrs were replaced with 6-pdrs in 1942, and during 1944–45 batteries gradually achieved one troop with 6-pdrs and two with the much superior 17-pdr gun. The number of AT guns available to a division was inadequate, and in 1942 each infantry battalion's HQ company additionally received a platoon of six 2-pdrs, later 6-pdrs.

All too often the four 2-pdrs supporting an infantry battalion were employed in a straight line across the defensive front, allowing them only frontal shots at tanks they could not defeat. This made them easier to detect – when one was spotted the others were to be found immediately to its flanks. Whether in desert or woodland, it was found that they had to be employed in staggered lines with one or more positioned to achieve side shots.

The British began the war with a doctrine specifying a continuous frontline protected by an AT obstacle, and the dictate: 'Troops allotted to the defence of a locality must defend it to the end without a thought of withdrawal...' Positions were to be placed in depth. In North Africa this doctrine was largely replaced by a much more realistic 'box' concept of in-depth strongpoints on tank-proof terrain protected by minefields and screened by outposts and patrols.

Because of the inadequacies and insufficient number of 2-pdr guns, field artillery was heavily employed in North Africa to supplement them. The 2-pdrs were directed not to engage tanks until within 800 yards, and closer in wooded terrain. Opening fire at 600 yards was found to be too close, since tank machine guns were then within effective range. At 800 yards AT guns were as accurate as at 600 yards, while machine guns were less accurate and unable to penetrate gun shields. The field artillery's 25-pdr gun-howitzer had the advantage of 360-degree

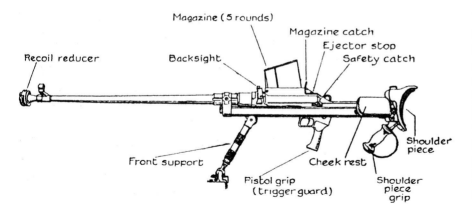

Magazine (5 rounds)

Magazine catch

Ejector stop

Safety catch

Recoil reducer

Backsight

Shoulder piece

Front support

Pistol grip (trigger guard)

Cheek rest

Shoulder piece grip

The 0.55in Mk 1 Boys AT rifle saw widespread use in British and Commonwealth armies; this round muzzle brake is found on British-made rifles. The Canadian-made Mk I* had a flat rectangular muzzle brake with vent holes in the edges; it also had a carrying handle, which the British model lacked. The Boys also saw limited use by US Marine Raiders and Army Rangers, as well as by the Chinese.

traverse and a 20rpm rate of fire with AP rounds; 25-pdrs opened fire within 1,000 yards, but were marginal tank-killers except at short range.

The 2-pdr guns were also positioned behind the frontline to protect artillery regiments, and their AT fires were integrated. The 2-pdrs might be positioned 100–300 yards to the flank of the artillery, or if all-round protection was necessary, as much as 500–1,000 yards to the front and flanks. The use of 25-pdrs as AT guns also provided depth to the AT defence. As more 6-pdr and heavier guns became available, along with self-propelled AT guns, the reliance on artillery faded. Guns were positioned to concentrate fires, as German tanks usually attacked in a mass that could not be engaged effectively by single guns.

In Burma and other jungle areas Japanese tanks were largely restricted to roads and Commonwealth forces concentrated AT guns along the roads in great depth. A definite forward line of the AT defence was specified, as was a rear line beyond which tanks were not allowed to pass. Rifle platoons relied on their single Boys AT rifle or PIAT and various AT hand grenades. Expedient means of attacking tanks were widely encouraged early in the war, but these proved to be only marginally effective. Camouflage and dispersed deployment were considered key factors in AT defence.

SOVIET UNION

The USSR began the war with the 45mm M1932 and M1937 AT guns for *protivo-tankovaya oborona* ('anti-tank combat'). These were rebarrelled 37mm M1930 and M1932 guns, almost exact copies of the German PaK 35/36, the identifying difference being wire-spoked wheels. In 1941 the short-barrelled 37mm was also still in use, though it penetrated only 40mm of armour at 500 yards.

Both calibres fired AP and HE ammunition. The 45mm M1942 was essentially an M1937 with a one-third longer barrel, increasing its velocity and thus penetration to 60mm at 500 yards; this was still inadequate, but the M1942 remained the primary battalion and regimental AT gun. A high-velocity round, based on a German design, was introduced in April 1942; this could penetrate 80mm at 500 yards. Apart from improved penetration the 45mm offered a more effective HE round than the 37mm.

Theoretically a platoon with two guns, either 37mm or 45mm, was allocated to each rifle battalion, and four or six guns to a regimental AT battery. In the event insufficient guns were available to continue equipping battalion platoons, and they were dropped between July 1941 and January 1943. The 45mm also armed divisional AT battalions, each with three four-gun batteries. The AT battalion was deleted from the divisional establishment in July 1941, but restored in January 1942. During that period the only AT guns were those assigned to regimental batteries.

Production of the 57mm ZiS-2 began in 1941, but it was halted when Soviet intelligence assessed German tank armour as thinner than had been believed. Production was resumed in June 1943, with an improved carriage. With a rate of fire of 20–25 rpm, it could penetrate 145mm at 500 yards; it fired both high-

The Soviet 45mm M1942 AT gun partly replaced the 45mm M1932 as well as 37mm guns. The 45mm began to be replaced by the 57mm ZiS-2 in late 1943, but earlier models remained in use. The long barrel coupled with a new high-velocity round made the 45mm a reasonably effective weapon for its calibre. The USSR was the only country to use 45mm guns.

velocity AP and HE rounds, and had the longest barrel of any gun in this calibre range. The 57mm was to replace the 45mm at divisional level, but often the necessary prime movers were unavailable, and divisions retained manhandled 45mm guns. From 1943 independent AT battalions and brigades were raised.

The standard divisional artillery piece was the 76.2mm F-22 of 1936 and the improved 1939 FS-22USV gun; the 76.2mm ZiS-3 was introduced in early 1942. The 76.2mm guns were long-barrelled weapons suited for AT use, and the Germans employed many captured F-22s in that role. The Soviets also adopted a massive 100mm BS-3 AT gun in 1944.

The Red Army was the war's largest users of AT rifles, producing some 400,000. Two models were employed, both of 14.5mm calibre, bipod-mounted, long and heavy, but capable of being broken down into two sections. The Degtyarov PTRD-41 was single-shot, bolt-action, 78.74in long, and weighed 38lb. The Simonov PTRS-41 was semi-automatic with a five-round magazine; its 84.25in length and 46lb weight, coupled with its complexity and cost, resulted in its seeing much less service. The 14.5mm B-32 AP-incendiary round penetrated 35mm of armour at 100 yards and 25mm at 500 yards, while the tungsten carbide-cored BS-41 AP-I punched through 40mm at 100 yards and 35mm at 500 yards.

Both weapons were adopted in August 1941, and a platoon of six was added to the rifle regiment establishment. They saw their first combat use only in November 1941, and the regimental scale was increased to a company of three platoons, each with three squads, each with three rifles – a total of 27 weapons. An AT rifle company was added to the rifle battalion in July 1942, with two platoons of four squads (16 rifles), as well as a four-platoon company in the

The Soviet 14.5mm Degtyarov PTRD-41 AT rifle, with a length of 6ft 6in, was actually reasonably light for its size at 38lb. The barrel could be separated from the action at the point where the assistant gunner's hand rests in this photo; on the march the No.2 carried the barrel and the No.1 the action.

divisional AT battalion (36 rifles). In January 1943 the battalion company was reduced to a nine-rifle platoon. AT rifles were also distributed to many other types of units. Although they were soon obsolete, AT rifles remained in Soviet use throughout the war. Tactics emphasized side and rear attacks, as well as use against the many light AFVs encountered on the battlefield.

With the acquisition of 8,500 US 2.36in M1 bazookas through Lend-Lease in 1942, the capture of various German rocket launchers in 1943, and their own vigorous *Katyusha* artillery rocket programme, it is surprising that the Soviets did not develop an effective shoulder-fired AT rocket launcher to replace the obsolete, heavy, awkward and costly AT rifles. They did make extensive use of captured Panzerfausts; and Britain provided 3,200 Boys AT rifles and 1,000 PIATs.

In 1941 the Soviets fielded an unusual weapon known as the *ampulomet* ('ampoule projector'), with six assigned to the rifle regiment's 'anti-tank mortar' platoon. This was a short 5in tube on a four-legged mount firing a glass sphere filled with jellied petrol/gasoline to a range of 250 yards; it had a crew of three men. Inaccurate and largely ineffective against tanks, it was withdrawn in late 1942. The use of man-portable flamethrowers against tanks was common, however.

The VPGS-41 AT rifle grenade was a heavy, fin-stabilized rod-type grenade, requiring no separate launcher attachment for the rifle. Its poorly designed shaped-charge lacked sufficient stand-off and had an almost flat nose, degrading its accuracy. It was phased out in about 1943 due to its short 50–75 yard range, limited armour penetration and damaging effect on rifles.

The Soviets employed three AT stick hand grenades. These were heavy, about 2.25lb, limiting throwing range to about 15 or 20 yards. All were stabilized by deployable ribbon drogues. The RPG-40 (*ruchnaya protibotankovyi granata*, 'hand anti-tank grenade') was a blast grenade penetrating 20–25mm of steel; it was more effective against pillboxes than armour. The RPG-42 used a shaped charge to penetrate 75mm; and the RPG-6 was a much improved design introduced in 1944, with 4in penetration. Apart from these grenades, 'Molotov cocktails' were produced in their millions, and self-igniting kits were provided to attach to bottles in the field.

*   *   *

Soviet AT defences emphasized depth: 1.25–1.75 miles in 1941, and four times that depth by the time of the battle of Kursk in mid 1943. Co-ordination between units, and a strong mobile AT reserve, were also major factors. Anti-tank units were called 'anti-tank artillery', and field artillery units were also trained to conduct direct fire on armour. Light AT guns were positioned well forward, but not beyond the infantry frontline, with progressively larger calibre guns in subsequent lines. Large calibre guns could be positioned forward to cover key avenues. Anti-tank guns were covered by infantry and AT rifles, and were positioned in pairs within 50 yards of each other. Sometimes guns were positioned 100 to 150 yards apart along the front. Camouflage and alternative positions were heavily emphasized, and fire was held until tanks were within

SOVIET AT DEFENCE IN BUILT-UP AREA, 1944

Despite the weight and bulk of the bolt-action PTRD-41 (1) and semi-automatic PTRS-41 AT rifles, the Red Army retained them throughout the war. The AT rifleman's dream shot was to be able to take a belly shot as a tank mounted an obstacle. Another weapon the Soviets retained was the AT hand grenade. The RPG-43 was the second Soviet design, and the first with a shaped charge (2). If it struck at right angles it could penetrate 75mm, so attack from above a tank was the optimum method. Pulling the pin allowed the rear cone of the thrown grenade to slide off the handle and act as a drogue at the end of the deploying streamers (3). Another weapon the Soviets used was the 'Molotov cocktail' (4). Submachine gunners (5) were deployed for close protection of AT rifle crews, and to shoot Panzergrenadiers (6) off tanks. TM-38 mines (7) are emplaced to catch a tank by surprise when it turns a corner. (Steve Noon © Osprey Publishing Ltd)

600 yards at most to avoid revealing positions prematurely. Four guns were often positioned in a diamond pattern to provide all-round fire.

Anti-tank guns and artillery were expected to fire until overrun; the destruction of large numbers of tanks was considered a successful defence even if the guns were lost. The Soviets calculated that 12 x 45mm rounds were necessary to knock out a tank, whether fired from one gun or several; this allowed for misses and deflected hits. Typically, one 45mm gun was lost for every tank destroyed. The 76.2mm required half the number of rounds to destroy a tank, and typically knocked out two or three before being destroyed itself.

The 'fire sack' was a pre-planned zone into which minefields, obstacles and fire would channel armour – a large-scale ambush. Several AT units would be positioned on both sides of the kill zone, to engage the tanks from different directions and ranges. Massed artillery fires were concentrated on the zone, and mobile AT guns would attack it. An AT reserve would be held, to manoeuvre into position to block escaping tanks even if the enemy changed direction.

Divisional and higher commanders established an AT reserve (*protivo-tankovyy rezerv*); at division level this was constituted from part of the AT battalion and one platoon from each regimental AT battery. Tanks and mobile obstacle detachments might be included – the latter laid hasty minefields on enemy tank routes.

The use of AT strongpoints was customary in the summer 1943 defensive battles. A typical strongpoint engaged in the battle of Kursk was built within a rifle company position; it might consist of three or four 45mm AT guns, two or three AT rifle squads, a sapper squad with demolition charges, a submachine gun squad and tank-hunter teams with Molotov cocktails and other close-attack weapons. Up to 1,700 mines were laid per 0.75 miles of frontage, along with AT ditches and other obstacles, all covered by pre-planned artillery concentrations.

At least ten AT rifles were to be committed against a tank platoon, and instructions provide an idea of their employment:

In all cases establish secondary firing positions; fire five to ten rounds from one position, then move to another. If the enemy tank is moving in a direction unfavourable to you, quickly and inconspicuously occupy another position to fire into the side or rear from 50 to 100 yards.

Manoeuvring on the battlefield, force the tank into the fire of another AT rifle; in those cases when you are operating with other AT rifles, and in a combat formation with our own infantry, co-ordinate your own mission with that of your neighbour. When supported by grenade and Molotov cocktail throwers, determine their positions and do not fire in their direction. If an enemy tank has halted, disable its weapons first.

A staged photo of a Red Army AT rifle crew taking on a PzKw III. Note that both men carry the haversacks containing 20 rounds of 14.5mm AP-I cartridges.

GERMANY

Despite all their emphasis on mobile armoured warfare, the Wehrmacht entered the war with marginal AT capabilities. The army was so oriented toward aggressiveness that anything smacking of defence was viewed with disfavour. *Panzerabwehr* ('armour defence') units were redesignated *Panzerjäger* ('armour hunter') on 1 April 1940, to play down their defensive nature. Anti-tank guns were increasingly mounted on tracked chassis to improve mobility.

The principal AT gun was the Rheinmetall-Borsig 3.7cm PaK 35/36 (*Panzerabwehr Kanone*, 'armour defence gun', model 1935/36). Nine guns were allotted to the three-platoon regimental AT company and 27 to the divisional AT battalion. Copied by many countries, the PaK 35/36 was an excellent weapon in the mid 1930s, but by 1940 it was obsolescent – as acknowledged by its army nickname of *Türklopfer* ('doorknocker'). Operated by a six-man crew, it originally fired an AP round that could penetrate 40mm at 400 yards; in 1940 the AP40 round was introduced, penetrating 50mm at 400 yards. In 1941 a massive muzzle-loaded shaped charge 'rod grenade' was developed to extend the gun's life; this Steilgranate 41 had a 159mm warhead that rested outside the muzzle, capable of penetrating 150mm of armour with an effective range of 200 yards, although much longer ranges could be achieved.

The 5cm PaK 38, a scaled-up version of the 3.7cm, was fielded in late 1940 to replace the 'doorknocker,' but supply was slow. With a good shot it could knock out a T-34 with the AP40 round, which penetrated 85mm at 500 yards, while the standard AP penetrated 60mm at that range. The Germans were so

The German 3.7cm PaK 35/36 AT gun was extensively copied by other countries including the US, USSR and Italy, as well as being exported to the Netherlands and China. The shield was usually high, but the upper portion was hinged (level with the loader's helmet top in this photo) and could be dropped forward to lower its profile.

badly in need of AT guns that they employed just about all captured ordnance in this role, but numbers were still insufficient. They also built several hybrid designs mating AT guns to artillery carriages.

GERMAN *PANZERKAMPFGRUPPE* IN COVERING POSITION, 1944–45

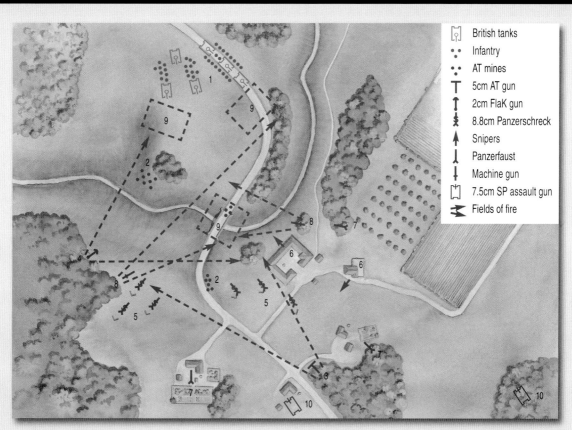

[⌐]	British tanks
⠐⠂	Infantry
⠐⠂	AT mines
T	5cm AT gun
↑	2cm FlaK gun
⚡	8.8cm Panzerschreck
↑	Snipers
↓	Panzerfaust
↓	Machine gun
[⌐]	7.5cm SP assault gun
➤	Fields of fire

The mission of this small armour battle group is to delay the approach of British tanks (1) on a secondary route into a defended village (off the edge of the picture). Point AT minefields were laid at chokepoints (2), intermingled with anti-personnel mines. The few AT guns available at this date were often employed singly, like this 5cm PaK 38 (3), rather than in larger groups; 2cm FlaK guns were positioned on flanks (4) to help make up for the lack of AT guns. A single squad with six 8.8cm RP54 Panzerschrecks has taken up positions in a typical pattern (5). While there are farm buildings in the area, only a few snipers occupy them (6); buildings attracted suppressive fire and allowed the enemy to pinpoint German positions quickly. Scattered pairs of grenadiers hide on tank routes armed with a few Panzerfausts, ready to engage tanks that might slip through (7). With rifle strength reduced in many grenadier units, higher allocations of MG34 and MG42 machine guns (8) were made to increase firepower. These were put to good use separating infantry from the tanks they escorted. As the enemy approached the position 8cm and 12cm mortars from the main battle position would fire on pre-registered barrage areas (9). Assault guns (10) might be positioned to the rear, usually dug-in or hidden in buildings to further deter the advance. (Steve Noon © Osprey Publishing Ltd)

This 7.5cm PaK 40 is typical of World War II AT guns: it has a long barrel for high velocity and range, a muzzle brake to reduce recoil (since the guns were kept as light as possible), a shield to protect the crew from tank machine gun fire and fragmentation, rubber tyres for high-speed towing when repositioning, split trails, direct-fire optical sights, and a means of rapid traverse. To be successful and to have any chance of surviving, AT guns also needed camouflage and protection. This gun appears to have been well camouflaged, though most has been pulled away to allow the position to be photographed. The low-profile gun has been dug into a pit, and a slit trench dug for the gunner and loader immediately beneath the breech. This view illustrates the double, spaced shield typical of many German AT guns; it required the use of less steel and reduced weight, while equating to the protective effect of a solid shield approximately one-third thicker.

A further scaling up of the PaK 38 resulted in the 7.5cm PaK 40, also fielded in late 1940. This became the main divisional AT gun, but some were assigned to regimental AT companies as well. Heavy to manhandle, it nonetheless proved to be an effective weapon. It could knock out most tanks, penetrating 105mm at 500 yards with standard AP, and 115mm with AP40. Many captured Soviet 76.2mm FS-22 guns were rechambered for German 7.5cm and further modified for AT use as the 7.62cm PaK 36(r). The 3.7cm, 5cm and 7.5cm were all provided with HE rounds.

From 1941 the Germans made limited use of two Gerlich-type tapered or 'squeeze' bore guns, the 2.8cm (tapering to 2cm) and 4.2cm (actually 4.5cm, tapering to 2.94cm). The 2.8cm sPzB 41 was a small, wheeled weapon meant to replace 7.92mm AT rifles, and the 4.2cm lePaK 41 was mounted on a 3.7cm carriage. These guns used a special projectile that was 'squeezed' down to a smaller calibre when fired in order to achieve a higher velocity. Guns and ammunition were expensive to produce – the rounds required scarce tungsten carbide cores – and production ceased in 1942. Penetration was good: the 2.8cm achieved 60mm at 400 yards, and the 75mm, 76mm at 500 yards. Their usefulness was limited by their lack of HE rounds.

The 2cm FlaK 38 single and quad anti-aircraft cannon were integrated into AT defences and provided with AP and AP40 ammunition, as were the 3.7cm FlaK guns. The Germans had small numbers of AT rifles in service in 1939, the Panzerbüchse (PzB) 38 and 39. Only 1,600 examples of the complex and expensive PzB 38 were produced, but 39,232 of the PzB 39. Both models were 7.92mm calibre, taking a necked-down World War I 13.2mm AT rifle cartridge, capable of penetrating 1.2in at 100 yards. The bullet was too small to do much interior damage; a larger round would ricochet around and hit different crewmen, but the little .31-cal bullet would usually stop when it hit the first man. The early rounds had a tiny tear gas pellet, but this was too small to be effective. Later ammunition had a carbide core – something learned from the Poles. Both rifles were single-shot and bipod-mounted. The PzB 38 weighed 35lb and the PzB 39, 27.25lb. Several other 7.92mm AT rifles saw limited use, along with numerous captured weapons including Soviet types, and various Swedish-made 20mm rifles such as the Solothurn s18-1100. A rifle company had a seven-man AT section with three weapons; one might be attached to each platoon, but it was preferred to keep them grouped for concentrated fire.

Recognizing that AT rifles were outdated, in 1943 the Germans modified the PzB 39 into the Granatbüchse (GrB) 39 AT grenade rifle, shortening the barrel by 2ft and attaching a grenade discharger cup. Capable of firing any German AT grenade, it was still heavy at 23.15lb, and its range of 150 yards was not much further than the same grenades could be fired from a standard rifle.

The Gewehrgranate zur Panzerbekämpfung 40 (GG/P40; 'rifle grenade for anti-armour combat model 1940') used a spigot-type launcher. The grenade, copied by the US, was ineffective even though the Germans used a base-detonating fuse; it lacked stand-off. It was withdrawn in 1942 and replaced by a 30mm cup discharger system. The first *Gewehr Panzergranate* ('rifle armour grenade') was a 30mm shaped charge with 20–30mm of penetration and an effective range of 50 to 100 yards. By 1942 a 40mm over-calibre grenade was introduced, capable of penetrating 50mm at up to 150 yards. Almost 24 million 30mm and 40mm grenades were produced. The 46mm and 61mm versions were introduced in late 1942 and late 1943 respectively, with an effective range of 80 to 100 yards. The 46mm penetrated 70–90mm, and the 61mm pierced 100–120mm.

While a few AT hand grenades saw limited use, the principal German hand AT weapon was the magnetic hollow-charge 3kg Haft-Hohlladungen (Haft-Hl 3). This *Panzerknacker* ('armour-cracker') was adopted in November 1942. It was of truncated cone shape, with a handle holding the fuse, and three pairs of magnets around the base that allowed it to be attached to a tank, fortress gun cupola and pillbox doors or shutters. Early models had a friction-ignited 4.5-second delay fuse, which sometimes did not allow time for the attacker to seek cover; a 7.5-second fuse was introduced in May 1943. The charge could penetrate up to 140mm of armour or 508mm of concrete. Some 553,900 'armour crackers' were made in 1942–44; the Haft-Hohlladung was declared obsolete in May 1944, to be replaced by the Panzerfaust, although existing stocks remained in use.

The Panzerwurfmine 1 ('anti-armour thrown mine type 1') was a 3lb hand-thrown hollow charge mine issued in 1944. It consisted of a hemispherical-nosed warhead with a long tailboom and four folding cloth vanes. When it was thrown the igniter was armed and vanes opened like an umbrella to stabilize the mine. Its range was 20 or 30 yards and it was considered to be quite effective – penetrating 80–100mm – but somewhat unsafe to handle.

The 8.8cm Racketenwerfer 43 ('rocket launcher model 1943') or *Püppchen* ('Dolly') looked like a small artillery piece, a breech-loading tube on two wheels. Its HEAT rocket was effective to 230 yards against moving targets and up to 500 for stationary targets, to penetrate 160mm. The weapon was not recoilless and there was no back-blast. It was expensive to make, and insufficiently portable for infantrymen, its 325lb weight being broken down into seven sections for man-packing.

Captured American 2.36in M1 bazookas led to a new design, the 8.8cm Raketenpanzerbüchse (RPzB) 43, also known as the *Panzerschreck* or *Ofenrohr* ('stovepipe'). This electrically fired shoulder weapon was 65in long and weighed 209lb; it used the same 8.8cm warhead as the Püppchen, but with a redesigned motor, and had a range of 150 yards. The Panzerschreck was highly portable, low cost, and could be produced rapidly in large numbers. The almost identical RPzB 54 was produced in 1944; this weighed 24.2lb because an added shield protected the gunner from muzzle blow-back. Only a small number were produced before the RPzB 54/1 appeared, with a shorter 52.5in tube and its weight reduced to the former 20.9lb; this could fire an improved rocket to 180 yards. This was the most common model of the almost 290,000 of all models produced. (The RPzB 43 could not fire the new rocket, and was reissued to second line units.) Regimental AT gun companies were replaced by *Panzerzerstörer* ('armour destroyer')

The 8.8cm Racketenwerfer 43 or *Püppchen* was a non-recoilless rocket launcher. While its RPzBGr 4312 HEAT rocket (foreground) looked the same as the RPzBGr 4322 and RPzBGr 4992 fired from the Panzerschreck RPzB 43 and RPzB 54, and RPzB 54/1 respectively, they were not interchangeable. Most R-Werfer 43s were sent to North Africa and Italy, though a few were seen in Normandy.

companies with up to 54 Panzerschrecks in three platoons, each with 18 launchers in three squads. Some companies retained a platoon with three 7.5cm guns.

The Panzerfaust ('armour fist') is the best known of the new German anti-armour weapons, and was genuinely revolutionary. The 'Faust' was actually a single-shot recoilless gun launching a fin-stabilized shaped-charge warhead with a propellant cartridge. It consisted (for the *klein*, 'small' model) of a 35in-long steel tube of 44mm bore. An over-calibre shaped charge warhead was fitted to the muzzle. It was held under the arm or over the shoulder, and fired by a percussion igniter, which was exposed to the rocking trigger when the gunner flipped up a folding sight on top of the tube. Looking through one of three apertures in the latter, he lined up a barleycorn sight on the top edge of the warhead with the target. Once fired, the non-reloadable tube was discarded.

The first Panzerfaust *klein* model, issued in July 1943 (aka Panzerfaust 1, or *Gretchen* – 'Peggy'), had a 100mm diameter warhead that penetrated 140mm of armour at 30 yards. The Panzerfaust 30 (aka Panzerfaust 2 or *gross*, 'large') followed immediately; it had the same range, but it and subsequent models employed a 150mm warhead capable of penetrating 200mm at an impact angle of 30 degrees. The *gross* weighed 11.5lb in total. This and subsequent models were designated by their effective range in metres, and had progressively larger propellant charges. The Panzerfaust 60 was introduced in the summer of 1944; with the same warhead and twice the range, it saw the widest use. In September 1944 the Panzerfaust 100 appeared, weighing the same as the 60. More advanced models were under development when the war ended.

More than eight million Panzerfausts of all models were produced. While short-ranged, they were effective weapons, mainly because of the sheer numbers available. They had no specialist crews, but were issued to individuals just like grenades; indeed, in the closing months of the war German propaganda made much of the fact that Hitler Youth teenagers, old Volkssturm home guardsmen, and even housewives could be trained to use them. Allocation to infantry divisions was 36 per rifle and pioneer company, 18 per AT company and other company-size units and 12 per artillery battery.

*   *   *

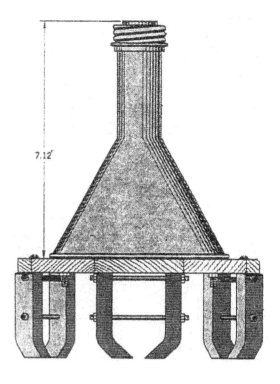

7.12"

The 3kg Haft-Hohlladungen was a hollow charge fitted with three pairs of magnets (*Haften* means 'to cling'). This hand-placed 'armour-cracker' actually weighed 3.6kg, being filled with 6.6lb of pentolite. The magnets were termed 'Alnico', which is often assumed to be a maker or designer name, but is actually a contraction: 'AlNiCo' for aluminium-nickel-cobalt, an alloy used for making magnets.

German anti-armour doctrine called for all units including rear services to prepare for tank defence by emplacing AT weapons to cover likely avenues of approach, to tie tank-proof terrain into the defensive plan, and to provide for early warning – a function of reconnaissance units and infantry outposts. Terrain was classified as *Panzerschier* ('armour-proof') – impassable to AFVs; *Panzergefährdet* ('armour-risk') – difficult for AFVs; or *Panzermöglich* ('armour-feasible') – passable to armour. The determination was made by map and ground reconnaissance of an area. Armour-proof terrain could include dense forest, swampland, deep mud, numerous large rocks and gullies, steep, slippery slopes, railroad embankments or deep cuttings.

Anti-tank guns were well dug in and concealed, positioned in twos and threes, and emplaced in depth throughout the regimental defensive sector. Selected single guns might begin picking off tanks at maximum range, but most held their fire until the target was within 300 to 150 yards. Close combat teams attacked tanks that reached the German battle positions. Once a tank attack was repulsed the guns moved to alternative positions.

The Germans learned that the massive effort expended in laying vast minefields was wasted, since they were so easily breached. They mainly laid small delaying minefields on routes and within their positions to knock out marauding tanks. Anti-tank ditches were no longer dug well forward of the frontline because they provided enemy infantry with jump-off cover; they were now dug immediately in front of fighting positions. The *Panzerabwehrgeschutz* ('armour

This Panzerfaust 60 was the most common of several models produced. The sight was folded down until the weapon was readied for firing. When using a Panzerfaust from a trench the firer had to be careful that the back-blast was not deflected into his confined position by a rear parapet. Most Panzerfausts were painted dark ochre yellow, but some field-grey. They were marked in red on the tube: *Vorsicht! Starker Feuerstrahl!* ('Danger! Intense fire flash!'), with an arrowhead pointing to the rear. Operating instructions were printed on the lower portion of the projectile.

defence centre of resistance') was established on the suspected tank approach route, where weapons were concentrated.

Tank-hunter teams (*Panzerjagdgruppe*) consisted of an NCO and at least three men well trained in AT close combat techniques and equipped with weapons to 'blind, halt, and destroy'. Such teams were employed only as a last resort, when there were no AT guns operational or a position had been overrun. Machine guns and mortars concentrated on separating enemy infantry from their tanks. Small arms were directed against tank vision ports, and the team moved under cover of smoke grenades. If possible they would lie in wait for the tank to come within 20 yards before attacking with close-combat and expedient weapons. After Panzerfausts became available they were the preferred method of attack, fired in barrages from multiple directions. Tank-hunter teams would move in close and attack from the rear or sides. Close-range ambushes were set up in woodland and built-up areas. Riflemen covering the close-in attacker would cease fire if it hampered him, but be prepared to fire if the crew opened a hatch to defend the tank. Once a tank was disabled and captured, its gun breechblocks would be removed and the tank set on fire.

In 1943 the Germans in Russia developed the *Pakfront* ('armour defence gun front'). This was an extension of the idea of emplacing AT guns behind the forward positions to engage tanks after they broke through, when their fighting formations were less organized and they might be separated from their supporting infantry; Soviet tanks often broke through in large numbers. The concept was for the divisional AT battalion (corps and army level battalions were also employed) to position six to ten or more well dug-in and concealed 7.5cm guns under a single commander, on favourable terrain blocking the main tank routes. Their towing vehicles were hidden close by, ready to relocate or withdraw the guns quickly. In effect, the Pakfront ambushed tanks at short range, with all guns opening fire simultaneously. Artillery and rocket projectors supported the *Pakfront* while available reserves and armour moved into a counterattack.

A US soldier examines 8.8cm RPzB 54 Panzerschreck rocket launchers. Late in the war the Wehrmacht regimental 'armour destroyer company' possessed 54 of these, which were typically employed in groups of six covering the same area.

JAPAN

Japan was dismally ill prepared for *taisensha sento* ('anti-tank warfare'), and suitable weapons were almost non-existent. Although they had been out-manoeuvred when they faced Soviet armour in Manchuria in 1939, they downplayed the decisiveness of armour, persisting in the view that tanks were infantry support weapons. There was no doctrine for massing armour or engaging in battles with enemy tanks. They expected their enemies to follow suit, and made the mistake of judging that only light US tanks would be committed to Pacific islands. In the event, from the November 1943 Tarawa assault onwards the US habitually employed M4 Sherman medium tanks, and later some tank destroyers.

The principal Japanese 'AT' gun was the 37mm Type 94 (1934) infantry rapid-fire gun. Originally intended to deliver direct fire to knock out machine gun nests, it was provided with HE ammunition. Although an AP-HE round was issued, it performed dismally as an AT gun owing to its low velocity and poor penetration – just 24mm at 500 yards. The Type 94 was light and could be broken down into six sections for animal or man-pack transport by its eight-man crew. Some units deploying from China were armed with more effective 37mm Type 97 (1937) AT guns; these were German-made PaK 35/36s captured from China, but were very few in number.

From late 1942 the 47mm Type 1 (1941) AT gun began to appear. While not as effective as similar contemporary weapons, it could knock out a Sherman, but seldom with a frontal shot. Its AP round could penetrate 50mm at 500 yards, and it was also provided with HE ammunition. Infantry regimental AT companies had three two-gun platoons with either 37mm or 47mm guns. Even late in the war they were often still armed with 37mm pieces, and most 47mm guns were found in independent AT battalions, which might possess a mix of the two calibres. There were no divisional AT battalions.

Machine cannon units were armed with 20mm Type 98 (1938) automatic cannon and 13.2mm Type 93 (1933) heavy machine guns. Both were capable of anti-aircraft fire, but were especially valuable as anti-boat and anti-amphibian tractor guns when provided with anti-personnel ammunition.

The 20mm Type 97 (1937) AT rifle was issued to some infantry battalions, with up to eight in the battalion gun company. This was an expensive weapon and few units actually received it; at 150lb it was cumbersome, requiring a three- to four-man crew. It was capable of semi- and fully automatic fire, an unusual feature for a weapon fed by a seven-round magazine. Mounted on a bipod and a butt monopod, it had a violent recoil. AP-tracer and HE-tracer ammunition was provided, the former penetrating 12mm at 200 yards.

Little use was made of AT rifle grenades. The Germans provided plans for their cup-discharged 30mm and 40mm grenades, and modified copies were produced as the Type 2 (1942) grenades – one of the few uses made of the

JAPANESE SELF-SACRIFICE, 1945

'Ten men for one tank'. The Japanese commander on Iwo Jima was much concerned by the USMC's M4A3 Shermans, fearing that his 47mm Type 1 (1941) AT guns could not defeat them (an exaggerated fear, as it turned out). He ordered preparations to use the Type 99 (1939) magnetic AT hand mine, a simple weapon that was moderately effective against hull side and top armour (1).

Sometimes two Type 99 mines were wired together to improve penetration. In other instances two pairs of mines were fastened together with small demolition charges sandwiched between them, and the four mines were wired between split logs (2). Though little used, the Type 2 (1942) rifle grenade launcher could fire 30mm and 40mm HEAT grenades, penetrating 30mm and

50mm respectively; the 40mm is illustrated at (3). One fallen soldier has attempted to throw a bar or 'yardstick' mine (4) with 6lb of explosive in front of the Sherman's tracks. As a last resort Japanese troops were encouraged to force tank hatches open and attack the crew with grenades – (5) is a Type 99 fragmentation – and even bayonets (6). (Steve Noon © Osprey Publishing Ltd)

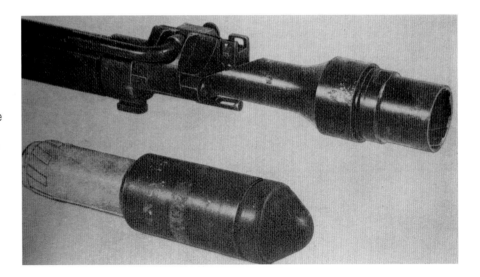

One of the few Japanese weapons employing shaped charges was the 30mm Type 2 (1942) grenade based on the German *Schiessbecher* cup discharger system. It could be fitted on Arisaka 6.5mm and 7.7mm rifles, and fired both 30mm and over-calibre 40mm (shown here) AT grenades. Their penetration was approximately 30mm and 50mm respectively, with a range of about 100 yards.

shaped-charge concept by the Japanese. Another shaped-charge weapon was the lunge mine, basically a hand-delivered AT mine attached to a pole. First used in the Philippines in 1944, it consisted of an 11.8lb truncated cone-shaped warhead fitted with stand-off 'prongs' and mounted on a 6ft pole. The attacker rushed a tank, slamming the charge into its side; he did not survive, but the mine could penetrate 150mm of armour.

The Type 99 (1939) magnetic anti-armour charge was a canvas-covered 2.75lb charge formed as a flat disc 1.5in thick x 4.75in diameter, and fitted with four magnets around the outside edge. Relying on blast, it was effective only against the thinner side and top armour, being able to penetrate 25mm of plate. The fuse was struck on a solid object to ignite it. Several types of expedient AT grenades and hand mines of marginal effectiveness were mass-produced in the Philippines in 1943–44.

*   *   *

Japanese AT tactics were characterized by their emphasis on offensive spirit, on efforts to offset their inadequate weapons, and on the close terrain in which much of the fighting occurred. The value of strength of will, to the point of self-sacrifice, in overcoming the material superiority of Japan's enemies was a powerful and prevailing belief. While Westerners tend to dismiss such intangible aspects, this suicidal aggression was nevertheless a viable factor, though with obvious limitations; 'one soldier for one tank' was a common credo, but the mathematics were usually costlier than that. Rugged, close terrain – either covered with dense vegetation, or broken ground with gorges, ridges, hillocks and sinkholes – provided AT weapons with cover and concealment, as well as allowing the

Japanese to concentrate on close attacks and to maximize the effect of their short-ranged weapons.

While organic divisional AT assets were limited, one to three independent AT battalions and machine cannon units might be attached to a division. Anti-tank guns were dug in well forward, though some would be positioned in depth, and others commonly protected flank and rear approaches. Secondary positions were prepared in the position's depth and on the flanks. Camouflage was excellent; anti-armour engagements were basically ambushes, as they would open fire at very short ranges with guns positioned for side and rear shots. Guns were often dug into ridges and rocky slopes inaccessible to tanks. In rough terrain numerous guns were concentrated on the few routes available to tanks.

Tank-hunter teams of six to eight men under an NCO were formed by each infantry platoon. The men sometimes worked in pairs: one with a Type 99 hand mine, a grenade and a smoke candle, the second with two each Molotov cocktails, grenades and smoke candles. Other tank-hunters organized into a diversionary team with smoke candles; a track team with hand-laid 'yardstick' AT mines or pole charges; a turret team with Type 99 hand mines or satchel charges; and a covering group of riflemen with hand grenades. The covering rifle platoon forced the tank to 'button up', while machine guns and 50mm grenade dischargers ('knee mortars') strove to separate the infantry as the tanks approached.

The fewer AT guns available, the more tank-hunter units would be formed. Each was given a sector in which to deliver its 'shock attack', as the tank entered an area where the unit was concealed. Attack sites were selected at points where the tank would have to slow down, such as when crossing a stream or gully. One Japanese document stated that attackers should 'voluntarily jump on the tank and throw a grenade inside or stab the crew with a bayonet.' Nevertheless, in April–May 1945 on Okinawa the causes of US tank losses were mines, AT guns, artillery and attacks with magnetic hand mines and satchel charges – in that order.

On Iwo Jima in February–March 1945, USMC tanks were hampered almost as much by the chaotic terrain as by Japanese AT defences. The soft volcanic sand caused many tanks to throw tracks or bog down. The Japanese tied tank

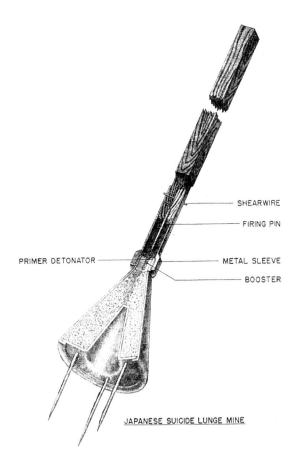

SHEARWIRE

FIRING PIN

PRIMER DETONATOR

METAL SLEEVE

BOOSTER

JAPANESE SUICIDE LUNGE MINE

The 6.4lb of explosives in the warhead of the *shitotsu bakurai* ('lunge mine') was pushed back with its detonator onto a firing pin when slammed into the side of a tank. Three 5.25in rods protruding from the base of the cone ensured optimum 'stand-off' for the hollow charge. US troops called this suicide weapon an 'idiot stick', but it did knock out tanks. Circular Type 93 (1933) AT mines ('tape measure mines') were also fastened to the ends of poles for the same purpose.

The Japanese Type 99 (1939) AT charge (99 *hako-bakurai*) was small (about 4.75in x 1.5in without the four magnets), but if two or more could be fastened together they caused a great deal of concern to tankers. It was issued in a canvas carrying pouch, with the fuse packed in a two-piece metal tube under the pouch flap.

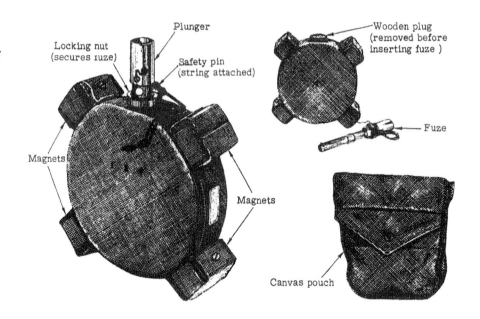

ditches and minefields into terrain features, to channel tanks into the fields of fire of 47mm AT guns, which proved effective at short range; in one such action three Shermans were immobilized within minutes by turret hits. Losses were high; by the operation's fourth day the 4th Tank Bn listed 11 of their tanks destroyed, eight damaged and 28 operational; the 5th Tank Bn had lost 13, with four damaged and 34 operational.

Losses continued to mount, and the battalions were hard pressed to field enough tanks. In some instances the Japanese use of non-AT weapons actually prevented the commitment of tanks. When tanks advanced with accompanying infantry the Japanese would barrage the area with mortars and grenade dischargers, causing infantry casualties; in some clearing operations the Marine infantry declined the use of armour in order to avoid the heavier fire they attracted, and painstakingly cleared pillboxes and caves with bazookas, demolitions and flamethrowers instead. The Japanese often sited pillboxes on terrain inaccessible to tanks to prevent flamethrower tanks from moving within range; these were particularly feared and hated, and often suffered close-in attacks.

CONCLUSION

It is said that while watching manoeuvres on Salisbury Plain between the world wars, Rudyard Kipling was asked his opinion of modern war. His reply was that 'It smells like a garage and looks like a circus.' For those who actually fought, the impression could be a bizarrely disturbing 'stream of consciousness', like that recorded by Capt Lewis Keeble of the 1/4th King's Own Yorkshire Light Infantry in Normandy:

> The troglodyte doctor; being lost in the dark and fired on by own troops; the mutineering signaller saved by his corporal; being shelled by Canadian mediums; the pacifist reinforcement; the drunken corporal; full body wash from a cup; a week in boots; tin hat lifted by a sniper; Tyneside Scottish rake our trenches; booby trap with football lace … cider in corroded jerricans; Callard's rum; the pioneer platoon massacred. And the battlefield is empty. One sees very few live, uncaptured enemy.

Many, like Sgt W. Virr of the 16th Durhams, felt that the frontline was a different world, and those there a 'different species'. Yet if there has been a message in book, it is that the frequently bloody and apparently random confusion of infantry combat was meticulously choreographed. Moreover, it is obvious that even in this microcosm there was change and development over time. New weapons were added, new ruses devised. Men changed: innocents and ideologues became veterans and victims of 'exhaustion', green replacements became officers and NCOs. Armies also changed, and not merely because they gained in experience or deteriorated in quality. The frontline infantry, though a numerical minority of the armies, generally suffered two-thirds or more of the total casualties.

'A people waxes and wanes according to the worth of its army: the army lives or dies on its infantry.' Such was the extreme point of view expressed in the German recruiting booklet *Offizier Im Grossdeutschen Heer* ('Officer in the Greater German Army') in 1942. Nevertheless, it was true that despite massive technological advances made between 1939 and 1945, success was still confirmed by the infantry: the men who finally seized the enemy ground and occupied it.

Pte Michael Swinkin of the 1st Infantry Division, US First Army, gathers his thoughts before crossing the Roer River near Kreuzau, Germany, on 25 February 1945. Fragmentation grenades are strapped to his chest ready for use. (©2006 TopFoto / Jon Mitchell)

BIBLIOGRAPHY

Ambrose, Stephen, *Band of Brothers*, Pocket Books, London (2001)

Balkowski, J., *Beyond the Beachhead*, Stackpole, Mechanicsburg (1989)

Biryukov, G. and G. Melnikov, *Antitank Warfare*, Progress Publishers, Moscow (1972)

Chamberlain, P. and T. J. Gander, *Anti-Tank Weapons*, Arco Publishing Co, New York (1974)

Doubler, M. D., *Closing With the Enemy*, University of Kansas (1994)

Ellis, J., *The Sharp End*, Pimlico, London (1993)

English, J., *On Infantry*, Praeger, New York (1984)

English, J., *A Perspective on Infantry*, Praeger, Westport (1981)

Farrer-Hockley, A. H., *Infantry Tactics*, Almark, London (1976)

Forty, G., *British Army Handbook 1939–1945*, Sutton, Stroud (1998)

Forty, G., *Japanese Army Handbook 1939–1945*, Sutton, Stroud (1999)

Fritz, S. G., *Frontsoldaten*, Kentucky University (1995)

Gabel, C. R., S*eek, Strike, and Destroy: US Army Tank Destroyer Doctrine in World War II*, Combat Studies Institute, Ft Leavenworth, KS (1985)

Gander, T. J., *The Bazooka: Hand-Held Hollow-Charge Anti-Tank Weapons*, PRC Publishing, London (1998)

Gudgin, P., *Armoured Firepower: The Development of Tank Armament 1939–45*, Sutton, Stroud (1997)

Jary, S., *18 Platoon*, Jary, Bristol (1944)

Knappe, Siegfried, *Soldat: Reflections of a German Soldier, 1936–1949*, Dell, New York (1993)

Koschorrek, Günther, *Blood Red Snow – The Memoirs of a German Soldier on the Eastern Front*, Motorbooks International, Osceola, WI (2006)

Marshall, G. C. (et al), *Infantry in Battle*, Infantry Journal, Washington (1939)

Marshall, S. L. A., *Men Against Fire*, Smith, Gloucester (1947)

McManus, J. C., *Deadly Brotherhood*, Presidio, New York (2000)

Sajer, G., *The Forgotten Soldier*, Weidenfeld, London (1971)

Shore, C., *With British Snipers to the Reich*, Greenhill, London (1997)

Weeks, J., *Men Against Tanks: A History of Anti-Tank Weapons*, Mason/Charter, New York (1975)

White, P., *With the Jocks*, Sutton, Stroud (2001)

Wigram, L. *Battle School*, Wigram, Chelwood (1941)

Winteringham, T. and J. N. Blashford-Snell, *Weapons and Tactics*, Penguin, London (1973)

Zaloga, S. J. and L. S. Ness, *Red Army Handbook 1939–1945*, Sutton, Stroud, (1998)

INDEX

References to illustration captions are shown in **bold**.